AT THE POLICE STATION:

DETECTIVE SERGEANT MARK WAREING: "You attended that house at three o'clock, and that's when you murdered this lady, and so much was your rush to get back that you went back to the [clinic] and immediately started altering this lady's records; and we can prove that only minutes after three o'clock on that date you fabricated that false medical history for this woman. Tell me why you needed to do that?"

SHIPMAN: "There's no answer."

WAREING: "Well there is, there is a very clear answer, because you've been up to her house, rolled her sleeve up, administered morphine, killed her and you were covering up what you were doing. That's what happened, isn't it, Doctor?"

SHIPMAN: "No."

IN COURT:

PROSECUTOR: "Not once in all these cases did you call an ambulance, did you?"

SHIPMAN: "I didn't call an ambulance, no."

PROSECUTOR: "Not once did you admit any patient to hospital?"

SHIPMAN: "That's also true."

PROSECUTOR: "And not once in all these cases did you permit a post-mortem examination to take place?"

SHIPMAN: "I did not inform the coroner at any stage that a patient needed a post mortem."

PROSECUTOR: "A simple explanation for the evidence in this case is your guilt?"

SHIPMAN: "No."

Dear Reader:

The book you are about to read is the latest bestseller from the St. Martin's True Crime Library, the imprint the *New York Times* calls "the leader in true crime!" Each month, we offer you a fascinating account of the latest, most sensational crime that has captured the national attention. St. Martin's is the publisher of perennial bestselling true crime author Jack Olsen, whose SALT OF THE EARTH is the true story of one woman's triumph over life-shattering violence; Joseph Wambaugh called it "powerful and absorbing." Fannie Weinstein and Melinda Wilson tell the story of a beautiful honors student who was lured into the dark world of sex for hire in THE COED CALL GIRL MURDER. St. Martin's is also proud to publish two-time Edgar Award-winning author Carlton Stowers, whose TO THE LAST BREATH recounts a two-year-old girl's mysterious death, and the dogged investigation that led loved ones to the most unlikely murderer: her own father. In the book you now hold, THE GOOD DOCTOR, acclaimed author Wensley Clarkson describes the terrible fall from grace of a kindly family doctor . . .

St. Martin's True Crime Library gives you the stories *behind* the headlines. Our authors take you right to the scene of the crime and into the minds of the most notorious murderers to show you what really makes them tick. St. Martin's True Crime Library paperbacks are better than the most terrifying thriller, because it's all true! The next time you want a crackling good read, make sure it's got the St. Martin's True Crime Library logo on the spine — you'll be up all night!

Charles E. Spicer, Jr.
Executive Editor, St. Martin's True Crime Library

THE
GOOD
DOCTOR

WENSLEY CLARKSON

St. Martin's Paperbacks

In memory of every single one of
Fred Shipman's victims
—may you all rest in peace.

AUTHOR'S NOTE

The central figure in this story, Harold Frederick Shipman, was always known to family, friends and patients as "Fred." In an effort to avoid confusion, throughout this book he will be referred to by that name.

Quotations from written material appear, with few exceptions, without the editorial "[sic]." When it seems that a word was inadvertently missing, it has been added for the sake of clarity. Mistakes in punctuation, grammar, and spelling have been corrected in certain instances, but in others it was felt that retaining an error helped convey the flavor of a document and the style of the person being quoted.

"If he came back this afternoon, I would be there on his doorstep. Dr. Shipman was wonderful with my second husband. He tried everything to save him. I will never believe he did it. He has been wonderful to me—and others. I am heartbroken."

—*One of Fred Shipman's patients, 1999*

"He wants to control situations. He likes to have control over life and death."

—*Detective Superintendent Bernard Postles, head of the team that investigated Fred Shipman, 2000*

"Lots of old ladies have died under Dr. Shipman. They say he's a lovely doctor, but you don't last long."

—*One of Shipman's oldest living patients, 1998*

I will use my power to help the sick to the best of my ability and judgment; I will abstain from harming or wronging anyone by it. I will not give a fatal draught to anyone if I am asked, nor will I suggest any such things.

— *From the Hippocratic Oath,*
taken by Fred Shipman when
he qualified as a doctor in 1973

INTRODUCTION

There is a kind of poetic injustice in the fact that Fred Shipman, the intriguing subject of this book, really does exist. He should be found only in horror fiction—the wiry, bearded, sharp-tongued medic who strode to the rescue of countless patients, only to cut short their lives with cold indifference.

Unlikely as his life story sounds, it is essential to examine it in minute detail in order to get a handle on the twisted mind of this extraordinary killer. You will read details here that will shock and amaze you. To be sure, Fred Shipman was no ordinary man, but a doctor whose superb bedside manner helped him gain the confidence of hundreds of patients before he cruelly cut them down. But was Fred Shipman psychotic, or insane? From his life and crimes I hope to reconstruct the development of his criminal brain—not only his nature, but even his appearance and personal idiosyncrasies, and in some instances, his charm and kindness. To watch Shipman at work is to imagine oneself back in a trusting middle-class world where the doctor is given god-like reverence and respect.

I first came upon the crimes of Fred Shipman in the summer of 1998, when I, along with millions of Britons, heard about the first excavation of one of his victims in the dead of night in a cold, isolated graveyard in Hyde, Lancashire, in the north of England. It soon became clear that police failed in their original investigation some months earlier. They, like so many of Shipman's patients, found it impossible to believe that such a respected, almost idolized, figure could be a cold-blooded killer. By the time investigators produced a criminal profile, it was way too late.

All Fred Shipman's victims deserve a mention, because each, in her—or occasionally, his—own way, is highly unusual. But I hope that most of all, this book will inform the reader about the doctor himself. What sort of man could stoop to killing on such a massive scale? How did he come to find a taste for death? What drove him to kill in increasingly large numbers? How did he hide these murderous instincts from the outside world?

I hope I can answer these and many other questions in an easy, non-technical style, but—and the reader should be prepared for this—in relatively explicit language. There is shocking material in this book, and I cannot gloss over certain disturbing facts. In some murders, Shipman was more successful in covering up the facts than in others, but I hope I have managed to get to the bottom of the truth.

There is a lesson to be drawn from the Fred Shipman case. What I have long found fascinating, and what I will underline so sharply, is the fact that the motivations behind the acts of a madman possess their own twisted logic. The psychotic murderer never acts with complete irrationality. There is a method to his madness: a rationale hidden behind what he has done and how he does it, however bizarrely and completely without reason it appears to be. The challenge to me, as an author, is to find that logic: and it is this hunt—this seeking out of the hidden mathematics of the disturbed mind, this reconstruction of the chess moves made by a madman—that I hope will unfold on the pages you are about to read.

I will also make this point: It is astonishing that so many of us are sane, and remain sane. That the human mind works at all—that anything so fantastically complex could even begin to operate as a unit—is itself remarkable. That most of us manage to keep this intricate and enormously variable mechanism under some sort of control most of the time, living with one another in tolerable harmony, is more remarkable still.

In *The Good Doctor* I have tried to probe the innermost feelings of a man now labeled one of the most prolific serial killers of modern times. Doctors play a very special role in our society. So often, people trust them without question. Doctors are rated as more "special" than the rest of us. Yet they are prone to guilt, depression, anger and—in the case of Fred Shipman—murder.

What makes Fred Shipman's crimes so extraordinary is the coldness with which he snuffed out people's lives, like the flick of a switch. But then, doctors are trained not to show their true feelings to their patients. In Shipman's case, he seemed to bottle up those emotions so much that his only means of "escape" was to kill.

I've interviewed countless people during the course of my inquiries into Shipman. But it was his colleagues and close friends who were to provide me with the ability to delve inside his mind and soul to explore the motives that drove him to kill. I have deliberately set out to inform and provoke in the hope that next time such a crime occurs, you will be alert to it. The tragedy of Shipman is that he carried on for so long without even being suspected of his crimes.

I have therefore tried to present the facts as vividly and realistically as possible. The result may be frightening. In parts, I have used dramatic techniques in adapting the Shipman story, occasionally making informed decisions about the details and emotional undercurrents of certain events. But the actual facts are as they ocurred.

Here then is the truth about Fred Shipman—the man, the murderer, the father, the trusted doctor. It promises to shake your trust in human nature to the core . . .

Wensley Clarkson, 2002

PROLOGUE

Hyde Cemetery, Hyde, North of England, November 1998

The rusting black-and-gold gates, proudly emblazoned with the town's crest, are rarely shut. Fresh yellow lilies lie alongside a gravestone inscribed, "TO LOVING DAD STAN." A few yards away fading daisies for a "MUM GONE BUT NOT FORGOTTEN." Elsewhere stand numerous ivy-choked tombstones of generations long departed. Wire mesh garbage cans hold old bottles of beer left by the people who sometimes slip into the cemetery to drown their sorrows. Across the way, a park worker with a rivet gun fixes tiny metal plaques to a stone wall in the garden of remembrance.

The 104-year-old Hyde Cemetery provides a backdrop more befitting a horror movie than real life. Gnarled old oak trees flash long thin shadows across the ground. Large ornate monuments erected in memory of some of the area's richest families create an almost gothic atmosphere. November is the month of the Holy Souls, when parishioners of the nearby St. Paul's Church pray for the dead at every Mass. If ever their prayers were needed, it is now.

Just one hundred yards away, residents sleep peacefully in their homes as cars and vans creep quietly along the cemetery pathway in low gear. In the starry sky, half a moon leaves long fingers of darkness across the grass. The smooth blankets of turf that covered the graves of Marie Quinn, Bianka Pomfret and Ivy Lomas have been peeled back and replaced with churned mounds of earth which now scar the once neat and tidy graveyard. The stark image of a white tent covering a desolate grave indicates that something is wrong. It's pitch dark. The grumbling sound of a generator cuts through the cold night air. Powerful spotlights strike beams of white across the gravesites. The old mill town of Hyde, in Lancashire, is about to unearth yet more evidence of the death and destruction wreaked by Fred Shipman.

A total of seven bodies would be exhumed from this same cemetery over the following months. A large white tent has been erected around the plot of Irene Turner. This once proud grandmother-of-four, described as "exquisite" by her family, always dressed to the nines, never a hair out of place. Yet she was about to undergo a final humiliating fate.

As the inquiry team gathers, Father Denis Maher whispers a prayer, his breath sending out small slivers of steam through the cold, damp air. Maher has been asked to attend by many of the families whose loved ones have been disinterred. Back in their homes they lie awake wondering what horrific sights are greeting the investigators and their hand-picked priest.

Each suspected victim has been assigned two detectives dedicated to her case, including the task of exhumation. All forensic officers wear green plastic department bodysuits. Just beyond them, uniformed officers patrol the perimeter of the graveyard checking for ghoulish onlookers, their flashlights flickering. It is a most distressing time for all the investigators. It's just as bad for the freelance workmen contracted at double-time pay rates to dig up the graves. They usually find most of their employment excavating roads.

Father Maher explains: "Nobody enjoys doing this. Nobody wants to do it, but they know it must be done, and they do it with dignity and sensitivity."

The priest repeats the prayers and service as each body is returned to its final resting place in a new coffin with a new name plate, usually within twenty-four hours. "It consoles the families," says Father Maher. But that reburial only comes after investigators have completed their grim task, in a far corner of the graveyard where the rows of new marble tombstones glisten like black, shiny teeth.

The Catholic section bore the brunt of it, with four exhumations. Flowers and a modest brown marble gravestone—inscribed, "A DEAR WIFE, MUM AND NANA, ALWAYS IN OUR HEARTS AND SADLY MISSED"—are removed from Mrs. Turner's well-tended plot as the mechanical digger starts up.

One officer stops by the fence and pours a cup of tea from a flask, while another lights a cigarette,

"I'm glad I'm not over there," he says.

The entire operation will take at least two and a half hours, the sodden ground and waterlogged grave making the task more difficult than in previous exhumations. At hourly intervals a church bell tolls. Eventually, lights begin to come on in nearby homes as early risers awaken.

An hour later the digger falls silent, leaving an unearthly hush; the operation is complete. The tent is removed to reveal the workteam carefully clearing away their equipment and debris from the grave and surrounding plots. But these exhumations have struck fear and horror into the hearts of the people of Hyde. One woman, whose house backs onto the cemetery, says: "You hear noises and half wake up, then realize what it is. It makes you shudder."

As Father Maher later pointed out: "It's pretty normal to die. You have the funeral, and that gives a natural completion to death. But this reversal—it has a profound effect on everyone involved. For a big town, Hyde is very close-knit. Everyone either is related, or knows someone whose death is being investigated. Quite frankly, I don't know if the place will ever get over it. It's like a cancer eating away at the heart of the community."

But where and how did that cancer begin?

1

In 1938, Harold Shipman and his young wife Vera were the first occupants of 163 Longmead Drive on the newly built Edwards Lane estate in the city of Nottingham, in the mid-east of England. The district they lived in was called Sherwood, after the nearby forest where Robin Hood, according to legend, robbed the rich to help feed the poor. Unlike many of the nation's Victorian cities, Nottingham had successfully diversified early in the twentieth century and didn't rely on the traditional trades of lace and frame knitting. New, vibrant industries such as bicycles and tobacco had emerged. The Edwards Lane Estate was a very close-knit community consisting only of two dozen roads lined with new red-brick houses.

Harold Shipman came from a poor family of eight children. His father was a hosiery warehouseman. Shipman was a quiet, unassuming man, used to a hard day's work driving his Bedford tipper truck, moving stones and broken tarmac for local construction firms. His idea of relaxation was to tend to his flowers in the back garden of his beloved home. Harold Shipman smoked a pipe and wore a trilby hat over his thinning, gray hair. His wife Vera, a small, slim lady with dark, saucer-like eyes, seemed exotic in comparison to her husband. The family was the epitome of working class respectability: a hard-working father, and a mother who ran a neat home and raised children described by neighbors as "a credit to her."

The couple's first child, Pauline, was born in March 1938. But when the Second World War began, Harold set off to fight with the Sherwood Foresters regiment. Vera, still in her teens, was left all alone to fend for herself and baby Pauline. So it was hardly surprising that her next child wasn't born until after the war, on January 14, 1946. It was just eight months after V-E Day, when the world had finally stopped fighting and the cities and towns of England were filled with young couples rushing headlong into building up their families.

The Shipmans' newest arrival was christened Harold Frederick, but everyone called him Fred, to avoid confusion with his father Harold. Fine, upstanding Vera tolerated "Freddie" and "Fred" for her beloved son, but had insisted that her husband—also known in childhood as Fred—change his name to Harold when they married.

The Shipman home was the middle house of a terrace of three. It had three bedrooms with a downstairs bathroom, a small front yard and a larger sixty-foot back yard. A good housekeeper, Vera stayed at home (only one in five women worked in those days), believed in discipline and considered that the family had no spare cash for gifts or vacations.

Having a sister seven years older meant, in effect, that Fred found himself with two mothers doting on him. Although there was a bond amongst them, the Shipmans were not an outwardly demonstrative family, but in those days they certainly qualified as happy and functional.

Vera Shipman's determination to move up the social ladder prevented her family from making a lot of close friends in their neighborhood. They did spend some time with the Cutler family, who lived opposite them on Longmead Drive, but one neighbor later explained: "The Cutlers said they weren't easy, by any means." Neighbor Hannah Cutler later recalled: "The family were rather insular. I think Harold and Vera wanted them to be different; they wanted something better for their family."

And there lies the key to Fred Shipman's upbringing; Vera led her children—especially Fred—to believe that they were better than those around them. Fred sometimes tagged along with other children, but he never seemed interested in joining in the usual street games played by most kids on the estate.

As one contemporary recalled: "He was sometimes with the lads, but definitely not one of the lads." Many of the local kids used to go down to the local movie theater on weekends. Their favorites were Roy Rogers, Tarzan and the Robin Hood movies, naturally. Fred rarely went because his mother insisted he stay home and do some extra school work.

Just outside the Shipman home, kids would squat down on the curbside and play cards. Others pinched apples from garden trees. But young Fred Shipman spent most of his time watching the world from his bedroom window. His mom preferred him to read a book in the bedroom he shared with his brother, Clive, two years his junior. And Fred didn't want to make a fuss, so he did what was expected of him.

At home Harold Shipman proved an extremely patient and sweet-natured "gentleman" of a father. Vera was devoted to her husband, but it was clear to visitors that she was the stronger personality. Vera herself had been born illegitimately to a local lace clipper. She wanted security and happiness for their three offspring, and was determined that they should have a better future. Nothing would stop Vera making sure her children were more successful than their peers on Edward Lane.

She wanted her children to grow up and beat a path off the estate. And during the mid-fifties she was proved absolutely right as the neighborhood gradually turned into the "Wild West," according to residents who still live there. The estate became livelier and noisier. Drunken brawls between teenagers, and wife-beating incidents were soon on the increase. It wasn't an environment that Vera approved of.

The Shipmans did not own a car, so Fred and his family would regularly walk across Nottingham to see their cousins. Uncle Reg Shipman later recalled: "They were nice kids. Fred was a quiet, clever little boy."

Fred first went to the Burford Infants' School, a short

walk from Longmead Drive, where most of the small children arrived from the estate holding the hands of their mums, brothers or sisters. In a photograph of eight little boys sitting around a table on a sunny day outside the school building, Fred is pictured wearing a bowtie while the others are not. It was Vera who made her favorite child dress more formally than other children. She wanted him to stand out—to be someone special.

When Fred was six, he should have gone on to Bestwood Primary School. But considered to be very bright, he immediately began busing to a new school called Whitemoor Primary, on the nearby Whitemoor council estate.

Classmate and neighbor Alan Goddard used to accompany him on a double-decker bus to Whitemoor Primary School. "We were outsiders when we first arrived, but there were a few of us, so we settled quickly," Alan recalled.

Fred failed to make the junior school soccer team, but he did excel at stool ball—a sport unique to Nottinghamshire—which is a cross between baseball and cricket, played with a large paddle which looks like an oversized table-tennis bat. Whitemoor topped the local schools league, and Fred was photographed in a school picture, dark-haired and dark-eyed, proudly dressed in the school T-shirts issued to the team. But as Alan Goddard later recalled: "Freddie would never say boo to a goose—he was quiet and kept out of the way of the rougher kids."

At Whitemoor, Fred studied for a very important examination which, if he passed, would qualify him for two of the city's finest schools. Young Fred's intensive school work helped him pass with such good results that he won a scholarship to High Pavement, the prestigious local grammar school. Getting her children into High Pavement—motto: *Virtus Sola Nobilitas* (Virtue is the only nobility)—was Vera's priority. She saw it as the key to young Fred's development. Vera was convinced that her favorite son was destined to go far in the world. He was one of a few boys from the estate to make it to High Pavement.

It wasn't easy for young Fred, carrying such big hopes

on his shoulders. Attending High Pavement meant that he had to get up before seven each morning to get to the school premises. Walking home at night, he was ridiculed by other boys on the estate because of his "fancy school uniform." It was usually dark by the time he got home each evening, and he spent all his waking hours poring over books.

High Pavement, founded in 1788, was built on a tradition of sporting and academic prowess. It provided a supportive and encouraging launchpad for working-class boys like Fred. High Pavement was a grammar school. The British Grammar School system (later abolished) was supposed to encourage more intelligent students, and such schools were considered almost on a par with the elitist, high-tuition "public schools" attended by the children of richer families.

High Pavement is so named because of its unusual original location between the city's castle and the middle of Nottingham. Amongst the buildings there was a Unitarian chapel, or "Chapel of the Society of Protestant Dissenters Assembling at the High Pavement." Originally the chapel had been a place of worship for nonconformist Christian intellectuals who challenged some of the orthodox teachings of the established church. Lord Byron's mother, Catherine Gordon, a Scottish heiress from Gight, near Aberdeen, worshipped at the chapel while her son, aged ten, was being treated for a deformed foot at the local hospital. More than a century later, D. H. Lawrence used the chapel as the meeting place for his fictional characters Paul Morel and Miriam Leivers in *Sons and Lovers*.

High Pavement was open to children of all denominations, the first non-sectarian school in England. It achieved another notable first a hundred years later, when it became the first school in the country to teach practical science. By the Second World War, the school was a boys-only establishment, while nearby Manning School provided education for girls. When Fred Shipman arrived in September 1957, a brand-new purpose-built premises had been constructed in Bestwood, less than a mile away from the Shipman family home.

By this time 60 percent of the pupils at High Pavement were working class. Fred and his neighbor Alan Goddard were accepted into the school together. They wore brown blazers trimmed with brown-and-yellow braid, brown caps, ties striped in brown, yellow and blue, school socks and, for the first year, short gray trousers. Not wearing a tie meant an automatic detention. After the first three years, caps did not have to be worn. On speech days and at the end of each term, the boys sang the school song, "*Una Voce Concanemus Omnes Paviores*" (translated it meant, "With one voice we Pavorians all sing together").

Alan Goddard, an only child, spent a lot of time with Fred's family. They invited him over for Bonfire Night (November 5) parties in their back yard, where they ate bonfire toffee and cakes baked at home by Vera Shipman. Alan later recalled: "They were a nice family. Mrs. Shipman was a lovely, sweet woman." Goddard even went to watch the local soccer team, Notts County, with Freddie and Freddie's dad. "I support them to this day, because they took me there for my first proper football match," he later explained.

John Soar, another friend from Fred Shipman's High Pavement days, later recalled: "Fred was old before his time. A wise head on young shoulders; always focused on something. We were in different classes, so I didn't know him that well, but he worked hard." As another classmate, Bob Studholme, later recalled: "No one really knew Fred Shipman. He was always in a crowd, but I couldn't honestly say that Fred had a friend."

Typical school days were carefully structured, with bells ringing at the end of the lessons, desks arranged in rows, strict no-talking rules in class, and masters flitting about wearing black gowns.

Headmaster Harry Davies came from a working-class background in Todmorden, West Yorkshire, a place which would become very significant for Fred Shipman later in life. Davies was a firm, but fair man, a committed socialist with a strong sense of social justice which he passed on to the sons of miners, truck drivers and factory workers who came to the school via scholarships from within the city of Nottingham. Eloquent and caring, he thought nothing of walking a problematical boy back to his home, there to put his mother and father at ease. Often he'd stay with the family well into the evening explaining any worries that might exist.

John Soar recalled: "Harry Davies was hard, but fair. If you crossed the line, you knew it, but if there was a glimmer of hope, he wouldn't stop giving all the encouragement he could."

Like most British schools at this time, corporal punishment existed, although Harry Davies was not a keen proponent of it. However he was capable at times of "giving a good stroke of the cane" when the punishment was required. Fred's High Pavement classmate Bob Studholme was beaten by Davies for throwing stones at the groundsman's tractor. Bizarrely, after inflicting the punishment on Studholme, the headmaster then shook the boy's hand.

Back at home, young Fred's homework was the most important thing in the Shipman household. His sister Pauline had left school at fifteen, and was working in the shipping department of a company that manufactured knitted garments. When younger brother Clive did not get accepted to High Pavement, Fred's academic prowess took center stage.

Fred Shipman's progress through school was marked, unsurprisingly, by his quietness. As Bob Studholme recalled: "We'd all be swearing, making rude bodily noises, getting into mischief. A couple of the lads had berets, and would do silly skits pretending to be French before the French teacher arrived. If you got caught being too silly, you got a detention, but I don't remember ever seeing Fred in detention."

Fred was so physically mature that he began shaving when he was just 13 years old. He also sported sideburns that were the envy of every other boy in the school. It gave him an air of superiority, and most students looked up to him. Bob Studholme remembered: "Those sideburns gave him real status, and he enjoyed that."

During the English equivalent of Shipman's eighth grade year, one of Fred Shipman's classmates told a filthy joke in the locker room. Bob Studholme looked in the mirror on the wall and noticed Fred sitting on a bench smiling faintly. "But he wasn't grinning like the rest of us," Studholme later recalled. "It was a condescending smile, as if he was looking at a gang of kids and thinking, 'You'll grow up one day.' "

The teenage Fred Shipman excelled at rugby, playing fly-half at first and later as a center or wingback. In October 1961, he even won the prize for most improved student—a backhanded compliment that was one of the few highlights of his school career.

Young Fred was well aware that his mother in many ways resented the fact that her husband was a simple workman. She dreamed of Fred making a successful career. Consequently, Fred always seemed in an odd frame of mind, with a total lack of interest in anything apart from his school activities.

But he was so proud to be able to wear the uniform of the best school in the area that he often passed himself off to strangers as a rich, well-spoken student. In a way he became a kind of con man—but without actually deceiving anyone for monetary gain. A good-looking and plausible young man, he enjoyed being accepted as this "other person," apart from the true Fred Shipman.

And Vera did little to dissuade her favorite son from his own self-delusionment. In many ways, she and Fred were cut off from everyone else in the family, inhabiting their own little world. Each always seemed to know what the other was thinking. Certainly, Vera pampered and protected Fred more than her other children, and eventually there was a growing resentment from the other family members, including hard-working Harold Shipman.

Most shockingly, it now seems entirely possible that mother and son became closer than is natural. Some believe that Fred was seduced by his mother—certainly mentally, if not physically—from the time he was about twelve or thirteen years of age. Certainly, Fred was in the habit of sneaking into his mother's bed at night if his father was out at the pub or working late. As one relative later explained: "Fred and Vera had this unusual telepathy between them. Sometimes we were all a little worried as to how close they really were."

As his rugby skills improved, young Fred even played rugby for Nottinghamshire Schools' Under-15s in the winter of 1959–60. He was stocky and tough, with an aggressive streak of utter determination once he got on the rugby field. During one inter-schools match, Fred showed a serious violent streak. "He carried out one of the most horrendous tackles I have ever seen," recalled classmate Phil Pallant. "It was not unfair, but he just cleaned this lad out, taking him round the waist. I remember everyone wincing, and I was glad that I was not on the receiving end of it."

And Bob Studholme recalled: "He could rattle people's teeth: he was an aggressive player. He was definitely not the same person off the pitch [field] as he was on."

On school cross-country runs, some of the boys would stop off for cups of tea at the home of one classmate named Michael Heath. "He'd come in, but never stayed for long," Heath later recalled. "He knew we'd be in trouble if we were caught, and he didn't like putting a foot out of line."

In the classroom, Fred Shipman may have lacked real flair, but he more than made up for that through sheer hard work and determination. Fred was a "plodder," often walking to school because he couldn't afford a bicycle and wanted to save the cost of a bus. He carried a huge backpack of books like a snail. Fred eventually became a Pavior–a prefect in charge of young students.

Mike Heath later recalled: "Some of us had it easy, but he really worked hard. I remember he had a long, loping stride, as he still does." Fred Shipman was always sheltering at the back of the class, absorbing the teachers' words, but seemingly immersed in another world. He was also just about the only student without a nickname. He preferred to keep out of the groups of friends who gathered in the school yard between classes.

In 1962, Fred graduated to the "sixth form," the English school system's version of America's tenth grade. Life in the sixth at High Pavement was more relaxed than in the lower grades. Although the boys still wore blazers, they were allowed to wear waistcoats of any style or color. Fred favored a bright mustard yellow one. It gave him the air of being quite a dandy, which seemed strangely at odds with his quiet personality.

Sixth formers also had more contact with the female students at the nearby Manning School, but Fred was so shy and awkward with girls that he barely spoke to any of them. Yet, physically, he remained far more mature than many of his contemporaries. With his sideburns he was often teased about similarities to Elvis, though most of the High Pavement boys enjoyed Buddy Holly, regarded as the "thinking man's rocker."

Studious, hard-working Fred Shipman had little time for pop music. He was more interested in pleasing his mom by getting good grades in his advanced Biology, Physics and Chemistry classes.

She was clearly the driving force in his life.

2

Just after Fred Shipman's seventeenth birthday in January 1963, something happened to him that would completely alter the course of his life; his beloved mother Vera was diagnosed with cancer. Rapidly, active, house-proud Vera Shipman became a mere shadow of her former self. She grew emaciated, gaunt and debilitated. Seeing Fred at the end of each day when he walked in from school rallied her, but as the weeks went by, she was soon struggling even to walk. With Pauline–now 25–and Fred's father Harold at work, and youngest son Clive just 13, it was only natural that Fred would become his mother's main caretaker.

The family's General Practitioner, Dr. Andrew Campbell, visited the Shipman house regularly, giving Vera welcome injections of morphine in ever-increasing dosages to try to ease the pain. Fred noticed how the morphine seemed to be the only thing that helped her. He would often sit and watch with fascination as the doctor injected his mother, and her pain-lined face positively lit up as the drugs kicked in. Vera Shipman now spent much of her time sitting in the front room of the family's immaculately clean council house, gazing out the window in a vain bid to ignore the agony that wracked her withering body until the next injection came.

Vera had undoubtedly been a very controlling influence throughout young Fred Shipman's childhood. She had originally set about isolating him, not letting him play with the other children. She'd encouraged him to go to grammar school, which isolated him further from those around him.

Even when he was good at sports, it somehow didn't provide him with a bridge to other people.

Now she was about to leave him—her pride and joy—just when he was beginning his life. Vera Shipman said little to the other family members, but neighbors recall her spending hours talking to Fred as he sat next to her in the front room. Vera got Fred to promise that he would continue his studies. She wanted him to escape from the poverty trap and make a real success of himself.

On the afternoon of Friday, June 21, 1963, Vera died. She'd said her final good-byes to the family the previous day. By the time Fred got home from school that evening she'd already passed away.

A strange silent stillness came over the tiny room as young Fred realized that his beloved mother had gone forever. The hush was only broken by the quivering of his father's voice as Harold tried to make Fred step outside, away from his mother's corpse. The atmosphere was unimaginable; it just didn't seem possible that such a thing could happen . . . it was so unfair.

A storm raged inside young Fred's head about his mother's death. It wasn't just an empty void he felt. He was shattered, mentally and physically, after staying with her through so many painful nights as she lay close to death.

It was to prove a harrowing weekend for the teenager—not that he dared show any of his emotions to the rest of the world.

Outside the Shipman house in the hours following Vera's death, a different storm raged as the sky poured with rain. Fred Shipman—the athlete who had played rugby for the city's under-15 team—now had distinctly unmanly tears streaming down his cheeks. He walked out of the front room, where his mother's corpse remained, and into the hallway, laced up his track shoes and rushed out into the deluge to run. Shipman pounded the streets, water streaking down his cheeks, diluting the endless flood of his tears.

The teenager was working out his grief alone, shedding

tears in the rain, torn by sadness and relief, running and running and running to escape the atmosphere at home. However, he was also pounding the pavement in order to gain mastery of his emotions, to take control and lose himself in psychical endurance. His mother had told him to be strong and not let her death ruin his chances of escape.

But he found it hard to suppress feelings of grief, loss, relief, guilt, anger, helplessness—and they all came out as he pounded the sidewalk through the driving rain. Fred Shipman ran right through that night and did not arrive home until three in the morning. He was emotionally and physically spent.

Heartbroken as they undoubtedly were, Fred, his sister Pauline and brother Clive tried to put on a brave face for the sake of their father, but it wasn't easy. Fred knew his mother would have expected him to be strong. His sister cried openly throughout the house at all times of the day and night, as did his kid brother. Somehow, it fell to Fred and his father to make the funeral arrangements; Vera's coffin was set up in the downstairs room where she had taken her last breath. The room was filled with flowers from friends and neighbors.

As Fred walked to school the following Monday, classmate Mike Heath asked him: "What did you do at the weekend?"

"Oh," replied Fred, a little nervously, "my mum died."

Mike Heath didn't even know that Vera Shipman had been ill. "I'm so sorry—are you all right, mate?"

"Yeah, I went for a run," came the reply.

On the morning of the funeral, Fred helped to carry the coffin, which was placed on a horse-drawn carriage. Fred didn't hold his brother's or sister's hands at all as the family stood in their appropriate place in preparation for the one-mile walk to the cemetery. As the carriage pulled out of Longmead Drive, the sidewalks contained a few neighbors and inquisitive residents, who wanted to give Vera a good send-off; some even joined in the procession and walked solemnly behind the family, but young Fred knew that his mother would never really have approved of that.

They first walked half a mile down the road to the church. A local policeman stopped and stood on the street corner and courteously raised his helmet as the procession passed by. On reaching the church, a small group of half a dozen other friends and relatives awaited the coffin. After the service the mourners followed the carriage another half a mile to the cemetery where Vera was buried alongside her mother and grandparents.

Fred hardly mentioned his mother's death to any of his other classmates, but he did wear a black armband over his blazer throughout the month following her funeral, and he couldn't stop visualizing her during those last few days of her life. He now knew that he had to become a doctor so he could try to save people like his mother from the sort of slow and painful, lingering death that she had suffered. No one should ever have to go through that, young Fred Shipman thought.

Fred's overall numb response was typical of his personality at that time, even though his dark broodiness made him a figure of respect inside the school. Because of that respect, most people considered Fred to be more mature than the other students at High Pavement, but in many ways he was actually very under-developed. He was shy and awkward around other people. Many recalled him being unable to make any conversation.

"I can't think of one really close friendship he struck up," recalled classmate Bob Studholme. Studholme also remembered that, despite being a handsome teenager, "I can't remember seeing Fred with a girl."

Pauline was the only other woman, besides Vera, whom Fred had ever known. But his mother was the one he felt most comfortable with. She was his driving force; the one person who seemed to understand what he was thinking. Now she was gone.

For the final month of that school summer term Fred continued wearing a black tie and armband. He even admitted to classmate Michael Heath, that taking that long run through the night following her death "was how I got it out of my system."

But the reality was that Fred Shipman never worked out his highly complicated feelings about his dearly departed mother. That image of her dying would stay with him forever. It wasn't just an occasional flashback. It came to him every single day without fail, and she dominated his dreams as well.

His father was a decent, hard-working man, whose only vice was that he occasionally gambled on horse races. Harold Shipman had simple tastes and few ambitions. He continued driving the local council's vans in the summer and their gritting trucks in the winter. It was Vera who had been the driving force behind Fred's success. In a sense he felt abandoned by her; but he also felt an obligation to fight on to show her what a success he would become.

Not surprisingly, the entire family was in a serious state of shock following Vera's death. They had to face the painful reality of life without her, knowing that they would never again come home from work or school and find her there organizing their lives for them all. She had been the mainstay of the entire family. How could they survive without her? To young Fred, it seemed so strange that people in the outside world were continuing to go about their business as if nothing had happened.

Fred must have felt that he did not have anyone to comfort him. His sister and brother had been well aware that he was Vera's favorite child, and seemed to share a much closer relationship with her. Fred was stuck in the middle, and could only have felt incredibly lonely. And the memories of his mother wouldn't fade.

Apart from going to and from school, Fred rarely ventured out in the months following Vera's death. He hated the way other people looked at him with such pity and sorrow. They didn't even know her, he must have thought. They don't know just how special she really was.

Both Pauline and Clive realized that Fred was taking his mother's death the worst. One day Pauline even knelt down in front of Fred in the house and looked at him with her sad, puppy-dog eyes and tried to get him to talk about it. Fred just got up and walked away. His only way to deal with the loss was to bottle it up. Remembering his mother, Fred believed there had to be something more than this humdrum existence, and his longing for it was obvious. His mother had been completely right: he had to get away.

Back on the sports field, Fred Shipman used rugby as an emotional outlet. He showed no fear on the field and that made him a frightening opponent. He would do anything to win a game, and he reveled in the rough-and-tumble aspects of this very physical sport. Bob Studholme explained: "We were all expected to behave in a proper manner. In assemblies, eight hundred boys standing up and sitting down, and you could hear a pin drop. That's why sports were so important. It was a means of letting off steam, and Fred certainly managed that."

Fred Shipman was also a very good long-distance runner, and became vice-captain of the school athletics team in his final year. He even merited various accolades in *The Pavior*, High Pavement's student magazine, for his contributions to school and house teams for both rugby and athletics. But many noticed that following the death of his mother, Fred Shipman became increasingly disassociated from his classmates. He refused to meet up with any of them at local pubs on weekends. Many presumed he had never even tasted alcohol.

However, Fred had an interest in something more intriguing than booze: he had become secretly addicted to sniffing Sloan's Liniment. Fellow cross-country runner Terry Swinn recalled that Shipman became obsessed with applying the pungent-smelling ointment, used to ease aching muscles; "Fred loved the smell of it. Some at the school suspected that he was addicted to sniffing it. We all used it, but he was addicted."

Fred Shipman adored the feeling of relaxation that came over him as he sniffed the ointment in a way similar to that of others sniffing glue. It was the only time he could forget about his mother and all the tribulations of his home life. Fred Shipman's addictive personality was already beginning to take shape. It was an ominous sign for the future.

Back on the rugby field, Fred's fearsome reputation began to fade as many of his contemporaries caught up with his height and weight. However, Fred remained aloof and very serious compared with most of the other sixth form boys. "We were often [playful] and stupid, running around twanging girls' suspenders and all that," Bob Studholme later recalled. "But Fred wouldn't take part. He was always on the edge of our group. He'd never demean himself with a dirty joke. Fred was serious; we were stupid. We thought he was old-fashioned."

Classmate John Soar agrees: "Fred didn't mix much, but he didn't suck up to authority, so people admired him." When the class went on a field study course to a nearby town called Slapton-Lee, Fred shocked his classmates by taking part in a massive beer drinking session. The legal drinking age in England is lower than it is in America, but this was the first time any of them had even seen him with alcohol. "He wasn't stick-in-the-mud. Fred was not in the inner circle, but he was not on the outside looking in. He just did his own thing and we admired him for it," remembered Soar.

Getting drunk—like sniffing that ointment earlier—enabled Fred Shipman to overcome his shyness. He liked having that brief respite from the relentless pressure to succeed. Shipman began thinking about alcohol and drugs and how they conveniently provided escape for people with emotional problems.

Bob Studholme, on reflection, believed that Fred was "too quiet. I was an open book; he was a closed soul. Fred never came to any of our houses, and we never went to his. We just didn't know his family."

* * *

Perhaps not so surprisingly, Fred Shipman got very poor grades on his exams, and agreed to stay on an extra year at High Pavement to take them all over again. Even then, there was something about Fred Shipman that commanded enough respect for him to be made head boy (President) at High Pavement during his extra year.

Fred took on such important roles as readings at the school's Unitarian church in Nottingham city center. He had been elevated to head boy when Terry Swinn left early in the new school year after passing his examination for entry to Cambridge. Swinn recalled that Fred Shipman was a firm-but-fair deputy. "Very straight-up-and-down. If you asked him a question, he would give a straight answer."

One of the most chilling things his contemporaries re-membered about Fred Shipman is what one later described as a "certain cold stare." It was a look of icy indifference which, years later, others would recall replacing the bedside softness of the GP when yet another elderly female patient was close to death.

Classmate Mike Heath recalled Fred Shipman appearing to be detached from the everyday pursuits of a typical bunch of teenage classmates. "I remember on a rugby tour it was someone's birthday, and we got him the Beatles' first LP. We were singing the songs; it was a time of music and spirit; a good time, a great atmosphere. But Fred wouldn't join in."

Not surprisingly, Fred's sister Pauline became a substi-tute mother back in the Shipman household. Fred's aunt, Dorothy Emerson, who still lives in Nottingham, recalled: "Fred was so young when Vera died, and it hit him hard. Pauline virtually took over as his mother. She did the iron-ing, the cooking, everything, for his father as well." Pauline even became young Fred's "date" at the twice-yearly rugby club dances in the school hall. "We found it amusing that he brought his elder sister and danced with her," recalled Mike Heath. Eight years older than her brother and some-what taller, they made a strange-looking couple. Fred re-mained ill at ease with other girls.

At the Shipman family home, the three children provided

the bedrock for grieving Harold Shipman to survive. Neighbor Ursula Oldknow still had fond memories of old Mr. Shipman. "He lived for his family. Most round these parts throw as much ale down their throats as possible, but not that family. They had real pride and determination."

And the family remained extremely proud that young Fred had made it to the top-notch grammar school. "Harold knew Fred wanted to be different," recalled Hannah Cutler, now 83, who knew the Shipman children well.

Fred left High Pavement in 1965, and never once revisited his old alma mater. His earlier feeling of pride at being there had been replaced by a gradual resentment about the formality of the school where he always felt a complete outsider. Few classmates were impressed by Fred. One, Peter Costen, later recalled: "What I remember about Fred was that he was just so ordinary."

Shipman's contemporaries believed that young Fred's seeds of resentment took root as he struggled to keep pace with the academic high fliers at High Pavement. Such fears of inadequacy followed him through life. It was only when he became a doctor that he gained standing and respect in the community and then began to show real self-confidence.

Fred's grades consisted of a B in physics, C in biology and D in chemistry, and he was accepted into Leeds University—seventy miles to the north of Nottingham—to read medicine (senior British Labor politician Jack Straw arrived at the same time to read law). In 1965 there was a serious shortage of doctors in Britain. Generous student grants were available, and because his truck-driving father was a low wage earner, Fred qualified for a full student grant that amounted to £340 (roughly $510) the equivalent of $6,000 in 2000.

Leaving home provoked mixed feelings in Fred Shipman. The family was still devastated by Vera's death, and the house had never been the same since the tragedy. It had become a joyless place. Old Harold Shipman rarely spoke except to bark orders at his offspring. He spent many hours sitting alone in the front room sucking on a pipe, staring into oblivion, thinking back to the happy days when his beloved Vera was alive.

Fred Shipman believed that medical school in Leeds would provide the escape his mother had so desperately wanted for him. It was the middle of the "swinging 60s." The Beatles were the biggest thing since sliced bread. The Who was pulling the more disaffected youth in with their anthem "My Generation." Miniskirts and mini-cars were all the rage in Britain.

Fred Shipman—who'd never taken a girlfriend to the school dance, and looked down his nose at anyone who told a dirty joke or served a school detention, and was even wary of sneaking a cup of tea during a cross-country run—was about to enter the real world.

Because of the extra year at High Pavement, Fred Shipman was nearly 20 when he enrolled at Leeds. The gap between Fred and the more academically attuned 18-year-olds again marked him out as different, making him even more of a loner. Moreover, Fred seemed strangely obsessed with casting off his former life in Nottingham. He never played rugby again. He buckled down to his studies, constantly driven by the thought that this was what his mother would have wanted. Fellow student Christakis Varnavides summed up the impression given by Fred Shipman: "Although I didn't know him very well, he certainly did not stand out in any way. He was just an average person."

By this time, Fred Shipman was thinner, but extremely dapper. One student at Leeds even went so far as to describe him as: "rather spivvy, wiry and dark." But Fred was still shy, introverted and definitely not "one of the boys" at med school, although plenty of girls noticed him because of his brooding, swarthy, almost Latin good looks.

Those who knew him in high school probably presumed that Fred Shipman would start enjoying life to the fullest when he got to Leeds University. But if he did hang out in bars and nightclubs, it certainly wasn't for long, because within a few months of starting his degree, the next major change in Fred's life occurred. Her name was Primrose Oxtoby.

3

Primrose Oxtoby was named after the beautiful flowers that line the steep Yorkshire lanes and blossom in the hedgerows with a startling whiteness. Her birth, on April 19, 1949, was supposed to represent new hope and new beginnings for the Oxtoby family. Parents Edna and George—who managed a farm at Huttons Ambo, near York, in the north of England— were already the parents of two other children, and, at thirty-nine and forty-four, were old-fashioned in both age and values. Baby Primrose was a classic example of the population explosion of the immediate post-war years.

By the time Primrose reached school age in 1954, the young Elizabeth II had been crowned Queen of England and the family had moved to the tiny hamlet of East Rigton, between Leeds and Wetherby, where father George continued his career as a farm foreman. They lived in a small cottage at the bottom of a lane near the farm where he worked. As a reward they were protected against eviction.

At primary school in nearby Bardsey, little Primrose rarely joined in with the other children. Her mother Edna disapproved of her playing in the yard with friends. Edna saw it as frivolous and unnecessary. She was furious if Primrose got her dress dirty. Edna was apparently convinced that her youngest daughter would be contaminated by other people's relaxed attitudes. If children wanted to play with Primrose, it had to be near her home, and the other playmates had to be personally approved by Edna.

One of Primrose's school friends from that era later recalled: "We had to play with Primrose—or else she would

threaten us with her mother, and we were all terrified of
Mrs. Oxtoby. If we made too much noise, her mother would
come out, and we'd all run off home instantly. With other
mothers, we'd take a bit of a telling off and then carry on
playing, but with Mrs. Oxtoby, we didn't dare wait around."

At the age of eleven, Primrose's life changed drastically
when her parents inherited some much-needed cash and
moved the family from their tiny tied cottage to a substantial
stone-built semi-detached house in the nearby town of
Wetherby. Primrose was sent to a new school, Wetherby
County Secondary Modern. When Primrose joined the
school in 1960, all classes were held in an old naval building
at her new school in Crossley Street, a five-minute walk
from the family's new home.

The Oxtobys' new house was set on a hillside overlooking the town center. It was an 1876-built property which
was part of a row of four matching pairs. Originally the
houses were part of a mushrooming development on the
western side of the town, and were referred to as "villas" to
attract professional, middle-class people who could for the
first time commute to the nearby city of Leeds on the newly
opened rail-line. The town of Wetherby was thriving by the
time the Oxtobys turned up, with the River Wharfe forming
a natural southern boundary for the town, and a racecourse.
The beautiful Yorkshire Dales nearby were a magnet for
visitors even back in the 1950s. And George Oxtoby had a
new job as a road laborer for the local council earning
around £10 ($15) a week. It was just enough to support his
family. Most times, George Oxtoby would be outside tending to his rows of vegetables in the back yard. He usually
wore a flat cap on his head and had a roll-up cigarette in
his mouth. Edna's homemade pies and cakes made their
mark on his physique.

Although Primrose was considered a bright child before
she hit her teens, she failed to make the grades to be offered
a place at one of the area's better schools. That meant Prim-

rose was destined to leave school at 15 without even taking any of the elementary British qualifications.

One school acquaintance, who lived near the Oxtoby family, says it was clear that Primrose was different. "She used to stare a lot. She wasn't like the rest of us." She had few real friends, and could often be found alone in the corner of the school yard.

In 1964 Primrose was nearing the end of her four years of high school education and had become a familiar figure on the streets of Wetherby. Every Sunday she attended the Methodist church on Bank Street with her mother Edna and older sister Mary—18 by the time Primrose began school—who was training to be a nurse as a local hospital near Wetherby. The family was always at the 10 A.M. service, after which they would head over to the church hall to listen to parables and sing cheerful hymns. On most Sunday afternoons, Primrose and her siblings would then attend Sunday school, sitting in a circle around their teacher to discuss the meaning of Bible stories. In the evening, there was another service.

According to Primrose's school friends, those fellowship meetings summed up Edna Oxtoby's attitude toward life; she wanted her two children to have fulfilled lives, but happiness wasn't her priority. She believed it was more vital to be proper and decent. Fun was self-indulgent, wasteful, ungodly; fun was for other, lesser mortals. That attitude must have spilled over into Primrose's development as a normal teenager. In those days, most of Primrose's classmates listened to pirate radio stations, saved up for Beatles singles, back-combed their hair, caked their eyelashes with mascara and went to dances in local village halls. Primrose was not even allowed to go with friends to the two local youth clubs where they played records by the Everly Brothers and Cliff Richard and practiced the jive and the twist. Primrose was even forbidden from going to the local movie theater just down the hill, and there was no question of her ever talking to boys. Apparently she never confronted her mother about these restrictions like most teenagers; instead it seems that

Primrose allowed her anger to fester. One day, she must have said to herself, I will get my own back.

Primrose met one of her few childhood friends–Una Ripley–at Sunday school. Una walked past the Oxtoby house most days on the way to school. Occasionally, Primrose's mother invited Una in, and she'd sit at a scrubbed kitchen table while Primrose finished getting ready. The atmosphere was austere, she later recalled. "It was almost as if there had been a death in the family. No one spoke out of turn. It was full of heavy old furniture. It was like a museum. Her parents were very strict." The inside of the Oxtoby house was dark and formal with heavy mahogany furniture. There was a piano, which Primrose struggled to play.

At the age of 13, Primrose obtained a newspaper route which enabled her to get free comics. She would pore over the girly stories of horses and fairy tale princes in magazines such as *Bunty*, the only comic her mother allowed her to bring home.

None of Primrose's classmates or friends knew what she did on the weekends, because she was so rarely allowed out to play. "I suppose she sat with her parents reading or doing needlework," said Una Ripley. But Primrose did have pet rabbits in a hutch in the garden, and the family had a small black poodle. "I think they replaced it with an identical one when it died," added Ripley.

Primrose's only real escape was the local Girl Guide troop (the British equivalent of the Girl Scouts). She adored the weekly meetings and days out, and occasional weekend camps. Another friend, Pauline Elson, recalled: "My mental picture of Prim is in her navy blue sweater, slacks and wellies [Wellington boots], lugging a large piece of wood for the campfire. She joined in, got on with things. She loved it."

At Girl Guides, Primrose was known as "the one who organized us all." Fellow member Esther Barnes recalled: "She was sensible, with short hair. Tomboyish in appearance. She was more into games, and she loved to take over the organization of the food for us all."

The most daring thing anyone can ever remember Primrose doing at Girl Guides was when she asked for a cigarette from a group of young police cadets whom they met while out hiking. But as her friend Una later recalled: "She only took a couple of puffs at it—and I never saw her smoke again."

Meanwhile Edna Oxtoby seemed to revel in her straitlaced, proud and very awkward manner. She reportedly never smiled at neighbors and if anyone upset her, she was extremely unforgiving. When neighbors asked the family to stop working on a fireplace they were building at midnight, they found a handwritten note from Edna pushed through their mailbox the next morning. It stated that from that moment on she would have nothing more to do with them. There was no confrontation. Edna's way was to cut people off completely.

When Primrose let her guard drop to one school friend, what emerged was a disturbing insight into her teenage mentality. "She was a real plain Jane back then," recalled Julie Goddard. "She wasn't happy about it, but I kept telling her it would change as she grew up. It never did."

Occasionally a sense of humor bubbled to the surface, but there were also many moments of stubbornness. "There would be a glint in her eyes," said Una Ripley. "And then you'd never get her to do anything she didn't want to do."

By the final year of school, Primrose was aged 15 and five feet, four inches tall, with a sturdy build that didn't exactly provoke admiring glances from the teenage boys of Wetherby. The boys weren't interested in shy, awkward Primrose, with her pudding-basin hairstyle, scrubbed face, twinset and pearls, pleated skirts and clumpy flat shoes. Most classmates barely recall her; she was the school nonentity. The only reason anyone remembered her was her unusual name.

But underneath the straight exterior, Primrose knew that

times were changing, and she was determined to show her mother that she was an independent spirit.

Primrose's attitude was in stark contrast to her chaste older sister Mary, who fitted the family's moral code much better. Mary had settled into a job as a nurse in an old people's home, but never married. She eventually developed multiple sclerosis and had to move into a care home because she could not look after herself.

Naturally, teenage Primrose would have become fascinated with sex as she entered puberty. Her parents' puritanical attitude meant that the subject was absolutely taboo in the house, and the family didn't even have a TV set to switch off if anything unsuitable came on screen. As was typical of the time, Primrose's sex education was extremely limited and it is unlikely that either of her parents ever discussed the facts of life with her. Without any explanation of pregnancy or contraception, or even what a period was, Primrose would have been left to try to glean most of her information from other girls at school.

In September 1964, Primrose was just fifteen and a half years old and about to start college in Leeds after winning a place on an art and design course. School friend Julie Goddard later recalled: "She did a painting of hats not long before the end of term. It was really good. I can remember it to this day. It showed she had some real artistic talent."

Primrose joined a group of her school and Girl Guide friends who met at the local bus station before riding into Leeds for their various jobs and colleges. There were always between six and ten of them, and they talked about clothes, make-up, music and . . . boys. Most of the other passengers took no notice of them.

Just being on that forty-minute bus ride was exciting for Primrose, especially since she knew it worried her mother that she was now out in the big, wide world. That year at college greatly helped her become more independent from her parents. Sometimes she even defied her mother by coming back late in the evening after stopping for coffee with a friend. At the end of that year, Primrose was awarded a college certificate and quickly found a job as a window dresser. Soon she was defying her mother by indulging herself in new, modern clothes and make-up. She even started going to the movie theater with friends, and each morning she continued to catch the number 38 bus into the center of Leeds. It wasn't much longer before she spotted a handsome, dark-haired young man sitting at the back of the bus.

Medical student Fred Shipman had just started living at digs in 164 Wetherby Road, Wetherby, in an area called Wellington Hill. Landlady Mrs. Copley did her best to put young Fred at ease. Taking in students was a sideline for her and her husband which supplemented the earnings of their greengrocery business. Fred and another student at the same digs, Peter Congdon, looked like smart young men compared to most as they traveled on the 38 bus to medical school each day.

Some time toward the end of his first year at medical school, Fred Shipman caught Primrose glancing flirtatiously across at him. Fred thought she was just another working-class moron, and looked away. For many weeks he didn't speak to her, but Primrose was becoming steadily infatuated. At home she told one friend in a giggly voice: "He keeps catching my eye on the bus . . ." By the end of that month, she told the same friend: "I hope he loves me, and we'll marry some day."

Without any encouragement from Fred Shipman, Primrose's infatuation grew on a daily basis. She didn't even consider going out with other boys. But frustrated by her inability to pull him into a conversation, she started to loathe this snotty young student with his wavy black hair. Primrose was on the verge of giving up her attempts when Fred suddenly asked her out.

Primrose's friends on the bus had watched with amusement and pleasure as shy, plain Primrose became transfixed by the dark stranger on the bus. But what none of them realized was that Primrose had no one to seek advice from about this blossoming relationship. She didn't dare tell her mother that she had met a boy. She was extremely dowdy and naive.

By all accounts, Primrose, just 16, really didn't know much about sex. As one of her contemporaries later explained: "You let them kiss you, but that was it. We didn't get anything in those days in the way of sex education at school, but we all knew we couldn't let our boyfriends go too far. And they knew it, too, and didn't try."

Back then most of the brides whose weddings were featured in the local *Wetherby News* were virgins. Their families expected them to be, as did their future husbands. Girls who "did it" before marriage were called "slags" and "tarts." The reality was that back in the mid-1960s fewer than 8 percent of all babies were born out of wedlock, compared with five times that amount in today's society.

In many ways, Fred and Primrose were made for each other. There were so many subjects they simply knew nothing about. They were both nervous—almost afraid—of the ever-changing world around them. Even photos in newspapers of scantily clad women brought embarrassed responses from Fred Shipman.

Fred and Primrose were both, it seems, lonely and frustrated. The secretive glances between them on top of a double-decker bus were founded on a subconscious recognition that they needed each other. Fred had been terrified of rejection. Primrose was just as scared, but she was also extremely excited by the idea of having a relationship with a man.

When losing one's virginity, said Queen Victoria, one must close one's eyes and think of England. Attaching a little more lyricism to the act, the great romantics, from Cervantes to Byron, saw virgins as roses and their deflowering a poem to passions that would saddle lions.

Fred Shipman's first and only taste of real romance—not necessarily the actual act of making love, but certainly a beginning—apparently came within a few days of meeting

his first-ever girlfriend, Primrose Oxtoby. After all those
brief exchanges on the double-decker bus, Primrose found
herself with no choice but to make the first move. Eventually she asked the shy medical student: "Are you going to
take me to the pictures [movies], or what?"

The night of their first date, Fred and Primrose met secretly at the end of her street before jumping on a bus to
the local movie theater in Wetherby. However, as Primrose
later told one of her few friends, they hardly touched each
other that night, and even conversation between the two was
strained because of Fred's shyness. But Primrose was not
easily deterred.

A few nights later she and Fred shared a few beers in a
local pub, and once again she had to make the first move.
She got things going by casually dropping a hand on the
seat beside him. Then she started playing with his fingers.
Minutes later, she later told a friend, they finished their
drinks, and lunged at each other in a nearby alleyway, sort
of kissing, only they didn't seem able to put their mouths
in the right place at first.

Fred's head was spinning and he could hardly breathe
from excitement. Primrose could hear, she recalled, her heart
banging away in her eardrums. Once or twice she opened
her eyes to make sure his eyes were closed, and they were,
so she reckoned he must have meant it. After that, the couple
felt as if they had already made love, and could talk more
easily together. Things apparently soon got pretty hot and
heavy between them. Fred and Primrose must have been
floating along, clinging to each other for dear life. They
knew there was no one or nothing else that mattered from
that moment onwards. Primrose quickly found herself con-
templating a future with this shy, awkward medical student.
Fred was still hiding the pain and anguish of losing his
mother, so being romantic was a welcome diversion, although he remained terrified of rejection.

One day Primrose astonished her parents by bringing Fred
Shipman home. She'd never had a boyfriend before, and

now here she was standing there with a fully grown medical student in the dark and austere living room of the Oxtoby house. Fred was usually silent and moody in company, but on this day he tried to be more animated, making small talk about his plans for the future. Primrose's parents were deeply suspicious of this handsome-looking young man with his wavy, jet black hair. He talked very quietly and properly, and his voice was so gentle they found it difficult to understand what he was saying at times.

When Fred had departed, Primrose's parents were united in their dislike of their daughter's first boyfriend. Mr. Oxtoby told his daughter they thought he seemed a little old for her, and that she should have nothing more to do with him. But within weeks the two became inseparable—although Primrose never again would make the mistake of bringing Fred back to meet her family.

Fred and Primrose now had the opportunity to experiment with each other in every sense of the word. Heavy kissing soon led much further. Making love must have provided them with a new-found freedom that neither thought they would ever experience. But despite Fred Shipman's medical training, he apparently made no attempt to use a condom, later admitting that he was too shy to go into a pharmacy and ask for one. It seems that Fred and Primrose were so swept up by the passion of their alliance that they felt no fear about the risks they were taking.

So, Fred Shipman's life-defining romance was with a girl who, although by no means stupid, was by his standards poorly educated. She was only three years younger than him, but that gap was huge when they were 19 and 16. (In Britain at that time, the legal age for sex was sixteen years.) No doubt Primrose was deeply impressed by Fred's university status. Meanwhile, his profound dislike of her parents was based entirely on their dislike of him. Perhaps they saw through him and were suspicious of him from the first encounter.

Back in the outside world, Fred and Primrose were going steady, and even invited two other medical students—boyfriend and girlfriend—back to their digs, where Primrose cooked them all a traditional Sunday lunch, serving Yorkshire pudding with gravy. The guests later recalled that the food was excellent, but the atmosphere in the house was depressing.

Primrose was evidently soon sleeping with Fred on a regular basis, so it was hardly surprising when she got pregnant. But, as one old school friend later explained: "She was the last person on earth we expected to get pregnant."

However, the prospect of a little baby presented Primrose with the perfect chance to completely escape from her mother's tightly knit world. And it has to be said that Fred Shipman did not need much pressure from Primrose to persuade him to get married.

Primrose first shared the news of her pregnancy with Pauline North, one of the girls she traveled with on the 38 bus. Leaning against the kitchen worktop in Pauline's apartment, Primrose came right out with it. " 'I'm pregnant. Out of the blue, no build-up—I nearly dropped everything," Pauline later recalled. "I'd never have even put them together in the first place, they were an odd couple. So when Prim came round to my flat and told me, I was shocked." Pauline continued: "I can't remember if she told me where it happened. My first and main thought was about her father and mother, because they were so old-fashioned and prim and proper."

Primrose still hadn't told her mother at that stage. "But she didn't seem worried, even though she should have been. Perhaps she was just putting on a brave front for me, but she genuinely seemed very relaxed about it," Pauline later recalled.

In fact, both families were horrified by the news. Harold Shipman even told his son that he was relieved his wife was dead. Fred was mortified, because he would never do anything to upset his dearly departed mom. Pauline Shipman simply refused to talk about the "scandal." Fred would never forgive them for their cruel response at his time of need. Things had been building up to this ever since Vera Shipman's death. Fred Shipman now felt completely and utterly alone. How he wished his mother was alive to give him some help and support.

Primrose's parents Edna and George were equally shaken to the core. Many of their friends claim to this day that the pregnancy "broke Edna's heart." A pregnancy out of wedlock was shameful even though the young couple were happily arranging a wedding. Edna even insisted that Fred and Primrose could not get married in Wetherby because people might see Primrose's "bump."

The Oxtobys already detested Fred, despite his bright future as a doctor. Most working-class moms would have been proud if their daughters came home with a quiet, caring trainee doctor like Fred Shipman. But call it what you will, there was something about young Fred that neither Edna nor George could put their finger on. They didn't like him. He seemed morbid and non-communicative. And there was something about his eyes that seemed very shifty.

But Fred and Primrose decided their wedding should go ahead, and they set a date for November 5, 1966, when Shipman would have just completed his first year at medical school.

Hand in hand, the young lovers climbed the steps of the Barkstone Ash Register Office on November 5, 1966. The bride wore a long blue dress. The groom wore a white shirt, a dark tie and an ill-fitting black suit that would have more befitted a funeral than a wedding. Once inside, streams of light from the stained-glass dome highlighted the shine of Primrose's dark pageboy-style hair. She was a tad on the plump side. Fred and Primrose clung to the iron-rail banister as they ascended the stone steps to the ground-floor office of the Registrar of Births, Deaths and Marriages.

From the large windows that spanned the spacious room, they could see the vast trees of the adjoining park, plus some of the civic buildings that dated from before Victorian times. Within minutes they were husband and wife.

Fred and Primrose pledged each other complete and utter loyalty before retiring to a nearby pub without any of their few relatives and friends, who had already dispersed. Primrose's mother and Fred's father were present, but they barely exchanged glances. That was it: the start of married life. No honeymoon. No gifts. No smiles from dozens of guests. No speeches. Just a functional marriage for a functional reason.

It hadn't exactly been the type of wedding that every young girl dreams of, but that wouldn't have mattered one iota to Primrose. She couldn't have been happier; all that mattered to her was that she had married the man of her dreams. To complete the day (and night), he took her back to his digs and carried her over the threshold.

Years later Shipman told one associate that it had all been an awful mistake. "I was a bright boy, I should have known better, shouldn't I?" he said. That associate got the impression that Shipman might never have married Primrose if the pregnancy hadn't happened.

Primrose was a shy, quietly spoken window dresser whose family came from similar working-class stock as the Shipmans. She might not have had the same high-flying ambitions as her young husband, but she was fiercely loyal. Some of Fred's fellow students at Leeds University recall Primrose getting "quite aggressive" whenever anything negative was said about her husband.

In some ways they were made for each other.

On the same day that Fred and Primrose married, the local *Wetherby News* featured a slew of white weddings. "Given away by her father, the bride wore a white satin dress with embroidered motifs, a bouffant veil and camellia headdress. Her bouquet was a pale lemon rose and white heather . . ." and on it went. For Edna Oxtoby, it must have further compounded the anger she felt about the shotgun wedding of her dearly beloved daughter. Primrose's pregnancy at the age of seventeen had opened a gaping wound with her strict Methodist parents which would never heal.

The final few weeks of Primrose's pregnancy, she lived at her parents' home in Wetherby. Fred rarely made an appearance at the house, and the couple usually met at nearby cafés.

On February 14, 1967, at Harrogate General Hospital, Primrose presented Fred with a baby daughter, Sarah Rosemary. Primrose's parents naturally adored their first grandchild, but their relationships with Primrose and Fred were very strained. The couple and their infant child eventually found an apartment near Blackman Lane, in the Woodhouse district of Leeds, a classic student area featuring narrow streets filled with small houses converted into flats and bedsits.

Fred and Primrose somehow managed to settle down and present a picture of contentment and normality to the outside world. Primrose truly admired her husband. She respected him for doing the right thing and marrying her when she became pregnant, and she trusted him implicitly. She believed he would make a fine doctor. She told him often enough, encouraging him not to let up when Sarah was a baby and he was laboring over lecture notes at night. They were going to have a fantastic life together and neither of their families was going to ruin that. Primrose already believed she and Fred could take on the world. Nothing else mattered.

Primrose, not yet 18, seemed to revel in her new life, despite the obvious financial hardships. She enjoyed the mechanics of running a home: she knew about cleaning and cooking, and she enjoyed baking cakes and pies. Bringing up a baby didn't pose any problems, because she didn't care about not going out with her friends.

Dr. Susan Pearson—also married with a baby while still in medical school with Fred—was one of the first students to encounter Mr. and Mrs. Shipman. She and a couple of other students had been on a placement at a nearby hospital when Fred invited them all in for tea. Primrose wasn't expecting them, but she laid out tea, sandwiches and cakes within minutes of their arrival.

Dr. Pearson later recalled it as a very welcoming home.

Baby Sarah was toddling around by this stage, toys were
scattered about the room, which was clean and well cared
for. "It was much more appealing than the usual student flat,
because of the baby's things. It was a relief to go there, you
felt cozy and welcome. Primrose said very little, but she
looked after everybody."

But what Primrose didn't realize was that her emotionally
immature husband's views about his own mother's death
had become completely skewed during the grieving process.
In many ways he'd felt abandoned and rejected by Vera
Shipman and he began thinking, "How dare you leave me?"
This helped explain why he rushed into the relationship with
Primrose.

4

Many might say that, because Fred Shipman's main guiding light—his mother—left him at such an early, impressionable age, he didn't know where certain behavioral boundaries existed. It meant he was capable of anything, whether ethical or not.

Fred Shipman was an impoverished 20-year-old medical student facing the intense pressures of being a husband and father. Occasionally, he escaped it all by slipping down to the local pub and downing a few pints of beer while Primrose stayed at home with their baby daughter.

At medical school though, Shipman became intrigued by other drugs following his interest in sniffing liniment at High Pavement. As part of their psychology studies, students were encouraged to carry out experiments on themselves, usually working in pairs. They performed such routine procedures as measuring each other's oxygen consumption. But there were also more unpleasant experiments such as swallowing tubes to monitor gastric juices, and drinking gallons of water to determine if it had an intoxicating effect. One grisly experiment involved blood being taken from earlobes.

It was during these tests that Fred Shipman encountered morphine for the first time since his mother's illness. Fred was fascinated with the drug, and decided to carry out his own "experiment" to discover whether his mother really had been "put out of her pain," as the family's GP had promised. Shipman was curious to know exactly what morphine felt like, so one night, after downing a few pints of beer at his local pub, he found Primrose fast asleep and decided it was the perfect moment to sample the potent painkiller.

The following morning, Primrose found her husband slumped asleep on the armchair in the living room. He said he'd fallen asleep after drinking a few beers. Shipman never dared admit to Primrose that he'd injected himself with one of the most powerful drugs known to mankind—and that the feeling had been out of this world. All his fears disappeared. He didn't get high. He didn't get stoned. He just didn't give a damn.

At the end of their second year at medical school in Leeds, students were put into specific groups, usually of four, on two-month cycles. This way they got to work with a cross-section of patients and specialists as they began the practical part of their studies in specific area hospitals. During this period of his studies, Fred Shipman's time was spent at the Leeds General Infirmary, but there were also stints at St. James's, in Menston, the Highroyd Hospital, in Leeds, and one stint in Wakefield, thirty miles to the east of the city.

At the end of that three years came a month of finals—the exams which would enable Fred Shipman to be provisionally registered as a doctor. Shipman was registered with the General Medical Council, number 1470473, on August 5, 1971. He'd graduated as a Bachelor of Medicine/Surgery.

While many in his class achieved honors degrees in that summer of 1971, Shipman scraped by with only a "pass" and immediately began looking for a position as a pre-registration, junior doctor. His registration would only come after his first "proper" job. While the majority of Fred's fellow students found proper placements in Leeds hospitals, for married students like Fred, the trick was to obtain a junior housemanship in one of the satellite hospitals, where there was more likely to be proper housing for a young family. With a stroke of luck, Shipman found a hospital in the nearby town of Pontefract with the perfect accommodation for Primrose and little Sarah, now a lively three-year-old.

*   *   *

Working as a junior houseman at Pontefract General Infirmary was tough for Fred Shipman; long hours, low pay, emergency room incidents. He was always accompanied by a more senior doctor, but was constantly in demand for non–life threatening injuries of patients. It was almost like a test to see if he really had what it took to be a devoted doctor. Many years later, Shipman joked that if you could cope with being a junior houseman, then prison was an easy ride in comparison.

Nine months into his first year at Pontefract, the Shipmans' second child, Christopher Frederick Shipman, was born at Wakefield Maternity Hospital on April 21, 1971. The family home in the grounds of the hospital was part of a solid, red-brick 1930s complex of houses. Because of the long hours he worked, living within the hospital made life much easier for Fred Shipman, and there were plenty of shops and amenities in the hospital complex for Primrose and their two young children.

The course at Pontefract was a tough round of theory and practical classes, leaving the eighty students with little time for energy or socializing, let alone bringing up a young family. The first two years at medical school had been half theory—basic science and lab work—and half practice, which meant visits to wards to meet real patients. But now Fred was out on his own. As one of Shipman's fellow students later explained: "You had to quickly learn how to deal with people, how to treat patients with respect, to be professional and polite and understanding and honest. How to be a doctor."

However, Fred Shipman wasn't exactly a medical high flyer. His leap into marriage and fatherhood had been made partly to help him avoid the more lively social scene favored by many medical students. Most junior doctors at Pontefract popped across the road to the Victoria, the local pub, for a chat and a pint of beer, while Fred would wearily pack up his books and shuffle home to Primrose. The only time he

drank was alone at another pub, where he knew he wouldn't
bump into any other medics.

Shipman never openly complained about his predicament. In fact, he proudly referred to his two young children
and wife in the most glowing terms. "It was almost as if he
felt a little superior to us, because he was already at a more
adult stage of his life," recalled one former student.

Fred Shipman retained that burning ambition to achieve
his mother's dreams of success for him. He was single-
minded. It wasn't going to be easy to succeed after coming
from an underprivileged background, but he intended to do
just that. Having a young family and keeping up his studies
required a very focused attitude. He was under severe pressure, struggling financially. But Fred Shipman firmly believed he could overcome such obstacles. He felt as if his
mother was always watching over him, and he would never
dare let her down.

At Pontefract General Infirmary, Shipman worked under
general surgeon consultant Mr. L. C. Bell, aural surgery
consultant Mr. K. Mayll and medical consultant Dr. J.
Turner. After two years, he would be qualified for full registration with the General Medical Council. Additionally,
while still living in the hospital accommodation at Friar-
wood Lane, Pontefract, Shipman also took a diploma in
child health and a Royal College Diploma in Obstetrics and
Gynecology.

Throughout all this period, Fred Shipman's interest in
drugs continued. Thanks to the long hours and grueling
work schedule at Pontefract, he started to use another easily
available narcotic called pethidine (known in the United
States as Demerol). It was a dangerous move for someone
who undoubtedly had an addictive personality.

Fred Shipman was first attracted to pethidine in order to
"come down" after his adrenaline-filled casualty department
shifts. He worked incredibly long hours before going home
to Primrose and the children. He needed the drugs to help
him sleep. He also enjoyed the sensation that pethidine produced; a "wide open" state of mind, as if he could not pull

down the shutters against the blazing light of reality that was beating through the window. And once he'd started, he needed more and more.

Pethidine, similar to another opiate, morphine, was known in the medical profession as a strong *narcotic* analgesic. Pethidine tended to be used mainly in hospitals to relieve severe pain during labor and after operations. Sometimes it was used as a premedication before surgery.

Shipman adored the rapid rush that pethidine caused. As one who has taken it frequently explained: "It takes effect quickly, but its effect lasts only for a short time. But it takes you to such heights that it's worth the ride."

This meant that Shipman, just before he knew he was going to have thirty minutes alone after work, could sit down, roll up his sleeve and deliver the injection, his nerves already tingling with expectation.

Pethidine quickly proved itself habit-forming for Fred Shipman. As one user explained very clinically: "Both tolerance and dependence can develop when the drug is used regularly." In other words, using pethidine for anything other than a genuine medical reason was highly risky.

As a legitimate painkiller, hospitals recommended using a maximum dosage of 150 mg every four hours. Shipman was soon taking doses every two hours. He knew only too well what to look for in terms of an overdose reaction. As one medical reference book pointed out: "Seek immediate medical advice in all cases. Take emergency action if there are any symptoms such as muscle twitching, nervousness, shallow breathing, severe drowsiness, or loss of consciousness." Driving under the influence of pethidine was extremely dangerous, and any use of alcohol could seriously increase the sedative effects of the drug.

If it had not been for the discovery of drugs, Fred Shipman later surmised, he might not have survived medical school and the pressures of being a father at such a young age. Pethidine seemed to remove the usual "filters" from his normal perception of life. It felt as if he were playing a record at full volume. But those "filters" he was removing were there to aid his mind to work and grasp at a strange kind of reality.

Pethidine weakened his willpower while undoubtedly strengthening his incoming stimuli, which meant that he immediately experienced an increase in intensified perception. It was the perfect drug to enable him to continue his long, arduous hours in Pontefract. But injecting himself with drugs was a risky business, because it weakened certain elements of his self-control. It was all a question of maintaining a balance.

Shipman rapidly became frightened and fatigued by his overuse of illicit drugs. He was subjecting his body to endless abuse, and with those drugs came a general mistrust of the world around him. Life was already becoming confused for Fred Shipman. Work was strange and impersonal. He wanted to simply withdraw inside himself, roll up in a ball, like a child in a warm bed, and pull the blankets up. But he couldn't do that; he had already burdened himself with so many responsibilities.

The strain of his job as an overworked, underpaid junior doctor was producing an inner revulsion for everything around him. Shipman talked to few of his colleagues and seemed guarded most of the time. He'd long since decided to mind his own business, which is, in fact, a mild form of schizophrenia. Shipman had self-chosen a state of isolation that was on the verge of turning into a complete alienation from people in general.

But his use of drugs also gave Fred Shipman the confidence to begin looking for a job as a general practitioner. He and Primrose both agreed that they wanted to stay in the Yorkshire area. Eventually Shipman spotted a job advertisement in a medical magazine for a position in the main medical center of Todmorden, a town near Leeds.

5

Todmorden is a quiet, unassuming market town sitting on the edge of the Pennines amongst countryside of high moorlands, limestone slopes, steep-sided valleys, and plunging waterfalls. Its plentiful supply of water provided the basis for a thriving cotton industry in the mid- to late 1800s, when much of the income from manufacturing was plowed back into the community. Todmorden lay in the shadow of vast Whirlaw Hill and at the end of day, the sun dropped behind the hill as gusts from the craggy slopes shook the red and pink seasonal decorations at the top of Halifax Street, the town's main road.

Todmorden was a self-contained town, a ribbon of dark Victorian millstone grit in a narrow defile where the River Calder cut deep beneath high, wild moors. There was barely enough room for the main road to Burnley and the Trans-Pennine railroad to squeeze through the gap. As a border town, Todmorden was governed by a Yorkshire local authority but had a Lancashire postal address. Up the valley was the once mighty cotton capital of Burnley, downstream was Halifax. In all other directions, nothing but bleak moor–the kind where Cathy Earnshaw might be found calling for her Heathcliff. Todmorden's damp, bronchial climate, exacerbated by damp mists that lingered in the steep valley, made it one of England's great cotton towns, with 1,800 looms clattering through the Victorian fog.

In Todmorden, as everywhere else in the industrial north of England, the basic industry set the pattern of life: steel in Sheffield, coal in Barnsley, wool in Bradford and Huddersfield. Up until the First World War, cotton had been Britain's most successful industry. That industry gave Todmorden a Lancashire way of working and living, carried over to Yorkshire's steep valleys. Red-brick mills rose across the horizon back then. Life centered on those mills.

Todmorden's physical decay in the mid-1970s reflected its industrial heritage of the 1800s and the early part of the 1900s. Yet there was a wealth of sturdy Victorian buildings and the once picturesque Rochdale Canal waterway flowed right through the town. The population of Todmorden had fallen by 50 percent and was standing at around 12,000 by the time Fred Shipman got his first GP job. There had been little investment in the town center for many years and the poverty of many residents had even attracted European and governmental funding for the run-down districts of the community. Todmorden needed a good rail link, a renovation of its canal, a stronger market town identity and the reoccupation of a lot of buildings in the town center if it was going to thrive as it had during those boom years of the cotton industry a hundred years earlier.

Civic pride, however, was still everywhere in Todmorden, thanks mainly to the Fielden family, a powerful and benevolent mill-owning dynasty who built tiny Todmorden a Grade 1 listed town hall that would not look out of place in a major city. By now its main use was as a ballroom, the venue for Monday afternoon tea dances. Todmorden remained a hard place in many ways; the churchyard contained numerous examples of child mortality. Many were laid beneath the earth in their twenties and thirties from climate, disease or the toil and danger of the Industrial Revolution. But the town had a long tradition of looking after itself. Maybe that is why newly qualified Dr. Fred Shipman found it so easy to blend in with the surroundings.

There was no movie theater. Just fifty pubs and a club. The streets of Todmorden were completely deserted by 5 P.M. A few modern buildings had replaced the mills, and the number of churches had shrunk to three. Yet much of the gray stone housing remained, as did many of the shops and businesses. In Todmorden, they liked to think that all their hard work in the cotton mills helped the south get even more prosperous—while they and the rest of the north of England fell further and further behind.

It was just the type of place where Fred Shipman would feel at home.

In March 1974, Fred was taken on as a junior GP at the Todmorden Group Practice run by Dr. Michael Grieve. The handsome young doctor and his family were initially greeted as a breath of fresh air. Within a month, "young Fred," as Grieve called him, was promoted from assistant to principal GP. He immediately rolled up his sleeves and began working day and night for the good of the practice. As Dr. Grieve later recalled: "Young Fred fitted in well. He was enthusiastic and interested in every stage of the medical profession. He was almost too good to be true."

The Shipmans purchased a picturesque greystone house on a street called Sunnyside on the hill overlooking the center of Todmorden. It was a comfortable four-bedroom semi-detached house commanding excellent views, yet within walking distance of the medical clinic and all the town's main stores.

According to Dr. Grieve, most patients adored young Fred. "He had a lot of fans. I remember there was one girl, whose baby he delivered, who still, to this day, thinks the world of him."

And Fred Shipman's treatment of patients went from strength to strength; When 10-year-old Karen Shepherd was diagnosed by another doctor as having blood poisoning, Fred Shipman stepped in and said it was osteomyetis. He was absolutely correct and, in effect, saved little Karen's life. Some months later, Karen's younger sister was diagnosed by Shipman as having a hole in her heart after other doctors had failed to pick it up. Senior partner Dr. Grieve later recalled: "He made that extra special bit of effort to find out what was wrong with a patient, and it paid off handsomely."

Another patient, truck driver Frank Scott, never forgot how Shipman rushed over to his home to deliver his wife's baby. A year later, Shipman repeated the delivery with a second Scott child. "The man was a saint, a really good person. He treated us so well. I'll never forget what he did for this family," Frank Scott later recalled.

"Young Fred" even helped teach his colleagues how to fit intrauterine devices, which were then coming into use for the first time. "He was very good technically and very good clinically," recalled Dr. Grieve. "He'd got all the right qualifications and worked well. Mothers thought the world of him. Mind you, he was good with everyone."

It was also noted inside the Todmorden practice that Fred Shipman was constantly pushing himself to the limit. "He was always rushing around like a maniac. Always everything last-minute. He never stopped," recalled one patient. "You couldn't keep up that pace without something happening. He was on course for a major burn-out."

Fred Shipman had continued using pethidine following his experimentation with the drug while at Pontefract. For the moment, no one in Todmorden had any idea that their new young doctor was an intravenous drug addict, but they did hear other rumors.

Around this time—1974—some of Shipman's younger patients were told that the handsome young doctor was willing to prescribe slimming tablets containing amphetamines—"speed"—even if the patient was clearly not overweight. The drug culture had been sweeping Britain's youth for the previous ten years, and many people under the age of thirty were willing to experiment with just about any chemical.

One local girl who was supplied with amphetamines (she's now a happily married mother of three) recalled: "We were all in our early twenties and you know what you're like, and someone said we could get these slimming pills off Dr. Shipman. It was only him at the practice who was willing to supply them. He'd give them to you. All we had to do was go in and just ask him, simple as that. He didn't even bother weighing you to see if you were overweight. I went to see him at least once a month. He used to give us a big bottle with 100 amphetamine tablets. I'd take one and be up all night doing whatever. I can't remember how many times I went to see him, but he never once bothered to examine me. Nothing. He was never awkward about supplying them, and never made any comment about what they were really for. I'd be in and out in a minute. He'd just say, 'How many?' Very cavalier attitude. When I realized afterwards what was in those tablets, I thought it was strange."

But it was the expression on Shipman's face that the woman never forgot. "It was a really weird look, a kind of smirk would wipe across his face, then it would return to doctor mode within a split second. He looked so satisfied with himself. I'll remember that look for the rest of my life. When I thought about it later, it was obvious he knew exactly what he was doing. He just didn't mention it directly. It's only afterwards I realized he must have known."

But Dr. Grieve wasn't surprised when he heard that Fred Shipman illicitly prescribed slimming pills to some of the town's youth. He said: "Most people prescribed sleeping pills easily at this time. He'd come from Pontefract, which was where there was a big drug problem."

The clinic was regularly patrolled by the local police following an incident when two men walked into the practice armed with a knife and demanded drugs. Moments later one of them tried to overdose in the treatment room. Virtually every doctor in the practice had been physically attacked at some stage.

Naturally, none of the patients or staff had any idea that Fred Shipman was himself a habitual user of pethidine at that time. "He never seemed out of it. He was very nice. He was very, very popular," recalled the woman who was prescribed the amphetamines.

She and her gang of friends used to visit clubs in nearby Wigan, where the speed tablets would help them stay up all night to dance. "There wasn't much to do in Todmorden at the weekends, so it was a welcome relief to get out to Wigan. It was mainly young girls who took them, but when

I decided to stop, I handed them over to a guy I knew who went and sold them off in one of the clubs in Wigan. I suppose Shipman might have thought he was living his youth through us."

But behind the drug addiction there was another "respectable" side to Fred Shipman's life. He'd become a much valued member of the Rochdale Canal Society, an organization specifically set up to help preserve the local waterway that ran through the Todmorden valley. Society secretary Brian Holden explained: "I was in awe of Fred in many ways. After all, he was a doctor, and they were treated with the utmost respect in a place like Todmorden."

Holden didn't discover until many years later that Shipman—who had begun to age at an alarming rate—was fifteen years younger than him. "I always presumed he was close to my age because he seemed to stoop and his reactions were like that of an older person." Only in his late twenties, Fred Shipman felt the pressures of responsibility as a father, husband and local practitioner. "He moved in a virtual shuffle, like a man approaching his fifties," explained Holden, then 45. "I had a great deal of respect for him. In fact we all tended to bow and scrape to Fred because he seemed such a caring doctor."

Shipman was extremely reliable at turning up with Primrose at the canal society's Saturday afternoon sessions by the waterway, during which volunteers helped clean out the canal and rebuild some of the worn-away brickwork. Holden also recalled: "Fred would do the digging and Mrs. Shipman would brew the tea, which was very nice of her. They certainly were not afraid to muck in and help out."

But Brian Holden found it difficult to call Primrose by her first name. As he later explained: "I couldn't bring myself to call her that, because, it seemed such a silly name. I always called her 'Mrs. Shipman' . . . she certainly did seem much younger than him, but I always found her perfectly polite."

Brian Holden and his fellow society members were, at

the time, working on a strip of canal between Todmorden and the nearby town of Littleborough. The waterway cut a northward line right through the middle of the town as it kept to the long thin valley. The society also held monthly meetings in the winter at so-called information centers between Manchester and Darby Bridge at each end of the canal. Fred Shipman paid £1 a year in subscription to be a member of the canal society.

Shipman was particularly interested in helping improve the riverside walk and specific buildings labeled "blots on the landscape." Some in Todmorden believed that with the right facelift, the community could be made an attractive destination for tourism. There was also a feeling that anything which improved the appearance of the town would help encourage new residents. "But in those early days we were still considered part of the lunatic fringe," Brian Holden later explained. "Most people in the town thought we were crackers. But Fred didn't seem to mind in the slightest. In fact, I think he rather enjoyed telling people he was a member of the society, because it made him seem more interesting."

Eventually, Shipman even purchased a small dinghy which he used in the society's occasional boat rallies, held to help raise money for the organization. "Anything from a canoe to an inflatable was used for the rallies. Basically it could be anything you could throw in the water and later recover."

The first Rochdale Canal Society regatta in 1975 was a huge success, and the supposedly "unsociable" Shipmans played a major part in it; Primrose provided numerous delicious cakes and kept huge brews of hot tea on the boil. Earlier, Fred Shipman had even sent away a sample of the water from a faucet by the side of the canal to see if it was clean enough to drink. "He was most concerned that we didn't end up poisoned by the water," Holden later recalled. "If anything, he was almost too helpful."

Fred Shipman was genuinely interested in the canal society because it presented him with an opportunity to do something "normal" and integrate himself and his family into the community. He was desperately fighting an addiction to pethidine on one front and with it, a series of strange urges he was beginning to feel toward his patients. Fred Shipman was in a deeply confused state. He wanted to rid himself of these demons and lead the life of a fine, upstanding citizen of Todmorden.

But the more pethidine Fred Shipman injected into his bloodstream, the more unhappy he became. The pressure of long hours at the practice and the confusing messages that had continued to haunt him ever since the death of his mother were converging on each other. He needed a release. The drugs were not enough to help him get through the day. Another type of urge was increasing its power over him, and he felt that the death of his mother lay behind it all.

6

Fred Shipman's attempt to retain a reasonably high level of self-esteem should have manifested itself in a preoccupation with the idea of intellectual and creative eminence in his field as a doctor. But at home he treated his wife and children in a mildly despotic manner, and expected total, unquestioning obedience, becoming highly abusive at the least sign of resistance. He was obsessed with being in the right all the time. He lacked self-criticism and would storm and rage about the most trivial matters, completely unaware that he was really just overindulging himself and wasting everyone's time. His attitude was that Primrose should truly respect him at all times and should not tell him when he was in the wrong. If she ever dared to do that, he took it as the ultimate insult.

"We used to hear the most dreadful shouting between Fred and Primrose," one neighbor recalled. "Fred sounded so demanding, he was always yelling, 'I am telling you . . .' as if his word was all that counted inside the house."

There were other aspects to Shipman's marriage to Primrose that augmented the already intense pressure, he felt. Fred Shipman apparently found intimacy with Primrose uninteresting, so the couple's sex life may have been characterized more by a lack of activity than anything else. Shipman only seemed capable of having a relationship that appeared normal on the condition that it was on his own terms. That was why he so desperately needed to dominate the world around him. Illicit vials of pethidine were not enough in themselves to help him overcome his mother's painful end.

At the clinic, Shipman spent longer and longer hours alone in his office avoiding going home until late most evenings. He'd increased his dosages of pethidine to 300 mg a day (most people could not withstand more than 100 mg) and gave himself a last "booster" injection at around 7:30 P.M. before it was time to walk home for dinner.

Between his strained marriage, exhausting work schedule and addictive use of pethidine, Shipman was clearly a man on the edge.

Authorities suspect that one of the first patients to find herself on the receiving end of Fred Shipman's rapidly deteriorating physical and psychological state was a 72-year-old woman named Ruth Highley, who lived on Maitland Street in the Walsden area of the town.

Her death on May 10, 1974, was unexceptional. On the death certificate, Shipman gave the cause of death as, "(a) Hypothermia and (b) kidney," which were incredibly vague descriptions.

But that first death may have been, in Fred Shipman's eyes, a "mercy killing." Significantly, it was the first death certificate he ever signed—he would sign another twenty-one during his eighteen-month stay in Todmorden.

On August 4, 1974, Fred Shipman—the friendly doctor already renowned as Todmorden's most popular baby specialist after delivering some very awkward births—found himself facing a medical dilemma. Susan and Marek Orlinski's baby son Christian had apparently been born with no problems at their home on Holme Street, in the Lydgate area of Todmorden. However, the following day the infant became extremely ill, and Marek, a local builder, called in the couple's GP, Fred Shipman.

Within minutes of Shipman arriving at the house, baby Christian was dead. The local coroner signed the certificate after Shipman told him the child had died of "sudden death in infancy syndrome." It would be another twenty-five years before it emerged that Fred Shipman may have deliberately killed the child.

Fred Shipman was supposed to be a doctor trained not to kill people, but to care for them. However, Shipman considered all medical treatment as a form of controlled violence. It was obvious in surgery as well as during medical treatment. Shipman knew that he administered drugs all the time which were poisonous if taken incorrectly. Investigators feel that Fred Shipman had now made the transition from being a caregiver to being a deliberate killer. He'd been put on a pedestal by the local community. He felt immortal. He was master of the universe. He was so invincible, he could do anything he wanted.

On August 21, 1974—just a couple of weeks after the death of the Orlinski baby—attractive Elaine Oswald decided to visit Fred Shipman because of a severe pain in her left side. The GP was immediately very concerned and diagnosed a kidney stone problem. He gave her a prescription for Diconal, a painkiller, and told her to take two tablets and stay in bed for three or four days.

Shipman insisted he would call on her personally to take a blood sample. "Leave your front door unlocked so that I can walk in without disturbing you," Shipman told 25-year-old Elaine, who later recalled that she agreed with the GP without even questioning his authority.

But she didn't feel that ill, so she ignored his advice and went shopping in Todmorden town center. Then she went home and rang her husband and her boss at the local Department of Social Security to let them know of her illness. "I curled up in bed with one of my novels. I was just getting drowsy when Dr. Shipman called 'Hello' and came upstairs. I sat up, we chatted and he told me he had just picked up his wife and child. They were waiting outside in his car. As we talked, he took blood from my arm."

Then Elaine passed out. Shipman told her later that she had stopped breathing for five or six minutes, although her heart did not stop. She later recalled: "All I remember is coming to on the bedroom floor, bruised, battered and bleeding from the mouth, surrounded by Shipman, two paramedics and Shipman's wife and child, who were watching the proceedings." Elaine was then dragged outside to the waiting ambulance and forced to stand upright and "move my uncooperative legs."

Shipman then accompanied his young patient on the eight-mile trip to the Victoria Hospital, in Burnley. "Inside the ambulance, someone's hand slapped my face every time my eyes closed," she recalled. Elaine's ordeal continued at the hospital, where she was thought to have overdosed on the painkillers and was forced to have her stomach pumped. As her mother, Mrs. Joyce Taylor, later recalled: "At the time, we believed that Dr. Shipman had saved her life."

In fact, Fred Shipman went to the hospital to ensure that he covered all his tracks. He told staff what he believed had happened. Shipman said that Elaine had suffered an allergic reaction to the painkillers. From that day onwards, she never touched any drugs for fear of an adverse reaction. Elaine Oswald remains completely traumatized by the incident, because she insists she only took two tablets. Her mother says today: "We now wonder what he did to her. Did he inject her with something, or what happened to her?"

It is possible that Fred Shipman's failure to satisfy his urge to kill on that occasion convinced him to stick to older, more vulnerable patients.

On January 21, 1975, 73-year-old widow Lily Crossley died in Todmorden half an hour after a home visit by the young GP. Her brother Douglas Redmond later recalled: "She was slightly ill and had anemia, but she was not ill enough to suddenly die like she did."

Lily was a retired weaver, and one of a family of seven brothers and sisters. "She thought he was a wonderful doctor and trusted him completely," added Mr. Redmond, who only linked the death of his sister to Shipman many years later. "I suddenly thought, 'Oh my God, did he kill her?' " The death certificate signed by Shipman stated that Lily had died from cancer and pernicious anemia.

Later that same day, Fred Shipman went out to visit 84-year-old Elizabeth Pearce. She died minutes later and Shipman put her death down as a cerebral hemorrhage. He then went to the Todmorden home of Robert Lingard, 63, who died minutes after the GP's arrival. Mr. Lingard was a heavy smoker and drinker, but his sudden death came as a shock. His daughter-in-law, Margaret Lingard, a nurse, later recalled: "It was out of the blue. Shipman said, 'He has had a heart attack.'"

And Mrs. Pearce's grandson, George Dobby, later said: "I was shocked to learn that Shipman signed two more death certificates on the same day that my grandmother died."

All three of these patients had been in reasonable health until Fred Shipman came calling. They all died on the same day—January 21, 1975—just seven days after Fred Shipman's 29th birthday.

Later in 1975, a patient named Hubert Dobson went to see Shipman after developing boils across his face and neck. Shipman told 44-year-old Dobson that he was suffering from diabetes, and prescribed 250 mg of Diabinese tablets.

The following day, Dobson, his wife and two children headed off on a driving holiday to the west of England, towing a caravan behind their car. Dobson recalled: "I was driving along some narrow country roads when my vision started going, and I was on the point of a blackout. My eyelids kept dropping and it then became a desperate struggle to stay conscious at the wheel long enough to find a lay-by."

Dobson eventually swerved off the road before collapsing across the steering wheel. When the family returned to Todmorden, he went to see Fred Shipman, who simply dropped the dosage of tablets after he heard what had happened. For the following ten years, Hubert Dobson continued taking the tablets on a regular basis, before finally getting such serious tingling and trembling that he stopped using them altogether.

Some time later, Dobson had to go to the hospital for a routine check-up, and a blood test revealed that he wasn't even suffering from diabetes. When other doctors told him that the GP should have taken all sorts of tests before diagnosing the disease, Dobson concluded that Shipman had taken a guess at his original diagnosis.

On August 9, 1975, Fred Shipman was called to the bedside of 89-year-old William Shaw at the latter's house on Stansfield Road. His daughter Eunice remembers: "Dr. Shipman came along, as our usual GP was about to go on holiday. It was the first time I had ever clapped eyes on him."

Shipman seemed in a hurry, and told Eunice his visit was a mere formality that would prevent the necessity for a postmortem examination. "He was saying all this very loudly in front of my dying father, and I shooed him away saying I didn't want him to hear things like that. I thought that Dr. Shipman was extremely callous in the way he behaved."

William Shaw died, supposedly of natural causes, shortly afterwards, but Fred Shipman's unpleasant bedside manner was never forgotten by other members of the Shaw family.

Following Shaw's death, Fred Shipman started blacking out at the clinic. Concerned staff presumed he was working long hours and was simply exhausted from his grueling routine. Primrose was so worried about her husband's "blackout problems" that she offered to chauffeur him to his house calls just in case he collapsed at the wheel of his car.

No one at that stage—including Primrose—realized that the blackouts were a direct result of the GP's addiction to huge doses of pethidine. Fred Shipman had rapidly used up all the available veins on his arms and legs in a desperate attempt to stay high enough to get through his day's work, which often began at 8 A.M. and didn't end until 9 or 10 in the evening. But suspicious deaths and heavy drug taking were the last thing on the minds of Fred Shipman's fellow doctors in the overstretched practice. Many just presumed the blackouts would stop once he learned to pace his workload more carefully.

In fact, the only serious problem about Fred Shipman as far as the other doctors at the practice were concerned was Primrose. She was still only in her mid-twenties and extremely defensive of her hard-working husband. Like Shipman's fellow students at Leeds, his colleagues in Todmorden noticed that Primrose took offense at even the most harmless of remarks about her husband. She even made it known that she reckoned senior partner Dr. Michael Grieve did not appreciate her husband enough. She claimed that Dr. Grieve preferred the receptionists to her husband.

On one occasion in 1975, Dr. Grieve's wife heard yet another of Primrose's bitter outbursts, and told her in no uncertain terms to "shut up or else." She concluded that Primrose would never last as a doctor's wife.

One of Shipman's other partners in Todmorden, Dr. John Dacre, later recalled: "Fred was a reasonably immaculate man, but the same couldn't be said for his wife. She was obese, scruffy and looked more like a bag lady than a doctor's wife. She was rather on the uncouth side, and we didn't really have much to do with her."

Investigators later surmised that, until his first few murders, Fred Shipman had a blurred self-image that was synonymous with feeling weak and passive. But as soon as he'd started killing other human beings, he experienced a sense of power and purpose, his self-image became clear and life suddenly had a true meaning.

Fred Shipman was not an excessively brutal man; he made a good impression of decency and efficiency in the outside world. But that social personality prohibited him from expressing the violent feelings that lay beneath the surface. By killing a patient, he could ignore his affected social personality and concentrate on the release of the desire to watch someone die. In some ways, Shipman saw his behavior as magical—a violent and unsubtle solution to an extremely subtle problem.

Shipman began to concentrate obsessively on killing people.

Back in the real world, Fred Shipman was trying to make a niche for himself in his first group practice while supporting an ever-growing young family on a modest salary. There was no support from his in-laws, who'd continued their feud with Primrose after her decision to marry Fred, and the couple rarely visited Harold Shipman Senior or Fred's brother and sister, all of whom still lived in Nottingham.

Fred Shipman desperately convinced himself that he'd been driven to drugs and murder after suffering depression. But the drugs were taking an appalling toll on his health. His blackouts became so serious that he had a nasty fall in the bath as he and Primrose were decorating the family home. Primrose had already been ferrying her husband to his home visits because of his ill health. For six months he had been constantly injecting pethidine into his arms and legs. He was also taking extra doses orally.

Eventually his drug use became so bad that Shipman had to announce to his colleagues at the practice in Todmorden that he was suffering from epilepsy. No one disputed his self-diagnosis, and his partners were most sympathetic. Fred Shipman assured them all that he would be fine, and that he'd deal with the illness himself.

Fred Shipman was now a full-time junkie. At least three times a day, he snatched a few minutes alone in the bathroom in order to "jack up" more pethidine. As the quantities increased, so did his desperation to mask his hopeless addiction. He would stay at the practice until long after all the other doctors had left for the day, and feed his habit in isolation, carefully calculating whose names he could continue to claim prescriptions from.

Shipman's veins were on the verge of collapse because he was using so much pethidine.

Fred Shipman saw himself as a modernizer in the practice. He encouraged use of computerized patient lists and a more carefully structured waiting-list system. But when some of those ideas met opposition he became even more disillusioned, or so he later said. And Shipman continued to claim that he was suffering from epilepsy and carried on working long hours despite the concern of his colleagues.

Then a local chemist noticed for the first time that Shipman was prescribing a vast amount of pethidine. Shipman had actually forged more than seventy prescriptions to feed his habit. Sometimes Shipman used part of those prescriptions on patients and retained the rest for his own use. But on other occasions, none of the drugs he prescribed actually went to the patients for whom they were intended. Shipman forged the signature of Nancy Harris, matron at the Scaitcliffe Hall Nursing Home in Todmorden, on many prescriptions. He even signed the backs of the prescription forms to obtain exemption from charges.

Nancy Harris never forgot how Fred Shipman dropped in at the nursing home one evening. "He rushed upstairs, and a moment later rushed downstairs and out of the building. I thought, 'Well, that's strange!' " she later recalled. "There must have been something wrong at the time. He was not like the rest of the doctors, he was like a flash of lightning."

Shipman had only been at the Abraham Ormerod Medical Practise since March 1974, but during his time in the Pennine town—population 15,000—Shipman signed a total of twenty-two death certificates, many more than any other doctor in the practice.

In July 1975, a Home Office drug inspector questioned Fred Shipman about discrepancies in prescriptions. He completely denied any wrongdoing and, for the moment, the inspector went away convinced that perhaps it was all a "misunderstanding" just as Shipman had claimed. The Todmorden druggist who'd first alerted authorities was furious. He had no doubt that Fred Shipman was fraudulently feeding his, or someone else's, illicit drug habit.

One morning, a receptionist at the practice telephoned the same pharmacy to mention that she would be coming by to

pick up a few bandages and dressings. The druggist decided
to leave the drug book open for her to see. She fell for the
bait, and was horrified to notice that it was filled with pages
and pages of entries, all in Shipman's name, all for pethidine, a drug rarely used in day-to-day health care.

Partner Dr. John Dacre later recalled what happened:
"The receptionist came hotfoot across to the surgery [clinic].
I went back and saw all the entries in Shipman's name.
There were thousands of ampoules. It was excessive. We
never use it, except for labor pains or as a painkiller before
you go on to morphine. Everyone was absolutely horrified,"
said Dr. Dacre.

Dacre and his colleague Dr. Lewin discussed the matter
later that day, and decided to investigate further and then
confront Shipman on the following Monday morning. When
senior partner Dr. Michael Grieve was eventually told the
news, he was stunned. "I was fed up, quite honestly. I knew
nothing of it. I had been sat in a surgery with him all that
weekend, then it was all sprung on me."

At a dramatic practice meeting that Monday, one senior
partner, Dr. John Baker, confronted Fred Shipman, who was
sitting to one side. Baker said, "Now, young Fred, can you
explain this?" Baker placed before him the evidence that
showed Shipman had been prescribing pethidine to patients
who never received it.

But from Fred Shipman there was no denial, no embar-
rassment, no remorse. He simply said softly: "I will stop—
can you give me another chance?"

The partners refused. That was when Shipman flew into
a complete rage. Dr. Dacre later recalled: "We were
astounded, amazed to find out what was going on. It was
shattering. It was the first time I had seen him lose his cool.
He stormed out, saying he resigned."

But that wasn't the end of the matter.

Less than an hour later, Primrose Shipman walked in on
the meeting of the GPs, who were still deciding what to do
next. She immediately declared that her husband would not
be resigning. "You'll have to force him out," she said.

It took the practice six weeks to dismiss Fred Shipman from the partnership for breaching practice rules by misusing drugs. In all that time, although not working, he remained on full pay.

Then, in November 1975, the same inspector visited the Todmorden surgery accompanied by a policeman. Shipman was told that it was alleged that he'd been dispensing drugs "in other than proper circumstances." Shipman stunned the two investigators by immediately standing up and saying that he had been injecting himself with pethidine for six months. He also said he was in the habit of taking about 600 to 700 milligrams a day, and explained that he had been depressed when he started taking the drug, and had taken more and more as he became increasingly depressed.

Dr. Dacre advised him to seek immediate help, or risk losing his license. Fred Shipman accepted the advice gratefully and went into the hospital after being given police bail following his arrest on charges of forging prescriptions and stealing drugs.

One consultant psychiatrist who treated Shipman at the time concluded that his drug habit was associated with the GP's feeling of "total failure in his personal and professional life." What none of those doctors or investigators realized was that Fred Shipman was already hiding a dreadful, dark secret which was tearing him apart. He was hooked on killing.

7

Primrose Shipman later admitted to one close friend that those two years in Todmorden were the best days of their lives, and she acknowledged that it was because of her husband's addiction to pethidine. "It turned him from being a morose, quiet, shy sort of person into a bubbly, funny man . . . He was like a different person in many ways. It was truly amazing," she said.

And Shipman's addiction to pethidine certainly improved the couple's social life. Countless party photos of Fred Shipman during this period show the GP drinking chilled wine and laughing with other guests.

For the most part, Fred Shipman had fitted perfectly into Todmorden. Its vast jurisdiction enabled him to go out and make numerous house calls—and he did not hide the fact that, unlike many of his colleagues, he liked making personal visits to patients. He relished the privacy of seeing them in their own homes, away from the prying eyes of receptionists and other doctors.

As Michael Grieve, the doctor who first appointed Shipman, recalled: "Everything was perfect. He'd been working very hard, then we discovered about his illness and periods of unconsciousness. It was a tragedy in many ways."

But Michael Grieve remembered: "A great deal of the pethidine was prescribed on our account. Most of these patients received nothing from Fred. It's easy to be wise after the event. How could I have been so dim? He was being driven around by his wife. She knew he was blacking out, but had no idea about the drugs. Looking back on it, Shipman was working very maniacally before all this was discovered. He got through an enormous amount of work surmising records and putting things onto the computer. The public don't seem to realize that GPs are expected to do the work of ten other people with appallingly inadequate resources. Even the practice computer was paid for by a charity, but all the work was done free of charge. Fred's day was spent getting up, walking to work and then coming home late. He even took the records home at night to do even more work. No wonder he caved in under the pressure."

Grieve is still full of admiration for the way Fred Shipman volunteered to work on the Rochdale Canal. "He'd even bought that little rubber boat so his family could enjoy the canal," recalled Dr. Grieve. "I had a boat at Skipton and I was touched by that, because he was so proud of his boat."

But he added: "Fred was playing a role in the community, except that he was fueling it with this bloody pethidine. Mind you, he probably couldn't have done any of these things without the drugs to keep him going. Other members of the practice were not well—two sick partners had to go part-time. It was tough by anyone's standards."

Dr. Grieve added: "How on earth is a doctor expected to work twenty-four hours a day 365 days a year to cover all his patients any time of the day or night? You drove your own cars. These days they go out with a man in a car with a mobile phone. There was a lot of snow back in those days, and it was so tiring. Even your medical bag was heavier in those days. It was an exhausting job."

Immediately after Shipman was fired, members of the practice went through all their medical records and found that pethidine had been, according to Dr. Grieve, "going out at a rate of knots." Dr. Grieve finds it impossible to this day to concede that Shipman's killing habits began in Todmorden. "I don't agree that he was killing people here. How could he have been doing that? It would have come out when they originally went through the books."

Grieve added: "Look, Fred Shipman was not easy-going

by any means. He was very uptight. Fred pleaded with us to cover him while he tried to get off drugs, but I said, 'You have to go into hospital. Everything must be out in the open. You cannot go around trying to conceal things.' "

Within weeks of Shipman's dismissal on October 10, 1975, a local real estate agent was instructed by Fred Shipman to put the family's beloved house on Sunnyside up for sale. The details were published in the *Todmorden News and Advertiser*. They stated: "PENRHYN, SUNNYSIDE, TODMORDEN. Excellent semi-detached property commanding good open views yet within walking distance of Todmorden town centre. Accommodation: Small hall, through lounge, living room, kitchen; 3 first floor bedrooms; de luxe bathroom, Garage space. Full central heating. Price includes many extras. Viewing by appointment."

Meanwhile, Primrose and the children headed over to Wetherby to try to reconcile with her parents while Fred was treated for his addiction to drugs in a clinic near his favorite city of York. Despite Shipman's addiction, his colleague Dr. Brenda Lewin still thought the world of him. She even visited him at the rehabilitation center, called The Retreat, numerous times after his dismissal.

On February 13, 1976, at Halifax Magistrates' Court, Fred Shipman pleaded guilty to forging prescriptions and stealing drugs, and asked for seventy-four other offenses to be taken into consideration. Remarkably, psychiatrists recommended to magistrates that he be allowed to continue as a doctor. Of course they had no idea that he may have already killed a number of patients. One psychiatrist wrote to the court: "It would be to his advantage if he were allowed to continue to practice. Conversely it would be catastrophic if he were not to be allowed to continue."

Fred Shipman, the small, bespectacled, shy GP, had brilliantly duped some of the most respected medical experts in Britain. None of them even got a hint of the fact that he was allegedly killing patients. Safe in the knowledge that he had escaped justice, Fred Shipman's self-esteem and arrogance began to re-emerge. Shipman wasn't even asked to appear before the British General Medical Council's Professional Conduct Committee. He was told by letter about the consequences of any further misconduct.

The court also heard how, on release from his six-month treatment program, Shipman was due to take up a post as a medical assistant in County Durham, where he would have no access to drugs. Health officials had been told of his conviction, and that he must remain under supervision while he worked under a district physician conducting baby clinics.

Presiding magistrate Dr. Maurice Goldin told Shipman: "It is indeed a very sad case, that almost at the beginning of your career you should find yourself in this position. It is something which, it seems, has been going on for a long time and no one could be more aware of the dangers involved than yourself."

In court, Shipman blamed the surgery for his crimes. He told the magistrate how he had taken drugs as he descended into depression caused by bad relationships with his colleagues. The court also heard from two impressive character witnesses—Ken Fieldsend, the managing director of a Todmorden engineering firm, and local musical conductor Dr. Ben Horsfall. Both said they had confidence in Shipman's ability. As chairman of the bench, Dr. Goldin advised Shipman to "get better and get out of medicine."

Shipman was fined £600 ($930) and ordered to pay £57.78 ($85.00) to Britain's National Health Service in compensation. By now he had lost his job, spent many months in "rehab" and was seeing a psychiatrist. But at least Shipman had helped the Home Office with their inquiries, said Dr. Goldin.

The *Todmorden News and Advertiser* reported Fred Shipman's court appearance in such a low-key manner that it did not even warrant a front-page mention.

Primrose Shipman's hopes of reconciling with her estranged parents were ruined by her husband's court appearance on the drug charges. The couple were once again outcasts, just

as they had been after their hastily arranged marriage. But
that isolation apparently helped them forge a much closer
relationship. It became an "us against the world" mentality.
Primrose remained unflinchingly loyal to Shipman, especially during the two years when he was suffering from
acute depression following his dismissal from the Todmorden practice. Their marriage was described by one psychiatrist, who counseled them in 1976, as "very happy and
stable."

But the highly respected psychiatrist Dr. Hugo Milne,
who examined Shipman while he was in the drug addiction
clinic in York, later claimed that Shipman's "melancholy"
state had put the relationship under immense strain. Dr.
Milne said that Primrose had been "quite unable to understand her husband's withdrawal from normal behavior."

Essentially, Fred needed Primrose desperately, despite
the huge gap in their intellectual capabilities. He wanted
someone to be dependent on him. He'd been overindulged
by his mother, who thought he could do no wrong, and he
needed his wife to adore him and bow to his every whim.
Because Primrose was undoubtedly overwhelmed in many
ways by her more intelligent husband, the relationship suited
Shipman perfectly. He didn't want anyone questioning him,
and he certainly did not take kindly to any criticism. Fred
Shipman needed women to be utterly dependent on him—
his mother, his wife and his female patients. To Primrose,
he was the provider and mentor. In many ways, they were
addicted to each other.

Back in Todmorden, Fred Shipman's former colleagues
were still stunned by the revelations about his "dark side."
Senior partner Dr. Michael Grieve even dismissed Shipman's claims about the other practice members. "He was
enthusiastic and hard-working, and we were pleased with
him. I had sympathy for him even after the case. We did
talk and listen to him. I think it was his own depression that
caused all these problems. He worked incredibly hard to
summarize our notes, harder than was physically possible.

Now we know why—to find out who was on pethidine. Being a doctor is a hell of a job, it's not easy. You get blamed for deaths anyway, even when you've tried to save them. That's why you get drug use with doctors and mid-wives, it can be because they have to try what they're giving their patients."

Before Fred Shipman could bounce back as a GP he had to suffer a few indignities. After his treatment for pethidine addiction was complete, he, Primrose, 10-year-old Sarah and 6-year-old Christopher moved into a small council house on the Burnhill Estate in Newton Aycliffe, County Durham. In many ways, Fred Shipman had come full circle back to the type of life he'd had as a child growing up in Nottingham. But at least the Burnhill Estate was brand new. The houses were designed in a modern, clean-cut way, and were spaced among wide grass verges and privately owned bungalows with pretty gardens. The estate was surrounded by thousands of acres of countryside.

Sarah and Christopher settled into the local schools, and one neighbor recalled: "They were friendly enough; they would say hello. They just seemed nice and normal." But Fred Shipman went out of his way to keep a distance from his neighbors. "I didn't even know he was a doctor," said another.

Fred Shipman only stayed on the estate about a year and another neighbor, Margaret Norms, said that residents were sorry to see them go. "They were a good family, and he was a lovely man."

On September 12, 1977, after a break of one year and 294 days, Fred Shipman landed a job as a clinical medical officer for children of the South West Durham Health Authority, where his role included liaison between the health authority, GPs and community groups.

But that job lasted just eighteen days, before he left for Hyde, near Manchester, and the Donnybrook House group practice. Fred Shipman wanted and expected to get a break back into general practice. He saw an opportunity, and even admitted to the eight partners at the Donnybrook group in

Hyde that he had a drug conviction, but insisted he was clear of his addiction. He got the job.

"All I can ask you to do is trust me on this issue and watch me prove my worth," he told the partners in Hyde. They were impressed by his honesty. They took him at his word and he repaid their trust by immediately throwing himself into the job with great energy and enthusiasm.

Within two years of his shameful expulsion from the Todmorden practice, Fred Shipman was back in general practice with the keys to the medicine cabinet once again.

How was the practice to have known they'd just employed a mass murderer who saw Hyde as the perfect killing fields to continue his sick and twisted habits . . . ?

8

Hyde is a suburb southeast of England's third largest city, Manchester, 200 miles north of London. This Lancashire community is located on the edge of the Peak District national park. Just a few miles down the road it's possible to cross the county borders into Derbyshire, Cheshire and Yorkshire. But there isn't much about the center of Hyde that could be called attractive. Many of the buildings sprang up during the town's rapid expansion in the eighteenth and nineteenth centuries, when the dark, Satanic-looking mills of the cotton industry were the key to the area's prosperity. In those days, Hyde was a mill town made rich by the boom years of the Industrial Revolution. By the time Fred Shipman and his family descended on Hyde, the city was far from prosperous, although it was not desperately poor, either.

The residents of Hyde watch their money and seek out the best bargains, and the town has always retained an intriguing element of old-fashioned dignity. It was a close-knit community where the same families had lived for many generations; where churches and chapels were always full on Sundays, and where respectability was still a priority. As one resident recalled: "I've been here thirty years, but I'm an outsider, not a local."

Hyde wasn't large enough or wealthy enough to support any of the major chain stores when Shipman moved there in the late 70s. The 1960s-built shopping mall contained local traders selling off mainly downscale products like cheap clothes and fruit and vegetables. Employment prospects for local youngsters were extremely limited, and most traveled into the center of Manchester to seek work. Overall, Hyde's claims to fame were few and far between: The local authority that covers it is called Tameside, and it has since been the birthplace of a couple of well-known soccer stars and rock singers, but there's not much else of any real note.

However, one pair of infamous former residents will never be forgotten. So-called "Moors Murderers" Myra Hindley and Ian Brady were living in the Hattersley housing project when they carried out two of their four sick and twisted killings of schoolchildren in the early 1960s. The couple even tape-recorded the pleas of some of their young victims. The crimes of Hindley and Brady shocked and sickened the world, and their atrocities were still fresh in the memories of many Hyde residents when Fred Shipman took up his prestigious post.

Shipman believed that Hyde represented his last chance to make it as a respected GP. The family immediately rented a pretty, semi-detached house on Lord Derby Road. The modern-style home, with its lawned gardens and nearby schools, was perfect for the young family. The property had vast picture-style windows that allowed plenty of light to pour in, and it stood on top of one of Hyde's many hills overlooking the old chimneys and dying mills in the distance. Here, the Shipmans believed they had a chance to settle down and put the past behind them, to wipe the slate clean and start all over again. The partners at the new practice at Donnybrook knew about Shipman's drug problems, but that was all in the past. They didn't even bother informing the local area health authority because they were convinced that Fred Shipman was no longer a liability.

But was he?

To the outside world, Fred Shipman's domestic life seemed relatively "normal." Babysitter Jenny Unsworth looked after the Shipman children during the family's first months in Hyde, including New Year's Eve when Fred took Primrose to a party in Leeds. Jenny found Sarah and Christopher to be very well behaved. They both went to bed without any fuss, leaving Jenny to enjoy the sandwiches and coffee provided by a charming Primrose. Jenny even noticed that Fred Shipman had set up home-brewed beer in vast plastic bottles behind the settee. He always enjoyed a pint or two at home after his long and exhausting days in the surgery. The Shipmans were so grateful that Jenny had agreed to babysit at short notice that they presented her with a plant as a thank-you gift some days later.

Another babysitter was Mary Burgess, whose daughter Jennifer was a receptionist at the Donnybrook practice with Dr. Shipman. Mary and Primrose began working together as registered childminders and became firm friends within months of the Shipmans' arrival in Hyde. Primrose's choice of jobs seemed bizarre considering that she had her hands full with her own children, but she seemed happy to utilize her skills as a mother and add some much-needed money to the family's weekly income. Soon she was minding at least a dozen children in the house each morning, but they never arrived until after Fred Shipman had left for work.

One who visited the house just after the children had arrived one morning described it as "disorganized chaos." The neighbor added: "The house was untidy, but it was hardly surprising considering the number of kids running riot there every day."

Ironically, Mary Burgess might never have started babysitting for the Shipmans or become Primrose's friend if it hadn't been for Fred Shipman's calming bedside manner as a doctor. Shipman had found her first husband dead at home from natural causes. During the visit, Shipman showed such kindness and sensitivity that he even gently advised Mary to leave the house rather than get further upset looking at the body. No one to this day knows if Mary's husband was one of Fred Shipman's numerous victims.

"The babysitting really helped me," Mary Burgess later recalled. "I could talk to them both at any time; they were wonderful. Primrose was bubbly then, we used to have a laugh. The children were lovely, very bright."

Later, Fred helped Primrose do the catering at Jennifer Burgess's wedding. Mary Burgess recalled: "I can still see them buttering bread. Fred is not one of those snooty doctors; I can't do with them, especially when you are not well. He was human, not stiff and starchy."

But many of Fred Shipman's colleagues speculated about Primrose's skill as a childminder. As one pointed out: "She wasn't exactly charming, and we all wondered how on earth she found the patience to look after so many children." But somehow Primrose continued to cope.

Not long after Fred Shipman joined the Donnybrook practice, he and Primrose went out for a meal with some of the other doctors from the surgery. Partner Dr. John Smith later explained: "It was a tradition when someone left or someone joined, as on the whole we didn't socialize at other times." Dr. Smith's wife Maureen asked Primrose if living in Hyde was handy for her in terms of seeing her family. Primrose replied coldly: "I have nothing whatsoever to do with my family."

Maureen Smith was shocked, because Primrose made it sound so extreme. A few months later, Maureen Smith bumped into Primrose in a local supermarket and asked her, "Have you made it up with your family yet?"

"No, and I never will," replied Primrose, curtly.

Maureen Smith never forgot that conversation. She disliked Primrose from the moment she first met her. "It all seemed so final," she later recalled, "as though she had made up her mind, and there was no way she would ever be friendly with them again. I thought that either they must have done something really terrible to her, or she was very stubborn and rather childlike." Maureen Smith also formed an aversion to Fred Shipman, deciding he was "sneaky and shifty."

It was also becoming clear that the Shipman children didn't exactly have the easiest of relationships with their parents. Shipman could be very rough with other children as well. One Sunday, a friend of daughter Sarah fell off a bicycle during a charity ride organized by the Shipmans' local pub, the Dog and Partridge. Shipman, who was called to the scene by a frantic Sarah, scrubbed away the dirt and loose skin with a viciously heavy hand. "He was awful," Sarah's friend later recalled. "I almost cried, he was so rough. It was bloody painful." Moments later Shipman walked off in a huff because he considered himself to be "off duty."

Yet Fred Shipman's children were obviously an essential part of his life. They provided him with a feeling of normality as his mind grew increasingly twisted. The pressure he felt to provide for them gave him the perfect excuse to work long hours. And despite his drug rehabilitation treatment, the stress was sometimes elevated by an occasional shot of pethidine.

Fred Shipman continued to seek forms of escape from the mundane nature of his life. He believed the evils of drugs were far preferable to the other instincts eating away at his mind; the urge to continue killing had to be quelled. If it meant going back into the dark abyss of drugs, then so be it.

By this time Fred Shipman was only in his early thirties, but he looked older, thanks to a gray beard and dark gray, thinning hair. He was smallish, skinny with a middle-aged paunch, and tended to wear gray-brown suits, conservative ties and thick-lensed spectacles. With his dry and narrow face, his scratchy, pedantic voice, and his tetchy manner, he was more like an old-fashioned schoolteacher or a middle-ranking civil servant.

In the hospital he often drummed his fingers impatiently in the presence of certain patients. His prescriptions were written with neat precision, which only he seemed to be able to decipher, but he had a tendency to frown irritably or sarcastically when someone was annoying him. All these characteristics made him seem as respectable and English as a rainy Sunday afternoon. Yet to his older female patients he was diligent and courteous, polite, a perfect gentleman; he was the embodiment of a good doctor.

Fred Shipman liked lists, he liked organizations, he liked order—and he was brilliant at Trivial Pursuit. His passion was clearly for objects, things; people became items in his catalogue. He was in urgent need of controlling. But the addiction to kill was once again rearing up inside him.

Shipman had become like a magician with his mysterious bag of tools and potions, his secret vocabulary, his impenetrable handwriting, his hidden knowledge. He could cure and listen. He understood people's pains and indignities. He knew about the bodies' intimate details and his patients' lives. However, some of those patients were getting on his nerves; they needed tidying. They were not real people in his mind, but symptoms and problems; a cold, a cancer, a heartburn, an ache, an irritation and a worry. For Fred Shipman, patients really were as meaningless as that.

Soon after moving to Hyde, Fred Shipman joined the St. John Ambulance Brigade, where he taught dozens of young members the importance of first aid. Through the organization, he also trained registered childminders. He was known as a charming, patient instructor. His very lighthearted teaching manner was supposed to help his "pupils" remember their lessons better. Amongst the audience of childminders was Primrose, whom many recall listening adoringly to every word her husband uttered with a proud smirk on her round face.

Some pupils also recall that Shipman occasionally belittled people who gave him the wrong answers to his "test" questions. One of them, Janet Redfern, recalled: "His attitude was just below arrogance. He had a superior air about him—'I know I'm better than you, but I won't rub your noses in it. I will let you know that, so you like me a lot.' But he wasn't really offensive, and we did learn a lot."

During one of Fred Shipman's first-aid lessons he claimed that he was allergic to bee stings. He told his audience that he always kept a syringe of antidote in his car at all times. In fact, it was a vial of pethidine, and Shipman had gotten into the habit of keeping the drug in his car in case his craving for a fix got too great. The secret life of Fred Shipman clearly had not ended when he was hauled before those magistrates in Halifax following his problems at Todmorden.

Meanwhile Shipman's professional work continued to thrive. He took on numerous roles in the hope of gaining gravitas. Besides the St. John Ambulance, he was also treasurer of the Small Practitioners Association, a national support group for surgeries with three doctors or fewer. He was also on the Tameside Local Medical Committee. Dr. Kailash Chand, secretary of the committee, later described Shipman as, "no diplomat, but a good doctor." He added, "I would have been his patient happily."

The Donnybrook practice where Fred Shipman worked had been a major innovation when it was established in 1967: fourteen doctors in two practices serving a whole town from one building. Fred Shipman was soon considered an important part of that set-up. "He was very assertive," recalled now-retired Dr. Bill Bennett. "He didn't like people opposing him very much, as I remember. But he certainly worked hard."

Dave Owen, chief officer of the Tameside and Glossop Community Health Council, explained: "Dr. Shipman could come across as abrupt and rather arrogant. This was no major concern, though; in fact it was a bonus when it came to negotiating services for his patients. He was very good at that."

But Donnybrook practice manager Vivian Langfield found herself regularly on the receiving end of Fred Shipman's "assertiveness." And she was horrified when the GP began snapping at her beloved team of receptionists, known as "the girls." When she defended them, he turned on her. She later recalled how he would literally turn white with rage—just because one of them had forgotten to get him a cup of coffee. Explained Miss Langfield: "I am always frightened of people who turn white, not red, with temper. He would be very calm, not raise his voice. That was even more scary."

One time, when Shipman was irritated by a particular member of the surgery staff he asked Miss Langfield: "Who was that girl?"

She replied, "You know who it is."

And then he responded, "Tell her to leave on Friday."

Shipman was in no position to hire and fire people, but Miss Langfield felt she had little choice in the matter. Numerous receptionists later claimed that Shipman created a very nasty atmosphere. He talked down to people, they said. And once Fred Shipman had settled into the practice, he turned out to be just as hard on his fellow doctors. He told one doctor in front of the reception staff, "If you can't show an interest in the practice, then leave it to those of us who can."

But other doctors found Fred Shipman the opposite of unapproachable. Donnybrook GP Dr. John Smith later recalled: "We mentioned Fred's rudeness to the staff to him at a group meeting, but not forcefully. You can't talk down to a professional man. We felt he was only doing his job, if a little forcefully at times."

Fred Shipman was also extremely sensitive about his junior position within the pecking order of the group practice. He felt he should have been promoted soon after his arrival at Donnybrook. He was so irritated by this oversight that he didn't usually even bother attending any of the surgery's social events.

In 1979, Fred and Primrose bought a modest three-bedroom semi-detached house in a leafy enclave called Roe Cross Green, in the village of Mottram, ten minutes' drive from Hyde town center. The Shipmans also added to their brood of children; on March 20 that year their second son David was born.

David represented a new start for Fred and Primrose: the children would provide a pathway into the community's heart. People liked the Shipmans. How could anyone dislike a large, happy young family working hard and keeping to themselves.

Primrose soon became known in Mottram as "The Child-minder," always trailing an entourage of children. She was also "the doctor's wife"—which meant that everyone gave her a measure of respect despite her obese, chaotic appearance. And Fred Shipman still kept that "bee-sting antidote" in his car—just in case he needed a fix.

By the turn of the new decade—1980—Fred Shipman had become, in the words of some of his staff, "a complete bitch" behind the backs of some of his colleagues at the Donnybrook practice. His favorite "victim" was Dr. Derek Carroll whom he regularly mimicked. Dr. Carroll was fifteen years older than Shipman. When head receptionist Vivien Langfield told Dr. Carroll about Shipman's sneaky mocking of him, he told her not to make a fuss. "It's better to let Fred have his own way," the doctor told Langfield. Some members of the staff had already come to the same conclusion. Miss Langfield later recalled an incident when Shipman was gerating yet another receptionist over some minor incident. When one of the other doctors walked in and began, "Hey, Fred . . ." Shipman turned on his colleague and snapped, "This has nothing to do with you. I would appreciate you keeping out of it." The doctor walked away without uttering another word. Shipman was a difficult, strange man in many ways, but there were no complaints about his work, and many of his patients adored him. He must have been doing something right.

Undoubtedly some doctors were scared of Fred Shipman. As he had done at Todmorden, Shipman put up many ideas for improving the surgery. Many were well received, but he would get very annoyed if anyone didn't like what he was proposing. Vivien Langfield says: "He was a bully who demanded that people look up to him and have regard to his position. If anyone queried anything to do with one of his patients he would say, 'I am a good doctor. I have all the qualifications from Leeds Medical School,' as if to say he should always be listened to."

But what really irritated Fred Shipman was if any female member of staff dared to challenge him when he was making rude and sarcastic comments. Answering back marked them down as targets for subsequent attacks. He rarely raised his voice; his favorite weapon was sarcasm. But as one former member of the staff re-emphasized: "That was far more chilling and sinister than shouting and screaming."

But Fred Shipman's control-freak mentality was most classically illustrated when he ordered the surgery's hard-working cleaners to move his desk to clean under it. They couldn't get it out of the office, so they left it in the doorway. Shipman returned the next morning and refused to put it back in its right place until they came back to the surgery and did it themselves. "It was remarkably petty of him, and from that moment on, I was very wary of Dr. Shipman," recalled one former receptionist.

On April 4, 1982, Primrose gave birth to the couple's fourth child—Samuel. A few weeks later Fred Shipman became an overnight local celebrity when he appeared on a national TV program. Interviewed at his desk in the Hyde surgery, Shipman gleefully enthused to the cameras about a new type of treatment for the mentally ill. He told British TV's *World in Action* documentary program: "If you can stay in the community, receive your treatment in the community with your family around you, and your usual friends, then this all adds to the speed of recovery from the illness."

Shipman also added: "In the past, if a patient has got a mental illness that required admission to hospital, the patient was formally admitted, undressed and placed in bed and was treated as though they had a physical illness. A consultant would come round—often in a white coat—and there was an invisible barrier between the patient and the doctor."

Fred Shipman also gave interviews to journalists from two medical journals, *Medeconomics* and *General Practitioner*, about the problems of dealing with alcoholic and drug-addicted doctors, but in both cases he made no mention of his own conviction. Shipman keenly advocated a much faster system of dealing with addiction and alcohol problems.

He happily pontificated to reporters about all aspects of his work as a GP, and was regularly quoted on a variety of issues. As a member of the local Medical Committee, Shipman appeared to thrive on his position of power and influence. Shipman clearly believed that others in the medical profession should be capable of his own high levels of knowledge. One time he attacked a drug company rep who addressed the local MC and got a small medical detail wrong in her speech. One of Shipman's oldest friends, Dr. Wally Ashworth, later recalled: "Fred tore this woman apart, viciously—he almost had to be hauled off. It was almost as though he had to prove himself superior, and she was not an easy target."

And it wasn't just work colleagues who were reprimanded by Fred Shipman. One of the receptionists at Donnybrook never forgot how hard Fred Shipman was on his two older sons whenever they called at the surgery for a lift home from school. They'd sit down, doing their homework in his room, and then troop out, "heads down, in tears" behind their father as he steered them toward his car outside. They were not even allowed to acknowledge the staff on their way out.

"They looked so miserable. I felt really sorry for them. He seemed to strike fear into them. It was really quite distressing," recalled the former member of the Donnybrook staff.

Back at home, oldest child Sarah was the one who was confident enough to challenge her father's stern and ill-humored mood swings. "Sarah often laughed off her father's bad temper, and that seemed to change his mood instantly," recalled one neighbor in Mottram. Shipman may have been afraid of Sarah in some ways, because she reminded him of his mother Vera. Fred Shipman found time to be a parent-governor at her school, Longdendale High, and even gave talks on family planning to some of the older students. School staff were naturally delighted to have such a distinguished member of the local community on the parent board.

Fred Shipman thoroughly enjoyed his positions of influence. He liked his children to know that he was always looking over their shoulders, ensuring they did well at school. That was how his own dearly beloved mother had been, and it had undoubtedly helped him to make a success of his life. Fred Shipman liked to remind his children that his childhood was a lot tougher than theirs and that they should be grateful for what they had. Hard work was the key to success, he believed. And his children were all expected to live up to his expectations.

Fred Shipman welcomed 1983 in at a drunken New Year's gathering complete with party poppers draped around his neck and a balloon raised in salute. A harlequin mask replaced the mask of sincerity he so often used with his patients. Shipman surprised many by still seeming capable of letting his hair down occasionally. He consumed many pints of beer, and was later remembered as the life and soul of the gathering.

At the time, Fred's star was still very much in the ascendancy. As one senior partner at the Donnybrook practice in Hyde later recalled: "Fred had terrific potential." He also had a chilling reputation as being "wonderful at getting into veins." This referred to his ability to administer injections with the least amount of pain—something that many of his patients truly appreciated.

The overriding impression from photos taken at the time is of a middle-aged doctor with a long, successful future ahead of him. There was no outward sign of the junkie who injected himself with pethidine. In the photos, Shipman even wore his favorite party outfit; an almost-fashionable velvet jacket.

But not all his patients were impressed; some of Shipman's younger ones began to despise the GP, who always seemed to have more time for his flock of over-60s than anyone else. Mother-of-two Lorraine Leighton was a nervous 17-year-old, deeply embarrassed by her problem—a lump on the breast—when she made an appointment after ignoring the situation for months. She visited Shipman at a surgery where he was working temporarily.

As Lorraine shyly explained her condition, Shipman made an "unsuitable comment" about the size of her breasts. Lorraine fled his surgery and waited many more months before returning to a different doctor, who immediately removed the lump. Fortunately, it was a benign cyst.

"He was horrible. He gave me the creeps. I was so upset by the way he treated me," Lorraine, who never forgot the incident, later recalled.

One of Lorraine's friends, a pretty young barmaid named Eve, also had a run-in with Shipman. When she visited him about problems over her nerves, he barked at her to pull herself together. "Go home and look after your kids," he snapped. When her husband went for the same reason a few weeks later, he got a two-week sick note. Eve continued to believe that Shipman had a severe "problem with women."

But behind Shipman's sometimes gruff manner lay a man in turmoil; he was fighting the demons that had first made their mark on him in Todmorden. He occasionally still used pethidine to try to kill the urges that may have led him to end the lives of a number of patients while he was in the small Yorkshire town. But he was losing the battle. It would only be a matter of time before the killing started again.

9

Six years after Fred Shipman arrived in Hyde—in April 1984—one of his 70-year-old patients died suddenly. Winifred Arrowsmith lived in an apartment in a fifteen-story tower block in the center of the town. The building even had a warden to check on its elderly inhabitants, plus a social club for mealtimes. Winifred had only moved to the block on a temporary basis because her own home was being renovated. She was fit, active and fiercely independent. Her apartment was immaculate and she doted on her pet budgie. Winifred adored reading, and always wore flowing floral dresses, whatever the weather. "She was a marvelous, sprightly lady for her age. She never seemed to suffer any real health problems," one old friend later recalled.

One day Fred Shipman turned up at the office of the block warden, Jenny Unsworth, and asked if Mrs. Arrowsmith was in, claiming he had knocked at the apartment door and there was no reply. Mrs. Unsworth let him in with a master key. Inside, Winifred Arrowsmith was dead, sitting in an armchair as if she had fallen asleep.

Shipman had been known to visit Mrs. Arrowsmith frequently at home, but that was usually only to give her a repeat prescription of arthritis tablets. "When they found her dead, she had just had her dinner," recalled her daughter-in-law Maureen. "The potato peelings were still on the worktop, and she'd had Fray Bentos steak pie, one of her favorites. I remember thinking that she couldn't have been gone long, because she always used to tidy up straight after her meal. It was all so sudden, and we were all very distressed."

But Winifred Arrowsmith's death seemed nothing more than the sad end to a happy, healthy life. There was no post mortem, as the death was, according to Shipman, from perfectly natural causes. No one said a word about it back at the Donnybrook surgery. Why should they? Amongst the inhabitants of Hyde were a vast number of elderly pensioners. Deaths of this kind were to be expected . . .

The efficiency of Fred Shipman's medical career was in strange contrast to the appallingly run-down state of the family home on Roe Cross Green. Bikes and children's toys lay scattered on the lawn outside the house. In the kitchen, the oven grill pan was thick with bacon fat from the thousands of rushed breakfasts for the six family members. The living room was scattered with coloring books and papers. Family life brought with it a measure of complete and utter chaos for the Shipmans.

Most mornings, neighbors were greeted with the sight of Primrose hurrying Sarah, Christopher, David and Samuel out to her battered Mini to ferry them to their local schools. Fred Shipman usually left the house at about the same time, clutching his doctor's bag as he dashed to his own rusting Ford for the ten-minute drive to his clinic. At that time, Primrose was still supplementing the family income by childminding for villagers in Mottram, but she was always careful not to let them into the house until after Shipman had left for work.

When it came to their own children's education, Fred Shipman remained in complete control. He offered little actual help with the children's homework, but always insisted they show him their completed work before they could sit in front of the house's only TV set.

At weekends, armed with a large bag, he would even knock on neighbors' doors collecting newspapers for the local scout group. He was trying his hardest to be a good father and husband. He so desperately craved a sense of normality, away from the drugs and death that seemed to haunt his professional life.

Fred Shipman also considered himself an expert in wine and cuisine, although his tastes weren't exactly adventurous. On the rare occasions that he did dine out, it was always at one of two local Italian restaurants, Ferrero's and Maestro's. Shipman loved flaunting his intellectual superiority to Primrose by making a big show of choosing the wine.

But Shipman found it difficult eating out, because he often bumped into patients or relatives of patients, and they always wanted a brief chat. He was a celebrity within a tightly knit community. Shipman was far too polite to ignore any of these familiar faces, but he grew weary of the constant approaches in public.

On family holidays to Brittany and Spain, Shipman adored playing the well-traveled European. During the summer of 1984, Fred and Primrose even accompanied Sarah on a school exchange visit to the Haute Marne area of France, parking their camper van opposite a house owned by Gilbert Thomas, also a doctor, and his wife Monique. The Thomases later remembered the couple largely because of Shipman's inability to speak good French and his wife's tendency "to be a bit fat." They said "please" and "thank you," but that was about it, the Thomases said.

Something happened to Fred Shipman on the twenty-first of September, 1984, which made it such a momentous day that the evil urges which had driven him back to murder exploded into multiple death and mayhem. That afternoon, Shipman claimed he found 76-year-old Mary Winterbottom "dead in bed." He recorded the cause of death as a coronary thrombosis. Later that same day, authorities believe, Shipman claimed a second victim, Elaine Cox, 72, who died at her home in Hunters Court, Dukinfield.

Then the suspicious deaths stopped again.

On January 5, 1985, Fred Shipman's father Harold died of a heart attack at the age of 70. He collapsed in the kitchen of the same council house in Longmead Drive, Nottingham, where he had lived quietly for forty-seven years. Fred's sister Pauline, who had always lived with her father, was too upset to stay on in the house after his death. Pauline and her father had remained so close that they'd gone to watch local soccer team Notts County together and shared the cost of buying their house from the local council in the late 1970s for £5,500 ($8,500). It was valued at £30,000 ($45,000) at the time of Harold Shipman's death. Pauline worked as a secretary, and was also involved in the local netball scene, rising through the ranks to become one of the main organizers in the Nottingham Netball League.

Pauline quickly sold the house and moved in with brother Clive, who had a large modern house in the nearby town of Long Eaton. Clive, three years younger than Fred, was a health inspector and father of two children. He lived in a semi-detached house, with a perfectly groomed yard, on a neat, modern estate. Clive was in many ways the picture-perfect image of middle-class respectability.

Fred Shipman had very mixed emotions about his father's death. He was still angry about old Harold Shipman's attitude toward his wedding to Primrose. He felt that things would have been very different if his mother were still alive. He refused to believe that she would have disapproved of his wedding. It may have been because of such mixed emotions that Fred Shipman almost suffered a nervous breakdown when his father died. He found it virtually impossible to handle the combination of guilt and anger he felt about his father. One district nurse who bumped into Shipman in Hyde at the time told one of her friends: "He's just hanging on in, just this side of a nervous breakdown. He's only just keeping himself together. He's clearly devastated."

The same nurse even talked to Fred Shipman about the pain of losing his mother at such an early age. She believed the loss made Shipman very good at handling his women patients, although others heartily disagreed with that sentiment. But what had most upset Fred Shipman was that the family house had been left entirely to his sister Pauline, who then sank the proceeds from it into a granny flat attached to the large house bought with her other brother Clive. Fred Shipman had been completely cut out of his father's will—and his affection.

When one receptionist at the Donnybrook practice heard about the death of Fred Shipman's father, she said to the GP: "I am sorry about your father, Dr. Shipman."

He turned toward her, grim-faced, and replied, "Are you? I'm not."

The death of his father and the continuing rift with Primrose's family certainly added to the couple's sense of isolation. That feeling of "us against the world" was still growing by the day, sending Fred and Primrose spiraling into a hole of self-sufficiency. They lived in a world they had created without any reference to the past. All this helped Fred to believe he was vastly superior to everyone else. Within the immediate Shipman household there were no challengers to that title. Fred Shipman relished being a very big fish in a very small tank.

Many who dealt with Shipman professionally say that around the time of his father's death, the GP became a much more isolated figure within the practice set-up. "He seemed more detached, less interested in the day-to-day workings of the surgery," one member of the staff later recalled.

In February 1985, just a few weeks after the death of Harold Shipman, the GP was making one of his routine home visits to patient May Brookes. He claimed he found her dead on arrival at her home in Hyde, but few doubt that Shipman murdered her.

Occasional visitors to the Shipman household continued to notice the appalling state of the place, and the strange way that Fred treated his children. The two older children had to share a cramped bedroom, while the two younger boys were virtually penned into their bedroom like animals. If Fred was ever in the house during the day, he usually insisted that the younger boys were placed in their bedroom and only let out once he had departed.

Inside the chaotic and filthy home, the culinary skills that Primrose showed at various public functions outside the family home were not apparent. As one other visitor later explained: "The place was a pit. It was dirty and in some places downright unhygienic."

One of youngest son Sam's school friends later recalled: "There were clothes strewn all over, and it was dirty and smelled a bit." Primrose always kept up a happy mood inside the house, but apparently dropped that façade the moment Fred Shipman arrived home, tired and hungry after yet another grueling day at work.

Even Fred's old friend Les Fallows conceded: "I live alone, but their house was messier than mine, more like a man-alone's house. I suppose that's families for you." Dr. Wally Ashworth, Shipman's own GP and a friend for many years, was even more blunt: "Your feet stuck to the carpet, it was so filthy."

Wally Ashworth also had some interesting ideas about Fred and Primrose's relationship. "He was a little man with a big woman. He was dominated at home; then he came to work. He was controlling and a perfectionist, a bloody hard worker, but not very intelligent. I have seen other doctors with God complexes and I think that's what Shipman had."

One of the rare occasions when Fred and Primrose actually entertained someone at their home was an eighteenth birthday party for daughter Sarah, in February 1985. The only memorable thing about it was that the house was unusually clean and tidy. But within days it was back to its old, familiar messy state.

In August 1985 a friend of one of Fred Shipman's male patients who had died of a rare disorder earlier that year made a complaint about the GP to the British General Medical Council. It concerned an alleged failure to treat the patient's condition and a breach of confidence about his disorder. Neither allegation was ever substantiated, and no one even bothered to see whether Fred Shipman had been involved in any other "problems" during his career as a doctor.

On January 14, 1986, Fred Shipman astutely invited some of his fellow doctors, including the bluff and popular Dr. Smith, to his fortieth birthday party celebrations at York House. "I had no problem with him then; he was a hard worker and the patients loved him," explained John Smith. "He had a lovely theatrical bedside manner that really worked with them."

Those who attended the gathering said that Fred Shipman appeared totally relaxed and "very full of himself." Recalled one: "Fred supped on a few pints of beer, and then switched to red wine. He was extremely merry by the end of the day."

So life wasn't all just work, work, work for Fred Shipman as he climbed the doctors' ladder in Hyde. He and Primrose even became regular fixtures at local cocktail parties, and one extraordinary set of photos later released showed Fred Shipman clearly enjoying himself at a fancy dress party. He was costumed as a Viking, much to the amusement of many of those present. He then proceeded to get so inebriated that he fell over.

At the same party, Primrose also wore a Viking hat made out of a colander and covered with silver paper. Alongside her, Fred looked resplendent in his toga. But the pictures show his eyes looking like huge black cesspits. The smile is there for all to see, but those eyes show none of his happiness. His pupils are so dilated, he may well have been high on drugs at the time.

Fred Shipman was clearly trying to be more sociable in an effort to "normalize" his life. He even hosted a couple of barbecues in the garden of his house, although those who attended later recalled that Shipman's favorite topic of conversation was his daffodils. To his neighbors and friends he looked as if he hadn't a care in the world. Yet Fred Shipman was continuing to use pethidine. The drug was the only thing that truly enabled him to relax.

Faithful, seriously overweight Primrose turned up with her husband at weddings and other gatherings in a particularly large, flowery dress and a jaunty pink hat. Fred Shipman tried to ease off his fondness for pethidine by using alcohol to help drown out the demons that seemed to fill his every waking hour. Drinking a few pints of home-brewed beer was tolerated with a certain degree of relief by Primrose, who may have harbored suspicions about her husband's continued use of drugs. It's unlikely she believed his story about being allergic to bee stings, but she would never have had the courage to challenge him about his claims.

Meanwhile, Fred Shipman's attitude toward the use of illicit drugs came to the surface in a bizarre manner. He was approached by two doctors in another practice who were very concerned that one of their partners was abusing drugs. Fred Shipman was extremely sympathetic toward the doctor in trouble. He even told the two partners that they should try to help the man. But they felt their primary duty was to their patients.

"A drug addict is always a drug addict—they don't change," one of the partners said to Shipman, not knowing anything about his background. Shipman stared ahead thoughtfully before replying: "Imagine, if you help him and it works, the satisfaction you will feel." There was no doubt whose side he was on.

At home, Fred Shipman rarely had time to read for pleasure, as he was always buried in paperwork from his surgery. But he did have a fascination with Britain's Victorian Era. He enjoyed books like *The Adventures of Sherlock Holmes*. And he was also fascinated by a non-fiction book about a doctor in the mid-1800s who specialized in killing his patients.

Dr. William Palmer had been a gambling man all his life. An arrogant and cavalier character, he was only ever charged with killing one patient, but there were at least thirteen others, including his own wife. And Palmer was only caught because he crudely forged the will of his final victim, leaving himself £4,000 (£240,000 [$400,000] by today's standards).

Palmer got away with killing for so long because he pre-

scribed the medicine and wrote out the death certificates. He
had the complete and utter trust of his patients and their
families, and he would often go alone to their homes before
lacing glasses of wine with strychnine.

On the final day of his trial, people lined up at 5 A.M.
for places in the public gallery, and when he was hanged,
the rope used was sold in small pieces to the crowd, desperate for souvenirs. But Palmer was a careless doctor compared with Fred Shipman; he killed people of all ages, not
just elderly ones who lived alone and whose deaths, while
lamented, would not be deemed suspicious. The Palmer case
sparked a few uncomfortable thoughts inside the increasingly twisted mind of Fred Shipman.

In November 1989, the General Medical Council received
a letter of complaint from the Family Health Services Appeal Unit about an incident involving one of Shipman's
epileptic patients named Derek Webb. Webb had been prescribed a drug called Epilem to control his fits. Fred Shipman had changed his prescription, effectively doubling the
dose. A month later, Webb was found in a dazed state at
his home, unable to recognize his own sister, Jean Wood.
He never recovered, having suffered irreversible brain damage.

His family sued Shipman, who fully acknowledged his
mistake and was found in breach of his terms of service as
a doctor. But despite this, Britain's General Medical Council
took no action against him. The case would continue to go
through the courts for the following ten years, and yet at no
time was Shipman's previous record uncovered.

Meanwhile, the Shipmans became even more active in the
parent—teacher association of their two eldest children's
school. Fred Shipman had the perfect cover in many ways—
the complete trust both of his patients and of the community
he lived and worked in. His image was, in everyone's terms,
that of the Good Doctor; a man who could always be relied
upon.

But the underlying urge to kill continued to grow within Fred Shipman. He tried hard to fight it off, but he soon found himself planning more killings with careful precision. By 1990, staff at the Donnybrook Surgery began to notice that Fred Shipman was becoming increasingly withdrawn, and when he was away from the clinic he became unsociable once again.

The back garden of the family house was Fred Shipman's pride and joy. It is featured in just about every photo taken of Shipman throughout the 1990s. He found it to be the only place where he felt he could truly relax. He'd lovingly built a rockery and garden wall, as well as planting numerous flowers that sprung into full bloom early each summer.

He adored ambling through the long back yard and then sitting at the garden table writing a letter with his cherished tortoiseshell fountain pen—the very same pen he always had with him when he was signing away death certificates. In many ways that pen had a mind of its own, as far as Fred Shipman was concerned. He was proud of it, and looked on it as a good luck charm. He became convinced that something bad would happen to him if he didn't have it with him at all times.

Sometimes Shipman spent hours in a white floppy sun hat, shorts and leather sandals, sitting quietly sipping wine, waiting for Primrose to join him on a warm summer's evening. But some photos of Shipman taken during this period show him squinting uncomfortably, looking as if he's feeling the strain of life . . . or death? Still only a relatively young man, his physique had become much bulkier, and that once-thick head of black hair had turned into a thinning gray thatch. Fred Shipman had the worries of the world on his shoulders. And his continued involvement with pethidine didn't help either.

10

Molly Dudley was a 69-year-old widow constantly beset with health problems. In the middle of 1990, she phoned her daughter-in-law to say she wasn't feeling very well and had called the doctor. But, she assured her relative, it wasn't anything too serious. She just wanted to be on the safe side.

Less than an hour later, Fred Shipman telephoned Molly Dudley's daughter-in-law from the elderly lady's house. "I'm afraid your mother-in-law only has about half an hour left to live," said Shipman in a coldly matter-of-fact voice.

Shipman also, bizarrely, insisted that she didn't have to rush over. "I promptly went round, but by the time I got there, she was already dead," Mrs. Dudley's daughter-in-law later recalled. Shipman told her that when he'd arrived at the house, the old lady was "cold, gray and sweaty, and looked as if she was having a heart attack." Shipman then added: "So I gave her a shot of morphine to kill the pain." Shipman later claimed he couldn't have killed Molly Dudley because he never carried morphine. But the recollection of her daughter-in-law suggested Shipman was a liar.

Back at the Donnybrook Surgery, the other medical staff continued to be baffled by the hard-working but increasingly anti-social GP. Senior partner Dr. Ian Napier insisted: "Although he could be an excellent clinician, he could also be volatile and bombastic; but when he was nice, he was very nice. He was well read, but he liked people to know it. He was a funny sort of devil."

Every few months Shipman's colleagues at the clinic noticed that he showed signs of violent and irrational mood swings, during which he would take out his anger on the staff. "He was not violent in any physical sense, it was almost like a childlike temper tantrum," explained Dr. Napier. "He would go completely over the top, and it was as if he had no control over it. He didn't do it with any of the partners. He would only talk like that to his subordinates. On the one hand, Fred was charming, urbane, pleasant with patients; but he had another side to him and, if crossed, he was capable of making people's lives a misery."

At one stage Shipman even refused to speak directly to the practice manager. "If he wanted to talk to her, he would write her a letter," explained Dr. Napier. "She was expected to do the same in response. Even though they worked in the same building and he had to walk past her every day, he would completely ignore her. It was totally ridiculous."

Behind the façade of their apparently happy, contented home life, Primrose must have suspected that her husband was hiding some dark secrets from her. Perhaps she wondered if Fred was having an affair with another woman. But such fears would only have made Primrose become even more insular. Her increasing weight—she had already ballooned up to a size twenty and weighed well over 200 pounds—also made her reluctant to step out of the house, except to drive the family van around picking up the children. Primrose seemed to be using food as a replacement for a lack of true love and affection from Fred.

The couple's sex life may well have long since ground to a halt following the birth of youngest child Sam. Shipman would have refused to talk about their situation, and it's likely that Primrose was, in many ways, too afraid to ask. No doubt she believed that whatever problems were driving a wedge between them would eventually disappear and they could get back to the way things were before.

Fred Shipman's mind was becoming increasingly immersed in the sick and twisted killing fantasies that were fueling his very existence. At the wedding of a close friend that he attended with Primrose in 1990, Shipman looked tired, and objected to having his picture taken by a photographer at the reception. "He looked dreadful. His eyes were constantly staring at the ceiling, even while I was talking to him. It was clear he had a lot of problems on his mind," explained someone who met him at the time.

When Primrose's father George died in 1991, he left some money to his four grandchildren, but nothing to his youngest daughter. The majority of his estate went to her sister Mary. But her father's snub simply reinforced Primrose's unflinching devotion to Fred. Her mom Edna—still living in Wetherby—heard nothing from her wayward daughter, who didn't even bother to show up at the funeral. Edna hadn't spoken to her daughter for many years, and didn't know anything about her life, apart from the fact that she was still married to Fred.

Fred and Primrose Shipman remained completely cut off from their respective families. It was as if they didn't want anyone getting in the way of the life they were leading. Fred had taken complete control of his young family. Friends of the couple later recalled how Primrose would instantly respond to his every request. She was completely reliant on him, especially since she had no one else to turn to. That was the way Fred wanted it to be.

As one friend pointed out many years later: "Primrose knew little about the outside world, and her husband was all she'd got. In many ways she was defined by him and, without him, it was difficult to imagine what she would do with her life."

Primrose was never strong enough to challenge her husband's overriding control of the family. When Fred Shipman lost his temper with any of the children, she wouldn't dare tell him to stop shouting at them. Instead, she'd nod her head in agreement as Shipman exploded in a tirade of abuse. None of the Shipman children have ever admitted to being physically assaulted by their father, but neighbors in Mottram recall hearing screaming and crying coming from the Shipman house. On a couple of occasions, one of the children was seen rushing out of the front door crying hysterically. One child even spent hours cowering in the front yard until Fred Shipman appeared in the doorway and ordered the boy to come in.

The key question is whether Primrose ever suspected, or actually knew, that her husband had started systematically killing his patients and putting their deaths down to "natural causes." "If Primrose did not know anything, and it's presumed she did not," one neighbor later said, "I feel very sad for her."

A doctor who has criminal or evil intentions toward patients has unique opportunities to exploit, harm and even murder them. In the privacy of a consulting room, or on a home visit, the trust that patients invest in their doctors can provide the setting in which a special relationship can be cruelly abused. A consultation is similar to a confession in church. Anything said or done is supposed to remain within the walls of the consulting room. The clinic, sitting room or bedroom of a patient's home is considered to be a place of privacy. Patients expect confidentiality, and doctors normally provide it.

GPs feel this particularly strongly, because they often develop a deep and lengthy relationship with patients and their families. But in Fred Shipman's case, it simply provided the setting for him to dispense not only care, but also death.

There are numerous patients who want to put their GPs up on a pedestal, godlike. When illness strikes, it is a natural human desire to hand over to a doctor who can take responsibility, make decisions and, if possible, even cure you. Therefore it is perhaps not that difficult to envisage a situation where a GP manages to cleanly and quietly commit mass murder. The opportunities were countless.

It was easy for Shipman to obtain the drugs he used as his weapon. Many chemists supply GPs with morphine and other drugs without batting an eyelid. Few would challenge the authority of a doctor. When a patient dies at home, the GP writes a death certificate indicating the cause of death.

If that patient is elderly, everyone feels that it is far more sensitive to avoid the fuss of involving a coroner and a post-mortem examination.

Even coroners are reluctant to get involved in the deaths of elderly people, particularly if they can be reassured by a GP that death was explainable. All these factors conspired to make it possible for the much-loved Dr. Fred Shipman to murder many of his patients without anyone taking much notice.

Death wasn't something Fred Shipman could take or leave. It had become an overpowering, maniacal urge that took complete control of his mind and body. One minute he would be impressing himself with his ability to act out the role of the good doctor, the next he'd be in a cold sweat as he quietly rolled up a sleeve and injected his deadly medicine.

But Fred Shipman knew that if he was to satisfy his urges to kill, then he needed to set up his own practice and be answerable to no one. By 1991, Shipman had been at the Donnybrook practice for more than fourteen years and his hard work and popularity with patients remained evident throughout that period. But his colleagues were getting in his way; they cramped his style. In front of them he had to show an assertive, caring manner, but without them, he would not have to pretend so much—and that might take the pressure off. He found it such a strain being so nice all the time.

Fred Shipman had never really been a team player, so he showed his true colors when he finally quit the Donnybrook practice to set up his own one-man operation at the end of 1991. In his original announcement about leaving the clinic, Shipman claimed that he was planning to move to Yorkshire, but had not yet found a suitable surgery.

Then, a few days later, he told the partners in Hyde that he was really leaving Donnybrook, and, because of a loophole he had found in his contract, was taking with him his list of 3,000 patients. "It left a big hole in patient numbers, and nearly decimated the practice," one partner later recalled.

The other six doctors in the Donnybrook practice were stunned by Shipman's move on four counts:

1. They now had no patient list to offer an incoming GP. This meant they'd lose his contribution to the running costs of the building and ancillary staff, about £20,000 a year ($30,000).

2. They would have to buy out Shipman's share of the building for £23,000 ($32,000). They had to do this with a bank loan, which they wouldn't finish paying off for many years.

3. They also had to pay Shipman's tax bill of almost £30,000 ($42,000). In those days (1992) tax was paid on the previous year's profits. He refused to pay his share when approached. The others discussed suing him, but they did not have a cast-iron case, even though they were morally right.

4. He took three receptionists and a district nurse from the Donnybrook staff after promising he would not poach any of the employees.

As former colleague Dr. Smith explained: "The first we knew about any of this was when he came to us and told us he'd been to a solicitor and found a technical flaw in our agreement, which meant he could take his patient list with him, and just pull out of our practice. It came like a bolt out of the blue. It was beneath contempt to exploit a loophole in a contract that he had been perfectly happy with when it was his turn to join the practice. Nobody had ever taken their list before."

Smith, furious about Shipman's announcement that he was going solo, fell out with the GP. His fury was further compounded when he realized that Shipman had been lying about his reasons for leaving. "He told me he didn't like the way the group practice was modernizing, getting in computers and that sort of thing," recalled Dr. Smith. "What's the first thing he does? He gets in a computer."

Fred Shipman had planned his departure for many months with virtual military precision. He had not told anyone else in the practice, because he felt he couldn't trust any of his colleagues. He wanted to be sure that nothing would prevent him from setting up on his own. Not for the first time, Fred Shipman was proving just how underhanded and selfish he could be.

But Shipman proved how much he cared about his patients by immediately holding an extra surgery session on Saturday mornings, when Primrose would stand in as the receptionist to save him the cost of paying his regular staff any overtime. Everyone—patients and staff—had absolutely no doubt that he had his patients' well-being at heart. And Primrose relished playing a subservient role to her husband by addressing him in a formal manner as "the Doctor" in front of other staff.

One staff member later recalled: "It was really weird. His own wife was calling him 'Doctor' to his face." In some ways, Fred Shipman's treatment of his wife summed up his role in the family and at work. He saw himself as "the Doctor" in every sense of the word. He needed that respect. He wanted to be looked up to.

Fred Shipman soon put his own stamp on his new clinic by starting a special fund for medical equipment that eventually raised £20,000. Shipman ran the fund with district nurse Gillian Morgan and his friend and patient Les Fallows, who organized raffles and social nights to try to raise cash. They eventually had enough to buy nebulizers, blood pressure monitors, even an electrocardiogram (EKG) machine and a sonic fetal heart detector.

Policeman Les Fallows was one of Fred Shipman's few friends at this time. The two men shared a love of rugby football. They often took Shipman's sons Sam and David to watch Sale Rugby Club on Fallows's season ticket. He also frequently gave Shipman's sons his tickets for the world-famous Manchester United soccer team if he was away.

Fallows felt sorry for the Shipman children because their father worked such long hours. His lasting impression of Shipman was: "I found him a quiet man who only liked to talk about sport rather than discuss any deeper issues." Fallows always felt that behind the friendly face lay a complex and intense individual. But Fred Shipman liked to use his "gentle" bedside manner to hide a multitude of confused thoughts.

The closest Fallows ever came to seeing an emotional side to Fred Shipman was when they cheered on youngest son Sam, who'd followed in his father's footsteps by playing rugby football for his school. The youngster also played prop forward for the Ashton Rugby Club schoolboy team as well as Lancashire's youth team, alongside the son of Billy Beaumont, one of the most famous rugby players in England when he captained the national side in the early 1980s.

For the first few months following his split from the Donnybrook practice, Fred Shipman continued to work from the same building, which he part-owned until the other partners could raise the finance to buy him out. Some of the other doctors warned Shipman that by working on his own he would be made an outcast. Fred didn't give a damn. This was what he had been working up to for many years.

As former partner Dr. Napier later explained: "When you are a one-man dictatorship, you can effectively do what you want. It is easy with hindsight to judge why he chose to move into practice on his own." Senior Donnybrook partner Dr. John Smith summed up Fred Shipman thus: "He was shifty, arrogant and treacherous."

It wasn't until after Fred Shipman departed the Donnybrook practice that one of the clinic managers pulled Shipman's CV up on the computer screen and realized that he had that drug conviction from Todmorden. So much time had elapsed since he'd first arrived in Hyde that virtually no one left on the staff had any idea about his past.

As one member of practice later recalled: "It's very odd,

really, because the only reason anyone checked out Shipman's CV was because we were all so angry that he'd left
so suddenly."

But no one thought to inform the local health authority
that a doctor with a serious drug conviction had set up in a
lone practice.

Fred Shipman's one-man practice soon became renowned
for his tireless effort and long hours. He gave people as
much time as they needed, and happily called at their homes
after hours, even on non-emergencies. Few other doctors
could match him with those sorts of personal touches. Fred
Shipman was pretty generous with medication as well; of
the 104 registered doctors in the Tameside area, he was one
of the top five highest prescribers.

When the West Pennine Health Authority's medical advisor called on the GP in 1992, she found him "strong
minded" with a robust defense of his methods. He insisted
he would control all his patients' needs and would treat them
himself rather than refer them to a hospital. Shipman's
words were like music to the authority's ears. The British
National Health Service was seriously over-stretched, and
needed more doctors as Fred Shipman appeared to be if they
were going to cut hospital waiting lists.

Moreover, Shipman always presented extremely rational
arguments as to why he prescribed so many drugs and usually recommended the most expensive brands. He was fond
of reminding anyone who was listening that this was simply
further proof of his dedication to his job, and no one
doubted the word of hard-working Dr. Fred Shipman. In any
case, the West Pennine Health Authority had no idea about
his previous drug conviction.

Fred Shipman set up his new clinic in a modest building
compared with where he'd previously been. But the location
was good, just 100 yards away from Hyde's market square
and the Town Hall, on the main street through the center of
Hyde. Number 21 Market Street was the second to the end

of a terrace of shops, with a well-stocked pharmacy on one side, two Indian restaurants within a few yards, a used car lot, and a pet-grooming parlor opposite.

Fred Shipman also saw nothing wrong with running a practice virtually across the street from the one he had just abandoned. The only buildings between his new one-man clinic and the Donnybrook practice were a tatty old gray bus station and an old bingo hall, where some of the good doctor's favorite, elderly patients were regular visitors. Fred Shipman took out a twenty-year lease on the property on Market Street, paying a rent of about £300 (about $500) a week. But the biggest irony was the name of the charity shop opposite his surgery: *Age Concern*. Fred Shipman saw it every single time he left his building. It was a timely reminder of his favorite type of victims.

Fred Shipman even decided to step up the number of house calls to his elderly patients, because he now had the freedom to do whatever he wanted. When a nearby bank shut down, Shipman immediately began negotiating with a young woman doctor, Dr. Lisa Gutteridge, to become his partner if he could expand into the larger property. But after just one meeting, the scheme fell through, and Dr. Gutteridge never saw Dr. Shipman again. Shipman dropped the idea because he was only too well aware of the difficulties of working in a shared practice.

In February 1992 an allegation was made to the General Medical Council that Shipman had failed to visit a female patient who'd suffered a stroke. Shipman disputed the facts, but the GMC's local medical service committee found him guilty of a breach of his contract, and he was fined £800.

But again, at no time was anyone at the GMC informed about Fred Shipman's drug convictions while he was working in Todmorden.

The GMC later claimed that the complaint it received did not suggest a pattern of performance sufficient to question Shipman's practice. "However, even if they had suggested a pattern," a GMC spokesman later recalled, "we only had the power to look at isolated incidents of serious professional misconduct. We did not have the power to investigate potential patterns of poor performance."

One of Fred Shipman's closest friends at this time was Dr. David Walker. The two met when Shipman was GP to Walker's elderly mother. "I also went to him a couple of times for an ear infection and once for insurance purposes on a medical," Walker later recalled.

Shipman and Walker reconnected when they found they were living in the same village—Mottram. Shipman's youngest son Sam was the same age as Walker's daughter Rebecca, and they both went to the village school together. "Fred was active in the community and the parents' association, and we were always bumping into him through those sort of things," recalled Walker, who lived around the corner from the Shipman family, on Hall Drive.

About six months after crossing paths again, the two men began going out for an occasional drink at a real ale pub inside nearby Stalybridge Station. Shipman and Walker would "sink five or six pints" on each occasion. Walker later recalled: "We'd meet about once every six months. I'd ring up and say, 'Do you fancy a drink?' " Amongst the others who regularly met with Shipman was John Davidson, a local police inspector whose own mother-in-law had recently died after a visit by Dr. Shipman.

Walker and Shipman's conversations in the pub during these get-togethers were, on the surface, painfully ordinary. "We would grumble about the health service, but Fred seemed to prefer more relaxed conversations," said Walker. One time Shipman made a brief reference to the appallingly untidy state of his family home. Dr. Walker recalled: "Fred was laughing about how he had a bag of socks under the stairs. He said it was the only place he could keep them and be sure they'd be in the same place the next day. He made it clear his house was a chaotic place."

Fred Shipman studiously made sure he always bought his

fair share of pints of beer. Said Dr. Walker: "He didn't need pushing. If six people went, there were six rounds. He was never [cheap]."

Shipman even admitted to Dr. Walker that he particularly liked the pub inside Stalybridge Station because he was not so well known in that area. "I think Fred didn't like to be seen out enjoying himself by his patients. He liked to leave that part of his life behind when he came out for a beer," recalled Dr. Walker.

But all the other men in the group noticed that Fred Shipman's character hardly altered even "when he got a bit tipsy." As Dr. Walker recalled: "The bar sold only real ale, which featured five good bitters. I think he tried them all as we all did, but he certainly knew how to hold his ale." The pub was located in the station's old waiting room area and people would walk through after getting off the trains.

Even when a pretty girl walked through the bar, Fred Shipman showed absolutely no interest. "Looking back, I suppose he was a bit guarded with his reactions. We'd all sit on the table at the back end of the bar, well away from the main area."

At the end of the evening, Shipman, Walker and their other drinking pals would walk the three-mile journey home, because they all realized they were over the drunk-driving limit. As Dr. Walker later explained: "Some of us would walk home faster than others. It was all uphill and took at least forty minutes. Fred was a faster walker than me, and he'd usually wander off ahead of the rest of us within the first mile. He seemed to prefer to be on his own."

On the local middle-class cocktail party circuit, the Shipmans never looked entirely at home, but they did turn up at a few gatherings after Fred opened his solo practice. Recalled Dr. Walker: "Primrose would often arrive first on her own. Then Fred would arrive late and sit sullenly in the corner. He'd always have a drink at these parties, but never as much as when we were out at the pub together. I think Fred liked to be in control when he was amongst a crowd of people."

Dr. Walker noticed that Shipman rarely made any effort to circulate amongst people at these cocktail parties. "He'd expect people to come to him and talk to him. Fred and Primrose usually stuck close together, and they were never the last to leave."

Primrose Shipman was virtually an enigma to neighbors and friends in Mottram. Said Dr. Walker: "I hardly knew Primrose at all. My daughter went to their house a few times, but never stayed for longer than a few hours." Walker's daughter was never invited to stay overnight and, rather strangely, Shipman's son Sam was never allowed to go over to the Walker household. The two childhood friends drifted apart after they left junior school. Years later, Dr. Walker asked his daughter what it was like inside the house, and she simply replied: "Nothing special."

Once, Dr. Walker did drop in at the Shipman house unannounced. "It was a Saturday morning, and I needed to borrow a stethoscope, because I was working as medical cover at a boxing match later that day. I got to the door, but Fred made a point of not letting me in. It was a bit strange." Moments later, Shipman appeared with the stethoscope and gave it to Walker without saying another word.

"I couldn't see what was going on inside. The house was like a cocoon, and few adults ever got in there." Dr. Walker would often pull up outside the house when he was involved in a school carpool with the Shipmans. "But Sam was always outside there waiting while Primrose was herding in a load of kids connected with her childminding work."

Behind Fred Shipman's attitude lay his bizarre relationship with the family house. "That property represented a different section of his life," said Dr. Walker. "And he clearly didn't want strangers in his home."

But Dr. Walker found it difficult to fault Fred Shipman's professionalism: "When he did a life insurance health check-up on me," Dr. Walker recalled, "he was most efficient. When I said no to something, he immediately pointed out I'd had an operation ten years before. He'd bothered to read my notes very closely and was able to pick up on that. He actually made me feel bad because I was lying."

Years later, Dr. Walker found it difficult to believe that Fred Shipman was capable of breaking the law. "I thought to myself, if he is that honest . . ."

But throughout the many years that David Walker and Fred Shipman were friends, Shipman never talked about his marriage. "I knew nothing about him and Primrose on a personal level," recalled Dr. Walker. The two men shared a similar background, grammar school boys from working-class families who'd worked their way into the medical profession, married young and even started families while still at university. "But we never really discussed any of this, even though we had so much in common."

However, Walker and the group of pub regulars were aware of Primrose's problems with her relatives—but only because she had mentioned them in passing to some of the other housewives in Mottram whose children she looked after. One of those women later recalled: "Primrose's problems with her own family only came out because some of us were naturally curious about her background. But she didn't exactly expand on what had happened."

One of the few memorable things about Primrose at this time was her driving skills, as she dropped and picked up her own children from friends' houses and, in some cases, dropped off children she had been minding during the day. "She was a very tense driver, hands clutching the steering wheel. Sometimes she seemed to leave braking until the very last moment," recalled one neighbor.

Occasionally, the Shipmans appeared at local functions—including a Mottram village hall show that featured a series of satirical sketches about local people, based on the national TV program *News of Ten*. The Shipmans' oldest child Sarah also appeared in the village hall in a local version of the musical *Grease*. Fred and Primrose were in the audience of at least thirty people. The show was hosted by the vicar of the village. Dr. Walker recalled seeing the Shipmans applaud their daughter politely, but "it was clear they were simply going through the motions. I don't think either of them had a very good sense of humor, to put it mildly."

Other Mottram village events summed up life in Middle England: church parties, horse competitions, fairground competitions, even light-hearted local community association quiz nights. The Shipmans turned up to watch the local junior school's parents' sports day, which featured events such as three-legged races and sack races. But neither of them took part. Dr. Walker recalled: "I particularly remember that Fred could often be found in the beer tent at these events. There's no doubt he liked a pint of ale."

And the Shipman children were certainly a credit to the family. As well as going to nearby college, the two eldest— Sarah and Christopher—both worked part-time at the local pub, the Dog and Partridge. Those who knew them at this time say they were bright and mature, with no qualms about hard work. Fred and Primrose occasionally turned up at the pub for Sunday lunch. The Shipmans adored the stodgy pub grub and regulars remember their favorite meal was roast beef and Yorkshire pudding.

Blonde, blue-eyed Sarah Shipman was immensely popular with the pupils at Tameside College, where she was studying to go into the catering industry. She eventually went on to run a hotel in the south of England with her boyfriend. Many of the family's friends and acquaintances insist that Sarah takes after her mother, especially when it comes to her culinary skills. Primrose's skills in the kitchen were so renowned that she had often done the catering for the practice's Christmas parties, even though her cooking skills at home seemed non-existent.

Back at work as a GP, Fred Shipman took on a completely different persona, as Dr. Walker later discovered while visiting him for a check-up. Dr. Walker's elderly aunt, Edith Brady, had died in Shipman's consulting room and was later counted amongst his probable victims.

"When I went for my medical, I said to Fred, 'Am I lying on the same couch my Aunt Edith died on?' "

Shipman replied very casually: "Yes, you probably are."

As Dr. Walker later pointed out: "There was no wry

smile on his face. He just said it flatly. I'll never forget it as long as I live. He seemed like a different person from the one I had enjoyed a few pints of beer with."

Back in the tidy, leaf-filled cul-de-sac of Roe Cross Green, Fred Shipman showed yet another side to his complex character. When one of his nearest neighbors fell seriously ill with lung cancer, Shipman became the doctor-from-heaven and showed extreme care and patience with the man's family. As another neighbor later explained: "This man wasn't one of Fred's patients, but he went out of his way to help the family. It was very touching, and Fred seemed genuinely upset when the neighbor died."

There is no doubt that Fred Shipman truly did love his job in a twisted way. He liked the feeling of responsibility that came with being a GP. Despite his shyness, he enjoyed being needed. The trouble was that some of his patients at his Market Street clinic were extremely demanding. They kept coming in for the most petty reasons, and it was getting to be too much for him. They needed him desperately, but all they were doing was pushing him to the edge.

Inside the sick and twisted mind of Fred Shipman, those omnipresent demons once again began surging to the surface. That's when Shipman began showing a distinct lack of patience with some of his supposedly beloved "flock." When one regular female patient showed up at the surgery complaining of a vague illness, Shipman snapped at her: "Stop disobeying me. There is nothing, I repeat, nothing wrong with you." That same patient later recalled: "He was so damn sure of his diagnosis, but then, that's why we trusted him so utterly. He controlled us all. I accepted his rudeness and left the surgery convinced he was right and there was nothing wrong with me."

That need to control his patients was a crucial element of Fred Shipman's urge to kill. Escalating the risk factor added to the thrill of the entire twisted scenario. Eventually the perils of pretending that one of his patients had phoned and asked for a visit—something that a technocrat such as

Shipman would know was easily checkable—added even more to the thrill of killing. Then he'd arrive at her home and administer a lethal injection. But each time, he felt the need to increase that level of risk with something even more hazardous.

Then Fred Shipman deliberately upped the stakes by risking killing a patient while a friend of the victim was in the next room. He'd already gotten away with murdering a patient in his consulting room. The boundaries had all but disappeared, and there was no stopping him now . . .

On the morning of April 17, 1993, Fred Shipman allegedly obtained a prescription in the name of Mrs. Sarah Ashworth for 30 milligrams of diamorphine. A few hours later, he was calmly and coolly filling a syringe with the morphine before squirting it gently into the air to make sure there were no blockages. Then, authorities suspect, Shipman leaned down and pulled up Mrs. Ashworth's sleeve. "You won't feel a thing, my dear." He'd uttered those words hundreds, if not thousands, of times over the previous twenty years.

As he pressed the needle into her vein, she thanked him. One wonders if by this time Shipman felt any pang of emotion or guilt. Did he perform his duties on automatic pilot? After all, he was just another doctor treating just another patient. Those feelings helped him block out the reality of the situation. Fred Shipman saw himself as merely treating a needy patient. But was he putting that patient into an irreversible spiral toward death? Soon, Mrs. Ashworth's body went limp. Her breathing became stilted.

The GP felt Mrs. Ashworth's pulse. It was getting weaker virtually by the second. She was fading into oblivion before his very eyes. Her skin color began to change to a slight gray. Soon she would be nothing more than a corpse.

Dr. Shipman leaned down once more and checked Mrs. Ashworth's pulse. She'd gone.

Shipman dropped his patient's limp wrist on her lap and stared into oblivion for a few moments. He kept telling himself he was only trying to help her. It was a weird, floating feeling; as if the entire episode had been a dream, and he would wake up to find that the devil hadn't infiltrated his mind after all. But then he looked at the corpse, still sitting in her favorite armchair, and the reality was there for him to see.

Shipman knew he couldn't turn the clock back. In any case, he felt strangely satisfied; like a cat who'd gotten the cream. There was no grim reality to face; his patient had died of natural causes and there was no question of him being held responsible for her death.

Not long afterwards, Shipman signed a death certificate for Mrs. Ashworth, stating that she'd died of "heart failure/ natural causes." Shipman even phoned her family on the morning of her death to relate the sad news. He told them that Mrs. Ashworth had called him out to her home after suffering breathing difficulties. Shipman said Mrs. Ashworth had "gone out like a light" as he treated her. He even claimed that he tried to save her with an injection, but he never said what was in his syringe.

11

Amongst Hyde's nurses and caretakers, gossip had begun circulating about Dr. Shipman "losing" increasing numbers of his older female patients. Some even called him "Dr. Death" behind his back. But no one ever considered the nickname to be anything more than a light-hearted jibe.

One of those who heard the rumors, but thought nothing about them at first, was district nurse Katie McGraw, who encountered Shipman that through her work at an old people's hall opened through the efforts of former Hyde mayoress Kathleen Grundy. Little did she know when she introduced Mrs. Grundy to Shipman that their paths would cross some years later.

McGraw had been a ward sister at the nearby Tameside General Hospital and had also met Shipman when they both sat on the area health authority. McGraw was the nurses' representative. Often Shipman and McGraw would share a cup of coffee before or after the AHA meetings, usually held in the hospital boardroom.

Recalled Katie McGraw: "Fred was quite open to me about certain things. We even discussed some very personal matters. He'd come out with the odd thing which surprised me at first. He was intense. Looking back, he wanted to tell me more than he actually did, but I didn't push him for more information."

Shipman even broke his own golden rule and talked about his family during conversations with McGraw. "He mentioned rugby and stuff like that, and kept referring to 'his boys.' He was obviously very proud of them. But he seemed a complicated man. Sometimes when you met with him he seemed very thoughtful, then at other times he could be extremely arrogant. He didn't suffer fools gladly, particularly colleagues, whereas I frequently saw him put on a very understanding look for his patients."

Although Katie McGraw never saw any evidence that Shipman was using drugs at the time, she did later concede: "There certainly was a darkness about him. But in many ways, Fred was a highly moral person, so I can't imagine him being involved with drugs." And Katie McGraw still believes to this day: "Fred was into preventative medicine in his own mind."

Shipman made a point of telling Katie McGraw that he was extremely worried about his children taking drugs. "He was really worried about that. He seemed to view the outside world as an evil, nasty place full of obstacles for his children." Katie McGraw frequently saw Shipman out in Hyde's busy town center at lunchtime going from one shop to another. "He was always in a bit of rush, but still noticed me straight away and said good morning. But I did used to wonder why he was out busily shopping during his lunch break."

Rumors circulated at the time that Primrose Shipman might have suffered some kind of nervous breakdown, because she was hardly ever seen out in the town, and she'd suddenly given up her childminding business without explanation. Katie McGraw recalled: "I knew Primrose by sight, and these rumors were very strong at one time, but I never got to the bottom of it. I met Primrose a couple of times at parties connected with the area health authority. She seemed a bit of a simple soul, education-wise. I expected Fred Shipman to have been married to a more dynamic lady, and they did make a strange couple." But Katie McGraw had no doubts that Primrose was "blindly loyal to Fred. He was her whole life. If Fred said, 'The moon is blue,' she'd say, 'Yes, Fred.' "

Katie McGraw concluded that Fred Shipman was "such a hard worker that he seemed to get angry with people who didn't put 100 percent into his practice like him." She added: "On the surface, Fred might have appeared to be an open person, but he wasn't really. I don't think anyone ever really got to know him properly."

Fred Shipman stuck to a rigid routine at the end of each day, especially after he set up in practice alone. He'd leave his surgery on Market Street at 6 P.M. on the dot and drive to the family home. Primrose would always be in the kitchen preparing the evening meal as he walked in. But Fred Shipman apparently never, or rarely, kissed his wife—instead he'd take off his jacket and say: "Good evening, what time is dinner?"

Then he'd carefully wash his hands and sit down in his favorite armchair while Primrose carried on cooking. Shipman would barely utter a word other than to complain about the patients who'd annoyed him that day. "They're wasting my time. The surgery is so busy. I've got too many patients to look after," was Fred Shipman's favorite moan and groan.

Then, with the family gathered around him at the dinner table, Shipman would bark out orders to his two youngest sons: "Samuel, serve the potatoes. David the carrots." They never dared answer back, and there was no conversation until they had finished eating.

Said one of the children's friends who attended one such meal: "It was very uncomfortable. None of the kids were allowed to speak unless spoken to by Dr. Shipman. It was easier just not to say a word. And neither of them asked me one question about myself."

And the food wasn't all that pleasant, either. "The sausages were undercooked and still a bit pink. The potatoes were hard and not completely baked, and there was some tinned corn. I didn't rush back there in a hurry," recalled the friend.

Most evenings after dinner, Fred Shipman would relax in his sitting room and bury his head in the business pages of a newspaper. He harbored a dream that his stock would go up hundreds of times in value and he would have enough

money to leave England and retire to a pretty cottage some-
where such as France.

By this time the once—pristine white interior walls of the
Shipman house were faded yellow. Three-foot-high piles of
unwashed clothes were left downstairs in the kitchen area
near a run-down, rusting washing machine, with shoes,
newspapers and magazines cluttering the floors. In the
kitchen, dirty saucepans and plates lay untouched for days.

When Primrose gave up her job as a registered childminder with Tameside Council, she began running a sandwich
shop in the nearby village of Hollingworth. "I think she
grew tired of looking after other people's children. It was
an exhausting job, and it caused even more chaos in an
already chaotic household," explained one friend.

Shipman's older son Christopher, definitely more like his
father, went on to university. The two youngest, David and
Sam, were still at West Hill High School. Both were known
locally as responsible, polite teenagers and both went on to
be captain [president] of the school.

While Fred Shipman was undoubtedly quite a stern father, he was not opinionated in the obsessive sense. He
craved to be regarded with respect and admiration, and this
dominated everything he did.

Shipman apparently felt his daily life was a sort of contemptuous lethargy, devoid of virtues or vices. He often simply did not feel as if he was part of the world he inhabited,
but an amused and sometimes disgusted spectator to it. Shipman detested the human race and its pretenses. To him, life
was a fine art and he was completely devoid of the ultimate
values or distinctions of right and wrong.

A Tameside Health Authority audit was carried out at Fred
Shipman's one-man practice in the middle of 1993. A full
computer system was to be installed within the following
few months, and the premises were being improved to provide new facilities—a staff room, computer room and mid-
wives' consulting room. The local authority report at the
time concluded: "An enthusiastic practise where we were

warmly received and an audit is clearly an integral part of the work."

That same year, Fred Shipman asked the Tameside authorities if they would award him £200 to support a survey of 16-year-olds in his practice. The aim of the project was to identify health problems and provide appropriate advice. Twenty-three of the thirty-two patients invited to take part were given advice about lifestyle, and also provided with facts and figures about cholesterol levels.

A second health authority visit to the Shipman practice in February 1994 was sparked by a much more serious situation. Officials were concerned about the amount of a drug called benzodiazepine which was being prescribed by Shipman to his patients. It was supposed to be used for congestive cardiac failure. Health authority officials urged their superiors to agree to a fresh audit on the Shipman practice, but the clinic was judged by officials to be "highly motivated," and was given the benefit of any doubt they might have because it seemed to be such a popular practice.

Yet again, Shipman's previous involvement with drugs did not come to light.

The only other real criticism of the one-man operation was that Shipman did not have a district nurse on call for patients to consult on the premises. Shipman told health authority officials that he held open access consultation sessions and dealt personally with patients who might otherwise consult a district nurse. He made it clear that he did not need any help.

In 1994/1995 Fred Shipman completed a questionnaire to assess the practice's all around performance. He referred to the problem of epilepsy in patients, the needs of those 16-year-olds and the repeat appointment situation again.

On a more practical level, Fred Shipman's skills as a doctor had clearly deteriorated. When one patient bumped into a surgery nurse named Jill, she told the patient: "I'm not in tomorrow. You'll have to see Dr. Shipman for your next jab." Jill then paused before adding: "He's not very good at injections, mind, so you'll probably have a huge

bruise for the next week." In fact, Fred Shipman—once renowned as a gentle doctor who could give an injection without the patient even noticing—had become much clumsier.
Or was it that he simply didn't care anymore?

Fred Shipman and his syringe were a popular subject of
conversation amongst his patients and staff. Yet despite this,
he continued to show great interest in his new patients. He
always sat them down and explained the workings of his
clinic. He made a point of mentioning that he was a "prescribing doctor" who kept abreast of new pharmaceutical
developments and didn't hesitate to use them. He was also
proud that the practice had access to its own counseling
service.

At least on the surface, Fred Shipman continued to appear avuncular, reliable, friendly and knowledgeable. Most
new patients were very impressed. Shipman's Market Street
practice seemed no different from any other clinic; a waiting
room filled with piles of dog-eared women's magazines,
ranks of senior citizens and subdued kids. The clinic was
never quiet, but it always seemed to be efficiently run.

Fred Shipman—not an ostentatious man by any means—
continued to drive a modest car and still live in that smallish
semi-detached house in the village of Mottram, a ten-minute
drive from his clinic. Money for the practice remained tight,
and Primrose still helped out at the reception on weekends
when she could. Fred Shipman gave the impression that all
his patients' problems were his own. He was revered by
many for his meticulous attention to detail. "He never forgot
anyone's name. It was remarkable, and it made his patients
feel so reassured," one former member of the staff remembered.

Fred Shipman even had a plaque on the desk of his consulting rooms which read: "EVERY DAY'S A BONUS." And he
remained a generous prescriber of medicine. "He always
said cheap medicine was not the best. That was why his
surgery was one of the most expensive in the country," re-

called Brian Dean, whose mother died while under the care of the GP.

All this made Fred Shipman as popular as ever. It also made his name very familiar with the West Pennine Health Authority, since he steadfastly refused to be constrained by the National Health Service underfunding that other GPs had learned to live with. Of West Pennine's 230 GPs, Shipman continued to be among the top five prescribers, exceeding his budget for seven years. Jan Foster, the area's directory of primary care, remembered Shipman as "always defensive, but he had rational arguments for his prescribing." And he usually won his argument, because he was an excellent GP. He performed high numbers of immunizations, had a good postgraduate education record and there had been few complaints from the public about him. He had 3,100 patients, well above the national average.

But there was another side to Fred Shipman's care and attention: whenever he came across a patient who wasn't completely forthcoming, he would place a tick alongside their name. He knew that such patients had to be treated with care. They might be on the lookout for any mistake he made, and that could prove very costly. For Fred Shipman was still stockpiling morphine by making out prescriptions to patients who did not need it, or who had died, and it was imperative that those "more difficult" patients did not have any suspicions about his "habits."

Fred Shipman falsely prescribed fourteen lots of 30 mg doses of morphine in 1993. The following year he prescribed even bigger amounts. One time he prescribed ten 100 mg ampoules for a woman patient the day before she died (her records later revealed that she did not need it). Another twenty ampoules of 500 mg were prescribed for a male patient on the day he died. It was more than Shipman would have needed to feed an addiction to morphine, if he indeed had one. Shipman would go on to procure a total of 22,000 mg of morphine—the equivalent of 1,466 fatal doses—during his six years running a solo practice.

Professionally, Fred Shipman saw computers and cutting-edge technology as the way forward in medicine. He could be irascible and even bad-tempered with those who did not share his enthusiasm. But it was his willingness to embrace the new that provided him with the confidence to drive forward in his quest to commit murder on a horrific scale.

Shipman had been a disciple of computer records from the moment he'd entered into general practice in Todmorden in 1974. At his one-man practice, he worked late into the night transferring records of patients from old buff folders into computer files. One member of the Market Street surgery staff later recalled: "Dr. Shipman was very meticulous, and had a computer system which he used all the time. He was very proud of what he could do with patients' notes in terms of auditing and things. In fact, he could be quite a bore about computers."

Yet for a man who prided himself on having the most up-to-date computer equipment, Shipman's sheer arrogance led him to completely ignore the safeguards that were built into modern hardware. He just couldn't come to terms with the fact that every single time he opened up the computer, it recorded the exact time and date. That meant that every time he put in new information on his MicroDoc software, a specialized program for GPs, he left a "shadow" on the hard disk.

The system at his one-man practice was even upgraded to allow for such an audit trail to be retrieved. Shipman was unaware of the facility, but anyone with a basic knowledge of computers could easily throw up a wealth of information on how Fred Shipman was tampering with the files of some of his patients in an attempt to make sure that their deaths seemed entirely "natural."

Fred Shipman's patient Renate Overton had always lived life to the full, working as a nurse at the Redferns rubber factory in Hyde. Even when she was laid off, she refused to feel down, as her world revolved around her family and friends. Then, on a February night in 1994, Renate, aged 44, returned to her neat terraced house after a night out with friends and soon suffered a minor asthma attack. Her 20-year-old daughter Sharon was concerned, but not overly worried, as the attacks happened two or three times a year. She phoned Fred Shipman, and he arrived at the house within fifteen minutes. Sharon immediately took him through to her mother, who was in the sitting room, having trouble breathing.

"I'll leave you to it, then, Doctor," Sharon told Shipman before going up to her bedroom.

Five minutes later, Sharon heard Fred Shipman yelling for her, and she rushed down the stairs. When she walked into the sitting room, her mother was laid out on the floor unconscious. Shipman immediately instructed Sharon to give her mother mouth-to-mouth resuscitation while he massaged her heart. "We tried it, but it didn't work," Sharon later recalled.

Then, without uttering a word, Fred Shipman reached inside his medical bag and brought out a syringe. "He sucked in liquid from a little bottle and shot a small squirt into the air just like doctors do on the television," Sharon later recalled. "Then he rolled up the sleeve on her left arm and injected the fluid into her."

"What is that?" asked Sharon.

To this day she cannot remember if he said "morphine" or "adrenaline." But he then told Sharon to call for an ambulance after saying that her mother was in serious condition. "It arrived quickly," she later recalled, "and the paramedics got out a defibrillator. After three goes, they got a pulse, and put her into the ambulance to rush her to the hospital."

Shipman said little to Sharon, and didn't accompany them in the ambulance. Moments later he left the house.

Within minutes of arriving at the hospital, Renate Overton was put on a life-support machine. One doctor even pointed out that Renate appeared to have been injected with morphine. "At the time it did not mean anything to me," Sharon later recalled. "All that was on my mind was my mother and her health. It never occurred to me that this [the morphine] was the reason that she was in this state."

For the following fourteen months, Sharon Overton visited her mother in the hospital virtually every day, and watched her steadily deteriorate. Sharon recalled: "She had asthma problems and also suffered from epilepsy. But it was not serious, and neither condition had prevented her from living a normal life. She was full of life before all this."

In April 1995, Renate fell into what doctors called a "persistent vegetative state" and died. When Sharon next visited Shipman as a patient, she hoped he might he able to offer her some kind of explanation. "But he didn't even ask me about her," Sharon later recalled. "I just didn't know what to say. I couldn't understand why he wasn't interested."

In fact, Fred Shipman knew only too well about Renate's fate. As far as he was concerned, investigators believe, she was just another notch on his belt—and all that mattered was that he'd once again gotten away with murder.

It wasn't until many years later that Sharon Overton discovered that morphine should never be given to people with respiratory problems.

Fred Shipman had an undoubted passion for order and neatness inside his professional life, even though the family home remained in a constant state of untidiness. And his compulsive list-making knew no boundaries. Not only did he assemble more than twice the number of patients any GP would consider sufficient, he knew exactly how many there were—3,200 at one point, 3,100 at another.

He'd even volunteered to work as secretary of the local Medical Council—a job of such overwhelming tedium that doctors normally did all they could to avoid it—in order to monitor his own performance as a GP. His love of lists meant that he could control without fear of intrusion or dispute. But sometimes he got angry that people seemed to fail to appreciate the accuracy of his skills.

In Shipman's mind it was all a question of efficiency— the cold, authoritative pride of a thing done well. Shipman relished issuing death certificates. They really were proof of his brilliance. But between the killings, Fred Shipman dipped back into deep, dark moods; an overwhelming emotion of helplessness like the feelings sparked by the loss of his mother. Taking pethidine had only been a brief respite. But killing had apparently eased the pain.

His mother's death had left Fred Shipman with a sense of self-preservation; he knew how to look after himself. But as a loner—despite his large immediate family—he tended only to do things for others that were convenient to him or to his benefit. He wasn't a "giver" or a "taker." He just didn't trust people much. After all, most of them had betrayed him at some time in his life. To the outside world he remained the perfect picture of respectability, but he was never content, and this made him moody and unpredictable. Shipman also suffered a serious degree of nervous irritation, due to the secrets he was holding inside himself, that further diminished his willpower.

Fred Shipman had lost his moral vision after his mother died. He wasn't really interested in conforming to the legal or moral ways of life, even though he wanted his family to grow up as "normal" as possible. He wanted his children to be successful in an honest, straightforward manner. A bit like a criminal who wants his children not to make the same mistakes he has.

Meanwhile, Shipman was prepared to continue to deceive other people to get his way. He liked acting out the impression of being open and honest, whereas in reality he refused to take any responsibility for his own actions. His arrogance would not allow him to look ahead as far as his medical work was concerned—unless, of course, he was covering his own tracks. However, Fred Shipman had been clever enough to conceal the truth for many, many years. He was a smooth and effective liar, leaving out essential parts of any story, even inventing facts or simply not telling the truth as it should be. He had the insight and the intelligence to spot opportunities, and the ability to turn them to his own advantage without caring about the dishonesty of his decision. He also loved to find excuses for his bizarre behavior and then blame others for his predicament.

Fred Shipman may have believed that the killing only started when his first victim-to-be was already slipping toward death and he simply gave her a helping hand. That had been exciting, because it gave him a role in life, as a ministering angel of mercy. He'd then wanted to try it again, and when he once more got away with it, he began to believe it was his God-given right to continue killing. Not surprisingly, it eventually became a casual, even habitual, event.

By the mid-1990s he saw his mission of mercy as a never-ending decimation of the geriatric population of Hyde. And Fred Shipman certainly couldn't imagine anyone being clever enough to stop him. He had the perfect cover, and he was convinced no one would ever dare question him; he was the good doctor; the life-saver; the man who *really* cared. He reckoned he was doing his patients a favor by killing them.

But there was something else as well. Fred Shipman so enjoyed the thrill of being there at the moment his patients died that his compulsion led him to kill one patient in her home, unaware that her best friend stood in the kitchen waiting for his visit to end. Shipman was visibly shocked when he found Marion Hadfield in Marie West's kitchen minutes after she died in her living room on March 6, 1995.

Shipman immediately said: "She's collapsed on me." Then he leaned down to his patient and tried to open her eyes. "Look, there's no life there."

Then Mrs. Hadfield asked: "What can you do, can't you do something?"

"No, she's gone."

At no time did Fred Shipman try to resuscitate Mrs. West, or contact the emergency services. Her collapse had been caused entirely by a vial of morphine administered by Dr. Shipman.

Primrose Shipman was never more proud than in January 1996, when Fred gathered his family and sixty friends, many of them patients, at Maestro's Restaurant, in Hyde, to celebrate his fiftieth birthday. He chose a menu of insalata di pollo, polla alla provinciale, salmone belladonna and bistecca alla boscaiola, and the finest wines. Each guest was given a menu card reading: "Happy Birthday 14.01.46. H. F. Shipman 14.01.96."

But one who was present at the gathering later recalled: "Fred seemed strangely subdued, although he still enjoyed ordering a pricey bottle or two of wine. But some of us did wonder if running his own practice was putting him under a lot of strain."

It was just three days after he'd signed the death certificate of pensioner Erla Copeland.

On July 11, 1996, Shipman visited an elderly patient named Mrs. Irene Turner at her bungalow on St. Paul's Hill Road in Godley, near Hyde. Neighbor Sheila Ward later recalled how Fred Shipman called her outside, asked her to wait five minutes, then go to the bungalow to pack a bag for Mrs. Turner, as she may have to go to the hospital while he did some tests. When Mrs. Ward went into the house, she found the 67-year-old widow dead in bed. "She looked beautiful," Mrs. Ward later recalled.

Mrs. Ward then ran to the house of Mrs. Turner's friend Michael Woodruff, and when he wasn't in, went home to find a telephone number for him. She then noticed that Fred Shipman had returned and gone back into Mrs. Turner's bungalow.

"Was it cancer?" Mrs. Ward asked the GP as she walked back in.

"No, diabetes," replied Shipman almost casually.

Yet when Mrs. Turner's son-in-law Alfred Isherwood saw Shipman the following day, he said she had died of ischaemic heart disease. Isherwood was baffled, but was too polite to question the doctor's verdict. Shipman even said he'd advised Mrs. Turner to check into a hospital, but she'd refused because she thought she was not ill enough. Isherwood immediately pointed out that she would have happily accepted any treatment recommended by a doctor. He later recalled: "He was very matter-of-fact, very businesslike. No compassion."

Mr. Isherwood went on: "She took Dr. Shipman's word. She thought he was a great doctor. She really liked Dr. Shipman. She took every pill he prescribed to her, because she trusted her doctor."

Alfred Isherwood never forget how Shipman explained to him that the veins in Irene Turner's arms and legs had collapsed and blood had rushed to the center of her body, putting too much pressure on her heart. Shipman assured Isherwood that Mrs. Turner would have fallen asleep before she died. But a post-mortem examination more than two years later showed that Mrs. Turner died from morphine poisoning.

On August 30, 1996, Fred Shipman paid a visit to the home of a patient named Sid Smith after he'd complained of feeling unwell. Moments after arriving at the house, on Garden Street in Hyde, Sid's brother Ken went into the kitchen to make them both a cup of tea.

Minutes later, Fred Shipman strolled into the kitchen to tell Ken that his brother had died. When the two men walked back into the sitting room, Sid Smith was still sitting in his favorite chair. "When the undertakers arrived twenty minutes later, they started talking to Sid, thinking he was asleep," Irene's daughter Sheila Marshall later recalled. "They were disgusted he had been left that way."

On December 17, 1996, just four months later, Ken Smith was also found dead, sitting in that same chair. A window cleaner had spotted him sitting motionless, and asked a neighbor to see if he was all right. She walked in through the back door, as usual, unlocked, and was unable to revive him.

Whether Fred Shipman even remembered that the two men were brothers will probably never be known.

*   *   *

Fred Shipman had gotten into the habit of standing by the side of many of his patients and watching them die. Lizzie Adams, was so active and in good health that, up until six months before her seventy-seventh birthday, she'd been a dance teacher, and danced regularly with her partner, William Catlow. But that didn't stop Fred Shipman from deciding that her time had come on the afternoon of February 28, 1997.

Shipman later claimed that Lizzie Adams died while he was in the next room looking for a telephone to tell her daughter she needed hospital treatment for bronchial pneumonia. It was at this point that he was disturbed by Mrs. Adams's dance partner Bill Catlow. He added: "I listened to the chest. There were no heart signs. Mr. Catlow said he felt something on her wrist, and I told him it was his own pulse."

But Mr. Catlow later insisted that he called at the house that afternoon and let himself in with his own key to find Shipman standing in the lounge looking at Mrs. Adams' collection of Royal Dalton figurines. In fact, Fred Shipman had been waiting for her to die when he was most rudely interrupted by Mr. Catlow.

Shipman turned to Mr. Catlow and asked, "Are you Bill?"

"Yes, that's right," he replied.

"Betty is very, very ill."

Shipman said he'd called for an ambulance, and Mr. Catlow rushed past him into the living room to find Mrs. Adams. Shipman followed him in and immediately pronounced her dead.

"She's gone. I'd better cancel the ambulance," Shipman told Catlow.

"Are you sure?" Mr. Catlow asked the good doctor. "She looks as if she's asleep."

"I'm afraid so," came Fred Shipman's reply.

Catlow later recalled that the GP then made a telephone call. He assumed it was to cancel the ambulance. But no telephone call was made or received that day requesting or canceling any ambulance. It was merely a charade performed by Shipman to help further conceal the murder of Lizzie Adams by his hands.

12

It would be a gross oversimplification to say that Fred Shipman's frustration was the result of an unsatisfied power-urge. But he certainly considered himself to be brilliant at his job. Members of the staff at his one-man practice often spoke of his fanatical attention to detail. As William Blake once said: "When Thought is closed in Caves/Then love shall shew its root in deepest Hell."

No doubt Fred Shipman found being a doctor a very numbing experience. He couldn't afford to care too much if he was to remain good at his job. When he'd first started, he'd found it difficult when patients died unexpectedly, but that feeling passed quickly. Fred Shipman could face death as long as he was in control of it.

In many ways Shipman didn't consider his victims to be human beings. He'd become completely desensitized. His version of caring for his patients was to want them all to die happily and peacefully without ever realizing that death was imminent. So, as the number of victims had increased, Fred Shipman felt a physical dependence on the act of killing. His addiction had turned into a physical dependency on watching people die.

The first few deaths had probably been unplanned. But now he felt a rush of adrenaline every time he had an opportunity to kill again. And, crucially, he still believed he was more clever than everyone else around him.

Fred Shipman—on the surface, a friendly if reserved local GP—felt completely alienated from society. He found it virtually impossible to function in normal situations. That's why he needed the outlet of death. His so-called normal life with a wife and four children helped overshadow his innermost fears. Now the strain of keeping those evil thoughts and deeds to himself was taking a punishing toll on his psyche.

But it was the godlike regard with which most of his patients held him that was the biggest clue to the warped and twisted mind that had already turned Fred Shipman into a serial killer. For he continued to harbor grandiose ideas about himself. He saw most other people as "stupid" and himself on another, higher plain from the rest. This arrogance made him believe that he was above the law. And his aloofness made him fixate on things that were not always the most intelligent choice. Morphine was a classic example of that. It could be traced in the body, easily detectable by anyone looking for it. Yet morphine had become the thread which ran through Shipman's life. He didn't seem to care that it would inevitably one day lead to his downfall.

Hyde really was an unlikely setting for mass murder. There was little to divert motorists as they hammered past on the nearby M67 freeway. It remained a distinctly low-key type of place. Even the biggest local supermarket boasted that it was a "No Nonsense Foodstore." Entertainment for the residents of Hyde still only consisted of that bingo hall near Fred Shipman's less-than-impressive surgery, and a few pubs. Two grim, concrete tower-blocks cast a shadow over the main shopping arcade. Shipman hadn't even bothered putting a brass plate up announcing his name and title, but it didn't seem to put off his vast list of patients.

Some years after starting his one-man practice, Fred Shipman got heavily involved with an attractive middle-aged female patient named Bianka Pomfret, who had recently divorced her husband and was suffering from a wide range of psychiatric anxieties. Her ex-husband, Adrian, later recalled: "Fred Shipman seemed to really care about Bianka. She was a very warm person underneath her very mixed-up exterior and she desperately needed guidance. She had a tendency to buy people," he added, "even to buy friends in a sense. She'd shower them with gifts, but she was extremely confused and terribly over-sensitive."

Born and raised in Germany, Bianka's life was filled with contradictions; she drove, but she didn't own a car; She rarely went out, but she was very outgoing when she talked to people. As Mr. Pomfret explained: "It was all a form of self-punishment. She even chopped all her hair off at one stage. She had a lovely head of strawberry reddy-blonde hair, but it was typical of Bianka to get rid of it—she was always trying to make a statement about her life."

It had all been very different when Adrian and the 26-year-old Bianka married more than fifteen years earlier. Adrian, aged 30, was stationed with the British Army in the German town of Munster. Bianka was unable to have children, and that had deeply affected the Pomfrets' marriage, but they adopted a baby boy and named him William. Bianka Pomfret knew she was highly strung, even during her marriage, and her ex-husband believes to this day that she had a deep-set fear of passing on that mental illness to any of her children.

Bianka's mental problems—manic depression—eventually cost her her marriage to Adrian Pomfret. Her condition would also cause a deep rift with their son. Just before Adrian Pomfret ended the marriage, he went to see family GP Fred Shipman to warn him that she might "go a little crazy" once he broke the news to her. Adrian had first encountered Shipman when he had problems with high cholesterol and had to get his blood checked regularly. "He seemed extremely good and trustworthy, and we felt very safe in his hands," Adrian later recalled.

That day, Mr. Pomfret told Shipman: "I've made this decision and I'm going to leave home. The situation is such that I can no longer live with her, and I've made the decision to move out in a month. The reason I've come to see you is to give you fair warning and make sure that she is looked after."

Fred Shipman responded by nodding his head thoughtfully. Adrian Pomfret later recalled: "He seemed genuinely concerned about Bianka's well-being, and I felt secure in the knowledge that he would keep an eye on her after I left home."

Shipman even made a point of telling Adrian Pomfret: "I think you're making the right decision."

Fred Shipman was even adamant that Bianka Pomfret was not as crazy as everyone else thought she was: "She is not mentally ill. It's just the way she is. She's a highly intelligent person," he told Mr. Pomfret.

But Mr. Pomfret also never forgot something else about Fred Shipman that day: "He didn't look me directly in the eye. He had the strangest stare. He never once blinked. It was quite the reverse. I'll never forget that stare."

Soon afterwards, Adrian Pomfret left the family home and set up with another, younger woman. But he so trusted Fred Shipman that a few months later he returned to the clinic on Market Street to give him an update about his marital situation. Shipman was already monitoring the pregnancy of the new woman in Adrian Pomfret's life.

That's when Shipman said to him: "Do you think Bianka will stay in the UK after the divorce, or go back to Germany?"

He later recalled: "At the time I didn't see the significance, but it was a very personal approach, and Shipman seemed to be crossing the line between patient and friend in his attitude."

Adrian Pomfret replied at the time: "Well, my honest opinion is that she prefers it here."

Fred Shipman snapped: "What d'you mean by that?"

"I'm going to give her 60 percent of my assets to ensure that she is okay," replied Mr. Pomfret.

"How d'you mean?" asked Shipman again.

"Well, she'll own her own property, her own home, and she will have money besides . . ."

All of a sudden Fred Shipman jumped in and said: "I don't want to know about that."

As Adrian Pomfret later recalled: "I remember thinking,

What d'you mean by that?' If you care about somebody, and as a GP, you would have thought one of the things that was important was that a woman with a serious mental illness was not going to be penniless."

After the shock of her marital break-up, Bianka Pomfret tried to mend her relationship with her son William. But her mental health was fast deteriorating. Eventually she agreed to visit the local community mental health center for more intense treatment.

Dr. Alan Tate, consultant psychiatrist at Tameside General Hospital, treated Bianka for manic depression. He'd encountered her some years earlier when, during her marriage, Bianka had asked Dr. Tate to commit her to a hospital because she was feeling suicidal and her husband was telling her to pull herself together. But, as Dr. Tate later explained, Bianka's condition was one in which "patients think about their death and about taking their life, but do not necessarily intend to do it." She was released within days.

But just after the divorce, Fred Shipman contacted Dr. Tate and asked him to see Bianka once again, because she had been suffering a "recurring depressive disorder." She was admitted to the hospital as a "crisis case" and stayed over Christmas and New Year's. By 1995 Bianka Pomfret's illness had become psychotic. She was hearing voices and believing her thoughts could be read by other people. She was rapidly "moving towards a high risk of completing her suicidal thoughts," according to one specialist.

It was then that Fred Shipman decided to take a much closer role in Bianka Pomfret's life. Adrian Pomfret later explained: "Some time later Shipman sent for me and said that Bianka's grandmother had suffered mental illness as well, and he was convinced Bianka needed to be hospitalized once again. They were obliged to get her treated."

Mr. Pomfret continued: "You have to appreciate that most people just gave Bianka a wide berth. They all acted as if she had something catching, but these sort of mental problems lurk in everyone. We all should be aware of that. And Fred Shipman seemed to really care about her."

Shipman told Mr. Pomfret that he was going to personally handle Bianka Pomfret's case from now on. "I never thought twice about it at the time. I thought he was a caring GP, so I went along with him. We all trusted him implicitly. And for some time, Shipman's decision seemed to help. He even gave her intensive counseling and prescribed her antidepressants. She seemed to get better."

Adrian Pomfret's relationship with Fred Shipman was then further cemented when his baby son Nathaniel, by his new wife, suffered severe liver problems—septicemia—and almost died at six months of age. "He was marvelous over that, and his quick thinking almost certainly helped save Nat's life. We both thought he was a fantastic man."

When Adrian Pomfret visited his former wife—now back at home after her spell in the mental hospital—he made a point of singing the praises of Fred Shipman. He soon noticed that Bianka was becoming more and more dependent on Shipman. Sometimes she'd visit his surgery three or four times a week for "counseling."

To begin with, Mr. Pomfret was relieved that his deeply troubled ex-wife seemed to have found someone she trusted to treat her and listen to her. "At that time she definitely improved," he later recalled. Shipman put Bianka on a course of lithium to try to end the vast mood swings she was suffering from. Bianka—a highly religious woman who attended Catholic church every Sunday—was deeply confused about the existence of God. "That used to get a grip of her sometimes, she found it difficult to handle," recalled Adrian Pomfret.

But Fred Shipman's propensity for prescribing drugs was not the main reason that Bianka Pomfret became so dependent on her GP. Shipman's "counseling" of Bianka was becoming increasingly personal. He found he could relate to Bianka's problems because she seemed to be coming from a direction similar to his. After some months she began turning up at Shipman's Market Street practice just as he was completing surgery. Then she would enter his office, sit herself down and pour everything out to him.

Eventually Shipman found himself revealing things about his own life to Bianka that he had never discussed with anyone else before. A close bond was forged between them. They shared a mental telepathy about certain sensitive subjects, and Fred Shipman made an emotional attachment to Bianka Pomfret.

In the middle of all this, Adrian Pomfret managed to sit down and have some reasonable conversations with his ex-wife. "But I learnt to be very careful not to criticize her. She didn't want her views questioned." Mr. Pomfret noticed that Bianka was receiving a large number of house visits from Fred Shipman. "There aren't many GPs who'd do the number of house calls he did," he later commented.

Shipman on occasion even visited Bianka Pomfret when she was in the hospital drying out from the high dosages of lithium that he'd prescribed to her. Lithium was known to damage the liver, so she had to go into the hospital to wash it out of her system on a regular basis.

Then one day Bianka Pomfret made a bizarre comment to her former husband: "Isn't it strange that Dr. Shipman is married to someone who looks so odd?"

Mr. Pomfret later recalled: "Looking back on it, that was a very strange thing to say. It made me wonder how close Bianka was to Shipman." But he added: "I do know that Bianka was the last person who could have coped with a sexual relationship with a man. You have to remember that her illness made her incredibly intense; she used to think about things far too much. The other side is that it can also make you bond with people who seem to understand where you are coming from. Shipman definitely came into that category."

But was Bianka Pomfret in love with Fred Shipman?

"It's possible," Adrian Pomfret said later. "She needed him, and he seemed to provide her with some kind of security. He was always there for her. I still wonder about their relationship to this day. But remember, she had very high morals, so she would not have entered into a relationship without a lot of thought and consideration."

And local district nurse Kate McGraw insists: "She clearly adored him. She had a lot of problems. I think Fred Shipman took advantage of her in many ways."

But did Bianka Pomfret and Fred Shipman really have a proper relationship? "Something happened between them," recalled Mr. Pomfret. "It was definitely on a mental level and might well have been something more. It was a cat-and-mouse game. One side of her tried to ignore it, but the other side of her would kick in and enjoy the attention. Bianka had this ability to look inside people's minds and she could see what Shipman was up to. She probably knew the truth behind what he was up to and it must have frightened and depressed her."

Adrian Pomfret believes that his ex-wife confided about the true extent of her relationship with Shipman to the people she met while attending counseling at the local health center. Mr. Pomfret later recalled: "Bianka got herself into situations where she had no other contact, no other friends apart from those people at Brindle House [the health center]. She spoke to them at some stage."

Mr. Pomfret added: "She may have fallen in love. I'll never forget how she'd come home from seeing her proper psychiatrist, who'd put her on a particular line of therapy, then one week later she'd go back and see Shipman, and she'd come back from him pushing a completely different line. I thought that was baffling at the time, but it shows how much control Shipman had over her.

"I believed Shipman was after something. As a GP he could get away with all sorts of things. I have no doubt you can be in love with someone mentally and you don't even have to go out with them. Certain people attract certain other people. Bianka needed feeding mentally and Shipman did that to perfection. I think he tried to make Bianka feel she was right about everything, but occasionally he did disagree with her and that wound her up completely. Bianka respected and needed Shipman so much, and he played that role so well for so long, but then the goal posts changed."

At one stage Shipman even told Bianka Pomfret: "Don't

worry about it [the illness]. We can't cure it, but at least we know what it is, and we can treat it."

In early 1997, Adrian Pomfret went to see Fred Shipman about his ever-increasing cholesterol levels, but ended up discussing his ex-wife. "He brought up her name first," recalled Mr. Pomfret.

"She's doing okay. Don't worry about her. She is a very strong person, and she will dance on your grave," Fred Shipman made a point of telling his patient.

"I'm glad about that," replied Adrian Pomfret.

He later recalled: "I thought, 'That's a strange thing to say.' "

After approximately two years of intensive contact, Bianka began to want more from their relationship. That was when Fred Shipman pulled the shutters down once more— leaving Bianka devastated. As Adrian Pomfret later explained: "She dived into a really deep depression suddenly. She was in such a terrible state that I advised her to start seeing a psychiatrist yet again. Something weird was going on."

Mr. Pomfret believed that Fred Shipman had so much control over his former wife that at first he urged her not to see a psychiatrist. "I took her twice to see a woman doctor and she refused to go back on each occasion. I know Shipman was urging her not to see this other doctor. He wanted to retain control over her."

He finally relented and Bianka went back to seeing Dr. Tate at the local hospital. Then another man came into Bianka's life whom she met during counseling sessions. Adrian Pomfret recalled: "I knew him as Czech Andy. He spoke fluent English and German. And he took a lot of Bianka's attention away from Shipman."

Fred Shipman was deeply offended when this other man came on the scene. He seemed almost jealous. As Mr. Pomfret explained: "You have to remember that Bianka was a highly intelligent person. In some ways she was flattered by the attention of these two men. She needed to feel she was in control sometimes, because of her own fears and her actual inhibitions about herself."

But it was Fred Shipman who really had the control.

THE GOOD DOCTOR

13

Fred Shipman might not have been regarded as the most charismatic of characters, but he had an ability to plug away at things, and that gave him his sense of achievement. Yet by this time he had become increasingly socially and psychologically isolated. His relations with his work partners had been far from successful. Beneath the surface, Fred Shipman was deeply afraid of what the future held for him. He wanted to believe he could do anything, just as his dearly beloved mother had predicted. But she was wrong, and coming to terms with that was eating away at his self esteem.

Fred Shipman's low threshold for irritation and anger came to the surface when he publicly tried to prove he was superior to other people. He desperately craved recognition, and the outside world was failing to acknowledge and reward his brilliance. Shipman had allowed himself to develop into a man who got twisted satisfaction from killing old and helpless people—it helped relieve the frustrations of his life, albeit on a purely temporary basis.

Shipman believed the killings were further evidence that he'd been in control of his entire life ever since the day his mother died, and that extended to all those around him. He needed that charge of having the ultimate power of life and death. But like any addiction, each "hit" lasted less and less time, and he needed even more regular "fixes."

In early November 1996, widow Irene Heathcote, aged 76, told her relatives and friends that she wanted to change her GP. His name was Fred Shipman. Mrs. Heathcote had been upset with Shipman for canceling one of her hospital appointments. "She felt he was giving her the wrong treatment," her daughter later recalled. "She said she was going to see him to 'have it out' with him."

But on November 20, 1996, Mrs. Heathcote was found dead in a chair at her home on Coronation Avenue in Hyde. Her neighbors alerted police when they couldn't get any answer from the house. Retired policeman William Trattles, who helped break into the house, later recalled what happened when Fred Shipman appeared at the scene.

"He arrived, examined the body and said she'd died the previous evening," said Mr. Trattles. "He said she suffered a stroke, and that he could issue a death certificate because he'd seen her the previous day. There didn't seem to be anything suspicious. He seemed a quiet, unassumed man, and professional."

But there was no evidence that Mrs. Heathcote had died naturally. The way she was found sitting "peacefully" in her chair was inconsistent with someone who'd died of a stroke. Authorities suspected that Mrs. Heathcote had been murdered by Fred Shipman.

Pensioner Charles Killan's wife died in 1984, and he'd planted a rose bush in his back garden in her memory. He spent hours tending to it each day. During the Killans' long marriage, the pair had enjoyed holidays away in north Wales and rides out on Charlie's motorcycle. In one treasured family photo he could be seen standing next to his beloved Bond three-wheeler car.

But on February 3, 1997, 90-year-old Mr. Killan died in the presence of Fred Shipman, who then called on a next-door neighbor to tell him that Mr. Killan "wasn't very well" and asked the neighbor to wait for the ambulance he claimed he had called. That neighbor then walked into Mr. Killan's house on Bagshaw Street in Hyde, and found the retired bus driver already dead. Moments later he watched as Fred Shipman put his hand around Mr. Killan's throat and said curtly: "You're right, he's dead."

Shipman then signed a death certificate saying that Mr. Killan had died of heart failure and heart disease.

On April 25, 1997, Shipman visited 59-year-old Mrs. Jean Lilley at her Hyde flat on Jackson Street, after she complained of chest pains. It was his first home visit to her. He later claimed: "She was a very interesting patient, and when she came to the surgery, I listened to her chest because I had never come across the condition before. When I visited her this time, there were far more noises, squeaky noises, harsh noises. I would say she had severe arthritis."

Shipman said he then decided she needed to be admitted to a hospital. He explained: "She was not very happy. She said, 'Couldn't I just have some antibiotics and see you tomorrow?' " Shipman claimed he then persuaded Mrs. Lilley to discuss going into the hospital with her family, including her husband, long-distance truck driver Albert Lilley. He said he left her alive sitting in a chair that afternoon.

Shipman claimed he was at the flat for fifteen to twenty minutes, not forty minutes as later claimed by Mrs. Lilley's neighbor, Elizabeth Hunter. He said he saw no one and spoke to no one as he left. Mrs. Hunter found Mrs. Lilley collapsed and rushed after the doctor as Shipman was driving off, but he completely ignored her.

Another neighbor, Janet Aldred, was looking out her window at the very same moment. She later explained: "I saw Liz on the path, shouting and waving and trying to attract his attention. He must have seen Liz. His head was out of the car window turned towards where Liz was coming down the path, but he just drove off."

Paramedics later told Mrs. Hunter that her friend had been dead "for some time." One expert, Dr. John Grenville, later explained that it was "inconceivable" that Mrs. Lilley could have been other than "in extremis"—or dead—when Shipman left her. While the ambulance crew was at Mrs. Lilley's flat, Shipman even returned clutching his dead patient's four-inch-thick medical file. Paramedic Sandra Smith later recalled that she thought it unusual that a doctor would bring a patient's medical file and then go over it in great detail.

Smith also noticed that Shipman became agitated and kept saying that Mrs. Lilley's pregnant daughter Odette was due to arrive. She later explained: "He did not want to be there when Odette turned up. You'd have thought a doctor would have wanted to be there to sympathize and help, especially as Odette was pregnant."

And during his return to the flat, Shipman hadn't even gone into the bedroom to examine Mrs. Lilley. Neighbor Mrs. Hunter later recalled that Shipman gave the impression that the death did not matter, "that it was irrelevant." A later examination of Mrs. Lilley's body revealed that, despite suffering from serious lung and heart problems, it was morphine that actually caused her death.

At 7:30 A.M. on May 29, 1997, one of Fred Shipman's elderly women patients died inside his own treatment room. Less than an hour later, he told the daughter of Mrs. Ivy Lomas that her mother had died of a "massive coronary." Mrs. Lomas did suffer from emphysema and narrowing of the coronary arteries—one by 70 percent, another by 50 percent and a third by 10 percent—but this did not kill her. Once again, it was morphine administered by the good doctor which sent her into another world.

Shipman had continued seeing other patients in his consulting room, even though the body of Ivy Lomas lay in his treatment room. Shipman later claimed that, after Mrs. Lomas's collapse, he immediately started heart massage and mouth-to-mouth resuscitation, but after what seemed like fifteen minutes or longer, he stopped, because there was no response.

Shipman then went into the reception area and told receptionist Carol Chapman that he had a "little problem" with the EKG machine, "but would see the next patient."

He later said he did not immediately tell Mrs. Chapman that Mrs. Lomas had died because: "To do it in front of three other patients, I thought, was inappropriate."

Ivy Lomas's daughter, Carol Dàlpiaz, had spoken to her mother on the phone a few hours before she died, because Carol was worried about her son Jackie. She later recalled that her mother had never even mentioned any heart problems. Shortly after Ivy Lomas's death, Fred Shipman met Mrs. Dàlpiaz at her mother's home on Thornley Street in Hyde. He explained how he'd left her in his treatment room to tend to other patients, then returned to find her collapsed. He insisted he'd tried to revive her.

(Later, under police interrogation, Shipman changed his story and said he had not tried to revive Mrs. Lomas.)

But what Carol Dàlpiaz did not realize was that Shipman had labeled Ivy Lomas one of his "nuisance" patients to other members of the staff at his surgery. Shipman even later joked that just a few hours before Ivy Lomas's death, he'd considered putting up a plaque in the seating area saying, "SEAT PERMANENTLY RESERVED FOR IVY LOMAS."

PC Phillip Reade, who went to the clinic, explained: "This lady had been left for a brief period of time, and Dr. Shipman was telling me that she could have taken her last breath as he left the room and been dead fifteen minutes, or she could have just taken her last breath as he went in. I was amazed, to be quite honest."

During 1997 another round of gossip circulated in Hyde that Fred Shipman's patients didn't always live to a ripe old age. A few patients took the rumor and gossip seriously and moved away from his one-man practice, but most simply laughed and shrugged their shoulders. The local health authority heard that some patients were quitting the practice, so they sent questionnaires to them to find out why. But they never followed up their own inquiries.

Meanwhile, Fred Shipman's need for a "death fix" continued. During one visit to the home of a patient he'd just killed, Shipman told the daughter that "morphine is a nice way to go." His words implied that he believed he was putting them out of their lives of misery and pain. It was important to Fred Shipman that his victims didn't feel the anguish of death creeping up on them. Vast doses of morphine meant they'd drift off into a happy oblivion called death. There was no struggle. There was no pain. Just a never ending sleep.

Despite his preference for quiet evenings at home with Primrose, Fred Shipman did attend class reunions with his fellow alumni at the Leeds University medical school. The get-togethers were organized by Dr. Colin Wilkinson, and held at the Bramcote Trust House, in Leeds. For Fred Shipman it was a relatively easy journey forty miles up the M63 freeway from Hyde. He even brought Primrose with him on two occasions. The reunions were amusing, gossipy affairs and Fred fitted in well. His dark sense of humor only came to the surface when talking about other people, but he seemed very passionate about his work. Shipman also breathlessly told other guests of his ambitious plans for the Market Street practice.

One other GP he met at the reunions later recalled: "Fred obviously deeply loved it in Hyde; he was very caring. He wanted to give a better service to his patients, do things his way, which he couldn't do before."

Shipman underlined that attitude by taking on even more work when he became the treasurer for the Small Practices Association, a support group for medical practices of three or fewer. His fellow graduates from Leeds were impressed: "And he was running an appeal for new equipment on top of that. He worked his socks off."

Primrose just about held her own at these reunions. On one occasion the couple even brought two of their children. One partygoer invited the Shipmans to his hotel room, as the Shipman children were of a similar age to his: "Fred spoke most, took the lead, because it was his reunion, but Primrose seemed pleasant and amiable. The children were very polite too, well brought up," the doctor later explained.

Fred Shipman was a considerable social success at these gatherings. Even the fact that the GP looked older than his years now seemed to work to his advantage. "While everybody else had aged, Fred always looked middle-aged. I suppose it's partly because he got married so young," said one old colleague.

When Muriel Grimshaw, 76, died unexpectedly at her home in Berkeley Crescent, Hyde, on July 15, 1997, her daughter, Mrs. Ann Brown, noticed that Fred Shipman didn't even bother to touch her mother's body before proclaiming her dead. "He just gave her a cursory glance," Mrs. Brown later said. She'd found her mother fully clothed on the bed with the television on after being alerted by a neighbor, and then phoned Shipman's practice. He arrived at her flat within twenty minutes. But Shipman didn't reveal to Mrs. Brown that he'd visited her mother the previous day. He even recorded in her computerized medical record that she had died of a stroke, but she had, like so many before her, died of morphine poisoning.

Shipman recorded the time and date of Mrs. Grimshaw's death as 6 P.M. on July 14. He also recorded on her death certificate that the last time he'd seen her was July 2, 1997, but he had actually called on July 14. "That was an error on my part," he later admitted.

Four years earlier Fred Shipman had taken a supply of heroin from the home of Mrs. Grimshaw's daughter, whose husband had just died. The GP removed it on the day that 54-year-old cancer sufferer Raymond Jones passed away. Following Mrs. Grimshaw's death, local undertaker Alan Massey questioned Fred Shipman after noticing how frequently he was being called out to deal with the sudden deaths of Shipman patients. Usually, there was little evidence they'd been seriously ill in the first place.

Alan Massey explained: "Anybody can die in a chair or drop down dead in the street, but Dr. Shipman's patients always seemed to be in the same or very similar positions. They'd be sat in the chair or a settee and 90 percent were always fully clothed. There was never anything in the house that indicated the person had been ill. Clearly something was not quite right."

When Massey asked Fred Shipman if there was "any

cause for concern," the GP responded: "No, there certainly isn't." Shipman then produced his death certificate record book and said, "There's nothing to worry about."

Alan Massey's daughter, Deborah Bambroffe, later recalled: "It was as if you were going and asking for a prescription for a cold or something. He just got up, got his register out where he gets his death certificates from, opened it up at different pages, and his exact words were, 'Anybody can inspect this book, there's nothing to worry about.' " She continued: "Shipman was calm and not in the least defensive. He invited Dad to look through the case notes of every death in his filing cabinet and said he had nothing to hide. That was good enough for Dad; he came back telling me there was nothing to worry about."

And Mr. Massey added: "Dr. Shipman's attitude was very friendly, considering what I was suggesting. I thought he'd hit the roof, but then, I wasn't making a specific accusation. We were just concerned about the actual number of deaths, and that was what we were really pointing out."

But at that time, reassured by Shipman's calm response, Mr. Massey decided not to pursue the matter.

14

In the middle of 1997, Fred Shipman's close relationship with patient Bianka Pomfret crossed all sorts of boundaries when she suddenly decided to make him the main beneficiary of her will. Mrs. Pomfret told her ex-husband about her decision when he dropped in on one of his twice-monthly visits to her home. "There was about £100,000 [$150,000] in property and cash. She told me she'd discussed it with Shipman, and how he could use it all to help improve his clinic," Adrian Pomfret later explained. "She just sat there and calmly explained to me that she'd made the decision to leave her estate to Shipman. I was so stunned I said, 'Suit yourself.' "

Two weeks later, Mr. Pomfret went to see his ex-wife again. "She was still going on about it. She asked me my opinion, especially in relation to our son William and the grandchildren. I told her I thought it was out of order."

Then Mr. Pomfret added: "Bianka putting Shipman in her will proved just how close he had become to her. You leave money to the ones you love and adore. There must have been a very intense relationship between them. I'd just like to know how he found the time to get so close to her."

The rest of the Pomfret family were stunned to discover that she was leaving her estate to her GP. Bianka even wrote a letter to her own mother back in Germany telling her about her decision. As Adrian Pomfret pointed out: "Bianka was a manic depressive and part of her illness was that she needed attention all the time, and that was what she was doing by changing her will. She thought he would give her even more attention by leaving the money to him."

Then, one day during this period, Shipman turned up unannounced at Bianka's house and found her in the company of another man. He was a fellow patient from the local mental health clinic. Shipman did not like the fact that someone else might be trying to influence the woman he controlled. Adrian Pomfret explained: "There was some kind of confrontation. That's all I know."

Mr. Pomfret believes that whatever happened during that encounter made Bianka decide she no longer trusted Fred Shipman. "Something obviously happened between them. It's such a shame, because for the first time in years Bianka seemed to be on the mend. The medication had been reduced. It must have dawned on her that Shipman was not to be trusted. He was losing his power over her. She was getting out more, and even became friendly with another woman from the clinic called Mary."

Shortly afterwards Adrian Pomfret made another of his regular visits to his ex-wife's home, and Bianka Pomfret immediately informed him: "Dr. Shipman is a horrible person." She refused to explain the reasons behind her outburst, but she asked him about the will. "She asked me what she should do," Mr. Pomfret later recalled. "She no longer wanted to leave all the money to Shipman. The way I put it across to her was that at the end of the day, the only lifeline she had left were the two grandchildren, no matter what the situation was between us. I said, 'You have to think deeply and sensibly, and leave it to the grandchildren.' "

A few days later, Bianka Pomfret saw her attorney and reverted the will so that everything was left to her son and grandchildren. "Shipman had lost his power over her," recalled Mr. Pomfret. "Something had come between them, but I never got to the bottom of it."

Sixty-seven-year-old Marie Quinn—a regular at St. Luke's Roman Catholic Church, in Hyde—had become a local celebrity overnight when she was seen by millions of television viewers talking about the rising problem of crime in the community: "Every day in our area you will hear of a murder being committed . . . We are just getting worse all the time. It's been forecast in the Apocalypse; there will be a cleansing."

The BBC-TV program *Everyman* filmed the widow sipping tea in the kitchen of her terrace home in Hyde, before she set off on a pilgrimage to a Catholic shrine in Medjugorje, Bosnia, where the Virgin Mary was reputed to appear.

At 6:30 P.M. on November 24, 1997—a year to the day after the program's transmission—Fred Shipman arrived at Mrs. Quinn's house to find her "breathing her last breath." Yet earlier in the day, she'd telephoned her son John and—as he later explained—she'd sounded "in very good spirits."

Shipman later claimed that Mrs. Quinn had called him at his clinic and said she was "feeling poorly." He said he then went to her house, where he found she'd apparently suffered a stroke and was partially paralyzed. Later investigations showed there was no record of a phone call from her home to the clinic that day. Fred Shipman's lies were all part of his deadly addiction.

Shipman then called Mrs. Quinn's friend Ellen Hanratty to tell her of the alleged stroke, and that Mrs. Quinn had died. That same day Mrs. Quinn's son John phoned Shipman from Japan. The doctor told John that his mother had tried to call him a few hours earlier to say she thought she'd suffered a stroke.

By this stage in his murderous career, Fred Shipman had become so confident—and reckless—that he thought no one would notice that he hadn't bothered calling the emergency services when he first found Mrs. Quinn. Also, Mrs. Quinn was found in the kitchen at the back of the house, even though the only telephone, from which she was supposed to have called him, was in the living room. Shipman immediately issued a death certificate stating the cause of death as a stroke, narrowing of the arteries, hypertension and secondary scleroderma.

The following day her son rang Shipman from Japan once again and suggested that he might have come more quickly or sent his mother to a hospital. But Fred Shipman calmly assured him that nothing more could have been done and, had she survived, she would have been paralyzed, with no quality of life, waiting for an inevitable second fatal stroke.

In fact Mrs. Quinn had no heart abnormality, and her coronary arteries were virtually free of any narrowing. She had died from a massive injection of morphine.

At 1:45 P.M. on December 9, 1997, Fred Shipman left an ante-natal clinic at his practice without explanation. Surgery staff only knew where he'd gone when he called them forty-five minutes later to say that patient Mrs. Kathleen Wagstaff had died. Receptionist Carol Chapman later recalled: "He telephoned me and said Mrs. Wagstaff was dead. Her name had not featured in any phone call or conversation that day."

Gardener Andrew Hallas had seen Mrs. Wagstaff earlier that same morning when she offered him a cup of tea outside her home in Rock Gardens, Gee Cross, near Hyde. Hallas later said the widow had gone into Hyde to do some shopping, and Shipman had arrived at the house when she returned after lunchtime. He saw Shipman knock on the front door and be let in by Mrs. Wagstaff. Thirty minutes later Shipman was spotted by Hallas in a nearby car park. Fred Shipman told relatives that he'd called an ambulance from her home, but there was no record of either a request for a home visit or any calls for an ambulance.

Shipman later claimed that he was just around the corner when a call from Mrs. Wagstaff came in, and he had gone straight to her house. Shipman said he found Mrs. Wagstaff looking very gray and sweating profusely. He then escorted her upstairs before taking her pulse. Realizing she was in a bad state, he immediately phoned for an ambulance and went downstairs for his bag. But, he later claimed, she died soon afterwards, so he canceled the ambulance. "We were relieved it had been a relatively easy death. It seemed right that she was with the family doctor we trusted and believed in," said her son Peter Wagstaff.

Fred Shipman had looked after three generations of the Wagstaff family of Hyde, and they thought the world of him. "We had a lot of respect for him," said Peter Wagstaff. "He was a gentleman, and seemed to do more than the normal doctor. Nothing seemed too much trouble for him. We often said we wished we had been younger than we were, because we would have loved him to be our GP when we were old."

The Wagstaff family was so grateful to the trusted GP that they sent a donation for £217 toward his surgery fund. The check was accompanied by a letter from the family to Fred Shipman in which they thanked him for all the care and attention he had shown their mother. They even praised his skills as a doctor.

The day after Fred Shipman murdered Kathleen Wagstaff, he drove across Hyde to see the very demanding Bianka Pomfret, who'd already upset him by deciding not to leave him all her estate after all. No one will ever know if she was pleased to see her GP walk into her house that lunchtime. But Fred Shipman already knew he was going to be the last person to see her alive.

With Christmas 1997 approaching, Bianka Pomfret had struggled to come to terms with spending yet another holiday period away from her family. Adrian Pomfret explained: "She was so worried about it, she even managed to get back on speaking terms with her son William by popping into the corner shop he owned just round the corner from her home."

Bianka had also made an effort to stay on good terms with neighbors Paul Graham and Jeannette Millward, who later remembered how kind and generous she was toward their young sons. "She was a nice person, very quiet, you didn't know she was there," Mr. Graham later recalled. "She was always talking to the kids; they thought she was lovely. Once she brought them a stick of [candy] rock back from a day trip to Blackpool, to thank them for looking after her dog."

But during the last few months of 1997, Bianka, still in

her forties, had begun to age with alarming speed. "She suddenly let completely go of herself. She looked about twenty years older than her age. It was really disturbing to see the change in her," one neighbor later recalled.

In December 1997, Bianka Pomfret became so distressed by her problems with Fred Shipman that she went to see her psychiatrist, Dr. Alan Tate, again. She told him she was feeling extremely depressed and lonely, and was still dreading being alone on Christmas Day, watching TV and smoking. She didn't go into any details about her clashes with Fred Shipman, but Dr. Tate was convinced that something specific had deeply disturbed her.

Over the next few days, Bianka Pomfret called Fred Shipman at his surgery on a number of occasions, but he refused to come to the phone. The GP was playing cat-and-mouse with a deeply disturbed middle-aged woman who was close to a major nervous breakdown. Then Bianka Pomfret made a very serious error: she left a message for Fred Shipman telling him she was no longer leaving her estate to him.

Shipman was so furious, he decided then and there that the blonde housewife would soon become just another statistic in his computerized medical records.

The second Sunday in December 1997, Bianka Pomfret went to Mass at her local Catholic church. Parish priest Father Denis Maher never forgot that day. "Throughout the service she was following my every movement with her eyes; her eyes were pleading with me constantly. Outside, after the service, she waited for me and asked me to visit her again. She wanted to have a long chat and I told her I could see her the following Wednesday or Thursday."

The one other person who saw Bianka Pomfret on that Sunday was Adrian. "She wanted me to take her out for a meal, which was unusual for her. It was as if she wanted to confide in something to me. But instead I gave her some money and said that she and her social worker—who was in the house that day—should treat themselves to a Chinese meal."

Then Bianka Pomfret mentioned Fred Shipman once again: "He's a horrible man. Not a nice person."

She repeated the words over and over again.

"She also made a point of saying she was going to see Dr. Tate the following day, so something was obviously bothering her deeply," Mr. Pomfret later explained.

Then Bianka Pomfret admitted to her ex-husband that she'd had a dose of flu earlier that week and Shipman had visited her home to treat her. She'd also been to his surgery.

"She hadn't actually dropped him. It was almost as if she couldn't let go of him," Mr. Pomfret later explained.

That Sunday evening, Bianka Pomfret also told her former husband that she was going to see Shipman again within the next few days to tell him she wanted to change GPs.

"She clearly didn't like him anymore. She'd gone from singing his praises to hating him." Mr. Pomfret pointed out: "But then, manic depressives are like that, although I still think her attitude was significant."

That evening as Mr. Pomfret got up to leave, his ex-wife turned to him and said, "I realize you were right, and I want to be with normal people."

"Everyone's normal. What is normal?" pointed out Mr. Pomfret.

"No, what I mean is, I want to be with normal people like I used to do with you."

Adrian Pomfret would continue to believe that his ex-wife was trying to escape the influence of Fred Shipman when she uttered those words. "I regret it now, but I had to leave that night because I was going to see our son and grandchildren to give them their Christmas presents. I just wish I'd stayed longer."

The following day, neighbor Paul Graham noticed Bianka sitting in her chair in the front room, gazing out the window. He thought she was watching him as he worked on his van in the front yard. It was only later that he realized she was waiting for someone.

Mrs. Pomfret received a visit from Fred Shipman later that day. "I was allowed into her house, and I asked what had happened to make me come and visit," Shipman later claimed. "She said she had not felt very well, and that she had chest pains which went right up to her jaw and into her left arm. She couldn't go anywhere fast, she had a small dog, and she said the dog ran while she walked. She recognized there was a limitation to her physical activity."

Shipman said that he and Mrs. Pomfret then discussed her history of chest pains. He suggested an EKG at his clinic that Friday, and also suggested she could take some tablets.

He said later: "She pointed to the multiplicity of bottles of tablets on her table and said she was taking a lot of tablets and didn't want to take any more. She was not happy about a referral to another hospital."

Fred Shipman later claimed that Bianka Pomfret had not taken her pain seriously, because it came and went. Shipman said he visited her home between 1:30 P.M. and 2 P.M. on Wednesday, December 10, and said: "I was upset by Bianka, because she hadn't trusted me enough to tell me about the pain earlier."

Shipman also later pointed out that Mrs. Pomfret smoked around thirty cigarettes a day. He said: "Any patient who has heart disease and who smokes is silly and looking to die."

Four hours later, 49-year-old Bianka Pomfret was found dead by her adult son and a social worker. As Adrian Pomfret later explained: "She was found in a casual position, like, with half a cigarette burning in the ashtray, half a cup of coffee and the TV switched on."

According to other eyewitnesses, Bianka Pomfret's body "looked relaxed"; she had her arms and legs folded. Parish priest Denis Maher was one of the first people to arrive at the house after the discovery of her body. "I was terribly upset," he later recalled. "She did suffer from depression, but I thought she was coming out of it."

That day, Father Maher took an instant dislike to Fred Shipman. "I opened the door to him and he just rushed in and almost knocked me over. I was a rival in a sense, because I was on his level, as a priest. He seemed very cold, arrogant and uncaring. There was no sensitivity in his voice. Nothing. He didn't expect to find me there, and was probably a bit annoyed."

Fred Shipman simply walked in and immediately asked: "Where is she?" before going to examine Bianka Pomfret's body sitting in her armchair. Shipman hardly looked at her and then said to her son William, "You know your mother had a heart condition, don't you? She wouldn't take the treatment, and she wouldn't go to the hospital. She's only got herself to blame."

Father Maher stood by getting increasingly angry. Then Shipman said, "Have you got an undertaker?"

Maher responded, "If you don't mind, Doctor, I'll help the family with that."

Shipman then snapped back, "Don't worry, there won't be an inquest. Just come down to my office in the morning and I'll sign off a death certificate." William Pomfret later insisted that he had no idea about his mother's health problems, but accepted the doctor at his word.

When Adrian Pomfret arrived at his ex-wife's house, he bumped straight into Fred Shipman walking out. "I was in such a state, I didn't even remember to ask him about an autopsy," recalled Mr. Pomfret.

Minutes later Adrian Pomfret concluded that perhaps Bianka had committed suicide. "There is a strong possibility that your mother took her own life . . ." he told their son William, ". . . and if she has, it's down to me, not you. I was the one who walked out on her, not you."

Close to tears, Adrian Pomfret later recalled: "I told William to go and see Shipman to ask him if there was any possibility she killed herself." When Adrian Pomfret later heard that Shipman was insisting it was death by natural causes, he concluded that the GP was being extremely humane by hiding the fact that she may have committed suicide.

"I thought to myself, 'He's playing the game here.' When the truth finally came out years later, I felt relief. That may sound odd, but I felt better about it because I didn't kill her. I thought I had killed her up until then."

Fred Shipman signed Bianka Pomfret's death certificate, giving the cause as a clot in the heart and heart disease, with secondary causes smoking and manic depression. When Bianka's psychiatrist Dr. Alan Tate telephoned Shipman after he heard the news, the GP reiterated that there was no need for a post-mortem examination. Shipman also informed Tate that he'd tried to save Bianka's life. "He said she had been resuscitated and defibrillated and then had died," Mr. Pomfret later recalled.

That day Shipman went back to his surgery and made three entries in the records of Bianka Pomfret. He later claimed that they would then provide a better picture of her medical history, including the angina he recorded on her death certificate.

He explained: "I backdated the entries because they showed the progression of an illness—because it showed something going back six to eight months. My practice was pro-active. I went out looking for illnesses rather than patients having to come in to see me."

Bianka Pomfret's funeral was a grim affair, held in pouring rain with a small number of people in attendance. One of her friends from the clinic—the tall, dark-haired Czech man who'd earlier upset Fred Shipman—unintentionally caused some of the family distress by taking snapshots of the coffin as it was laid to rest in the cemetery.

But as Adrian Pomfret later explained: "I told the priest not to worry about it, as it was quite common on the eastern side of Germany. They photograph the bodies quite often, and I have been in Polish and Czech homes where you walk in and there's the granddad laid out in a coffin."

Bianka Pomfret was buried on a rain-sodden day at Hyde Cemetery, her plot marked with a black marble gravestone inscribed, "SHE WILL BE LOVED AND MISSED FOREVER."

Adrian Pomfret was so concerned about Shipman's role in his wife's last years that he went to see Dr. Alan Tate and mentioned his concerns. Then, a few months later, Pomfret visited Fred Shipman in his surgery to pick up some blood-test results. "He said Dr. Tate had spoken to him, and that Bianka obviously was still suffering from mental illness. I couldn't understand why he was saying this, since before, he'd been saying the exact opposite."

Mr. Pomfret found that the year following Bianka Pomfret's death was "probably the worst twelve months of my life. I was still wracked with guilt. I had something worse than even depression. Even her family in Germany believed she'd killed herself. The only thing that stopped me accepting that she'd done it was that she was very strong morally. She had no time for people who took their own life. She thought they were weak, and I couldn't quite believe she would do it."

Bianka Pomfret's neighbor Paul Graham and his family have kept Bianka's Bible, which they found in the back yard after the house was cleared following her death. It was inscribed: "God loveth a cheerful giver, Corinthians II." The church had meant everything to Bianka. When she was feeling at her lowest, Bianka had even considered throwing herself from the freeway bridge as she walked to St. Paul's Church. But she'd always insisted to Dr. Tate, "I don't want to die."

Then she'd upset Fred Shipman . . .

15

At 1 P.M. on Christmas Eve 1997, 83-year-old Hyde pensioner Jim King was so ill from flu and an ear infection that he called up Fred Shipman and asked him if he'd come by his sheltered apartment. King was found dead in the chair of his front room just a few hours later.

The death of Jim King bore all the hallmarks of a Fred Shipman killing. As his son, Jim King Jr., later explained: "A healthy person dies suddenly. Found in a chair as if asleep shortly after a visit from Shipman. The only difference was that he was an old man, not an old lady."

Jim King's son had recently married and King had even escorted his son down the aisle. "My father was a quiet man and a gentleman. The week before he died, we did a five-mile walk along the side of the canal together. He was so fit, he gave me a run for my money," remembered Jim Jr.

It was only years later that Jim and the rest of his family became convinced that Shipman had also killed his 69-year-old Aunt Molly Dudley back in 1990. She had flu and was visited by Shipman. "He called her daughter to say he had given her an injection of morphine because she was in pain, and seemed to be going into cardiac arrest," Jim later recalled. "By the time they arrived, she was dead—he said she had died in his arms."

Not long after Jim King Senior's death, his son's Aunt Irene Berry called Shipman complaining about a severe case of shingles. She was found dead a few hours later. As Jim later explained: "Death was completely out of the blue. She only ever suffered from shingles. She was in pain, so she called Shipman."

That day Fred Shipman routinely telephoned Mrs. Berry's relatives with the news. When asked how sick Irene was after he'd been in to examine her, the GP replied: "Well, how bad d'you think it can get?"

"Has she passed away?"

"Yes," Shipman replied without a hint of emotion.

When Mrs. Berry's daughter Jean Darlington and her husband arrived at the house, Shipman was still there. He then told them, "She's very comfortable, cup of tea, the fire on. And she was just sat in the chair where she would normally sit with her book and half a cup of tea. She just looked as though she was asleep."

Jean Darlington's training as an accident and emergency nurse left her far from happy with what Shipman was saying. Shipman then claimed that Irene Berry called him out because she had chest pains. He didn't mention shingles. "I immediately wondered why he didn't do something about it," recalled Darlington. "He said he gave her a GCM spray, but that didn't work, so he'd decided to go back and see how she was later. He'd brought the ECG machine with him, which seemed odd to me, but he said that when he got back, she was dead and he didn't think it was a cardiac problem. But then why did he go for an ECG machine? Why didn't he just get an ambulance? I felt concerned about my mother, but I wondered how could he have done this? But I didn't think he did it on purpose. I just thought he'd been negligent."

However, as Jim King Jr. later recalled: "The strangest thing is that my father dies, and then my aunt dies in the same circumstances with Shipman in attendance." But Jim resisted the temptation to go to the police about the "strange coincidence." He recalled: "Basically, I trusted the doctor. I couldn't even consider he was guilty of anything."

Jim believed he was already indebted to Fred Shipman since his own brush with death.

*   *   *

Jim King had returned to Britain from the US in 1996 before marrying his wife Debra, in Hyde. A week later he began getting backaches and noticed blood in his urine. Fred Shipman immediately referred him to a hospital. A couple of weeks later he announced to King that he had cancer in his bladder, urethra and prostate.

"Dr. Shipman started prescribing me morphine and told me I had only eighteen months to live," he later recalled.

What Jim King didn't know was that the hospital consultant had informed Shipman that King did not have any cancer. But the doctor did not pass that vital information on to Jim King, because he was using King's prescriptions to help increase his own stockpile of morphine.

Jim King—once a highly successful engineer in Texas—recalled: "By having a patient like me on his books, he was able to draw Class A drugs for pain relief. He fed me massive doses of morphine—enough to kill me—but I don't know how much more he obtained in my name for use on other people. I was on as much as 360 mg a day—the normal dose for pain is 30 mg—and he was prescribing as much as 24,000 mg at a time. I became addicted to morphine. It was terrible, what he did to me. I didn't know what was happening for twelve months. I lost my job with an engineering firm, and the mortgage on our £56,000 home in Denton was withdrawn. I lost my company car, and we had to sell the Jaguar I had bought Debbie. We ended up here in a council house. Yet he seemed to be my savior in many ways. He was prepared to give me as much morphine as I wanted to help kill the pain."

Fred Shipman knew what a joy it was to have morphine running through your veins. But, of course, there was another motive: he needed the drugs to keep killing his patients, and was more than happy to let an innocent man believe he had a deadly disease in order to feed his killing habit. Recalled Jim King: "I thought I was dying anyway, so I kept taking it and he kept prescribing vast amounts."

Just before Christmas 1996, Jim King took a serious turn for the worse. As his American wife Debbie later explained:

"Jim was in a bad way, so I rang Dr. Shipman to have him come around and check him over." Jim King takes up the story: "He tested my chest and said I had a bad dose of pneumonia, and I'd got liquid on the lungs."

Then Shipman hesitated for a moment before saying: "I need to give you an injection to help all this."

Jim King looked over at his wife and noticed that she seemed concerned by the GP's suggestion. Mrs. King later recalled: "For some reason, I don't really know why, I said no, and said, 'Can't you just write out a prescription for him?' "

But Fred Shipman was insistent that Jim King needed the injection. "I kept telling him no. I didn't like the way he was being so arrogant about it. He had a real snotty attitude towards me," recalled Mrs. King.

Jim King believes that at that moment his life was saved by Debbie, who had worked with doctors when they'd lived in the United States. Debbie believed Shipman should be using antibiotics instead of morphine if his claims about pneumonia were correct. At that moment alarm bells went off in Shipman's twisted mind and he resisted the temptation to finish off Jim King. He knew there could be repercussions.

"I honestly believe that if I had that injection it would have killed me. He would have said it was cancer, Debbie would have gone back to the States and no one would have known any different."

It is suspected that Fred Shipman wanted to finish off Jim King because he could then offer to dispose of any excess medicines in King's house. Shipman already had a huge stockpile of diamorphine in his office, and even kept some at home "for emergencies," but he never wanted to run short of his favorite drug.

A few days later, Jim King discovered that he did not have cancer when he went to see a urologist about another matter. "He read my reports and said they did not make sense. I told him I was dying and he replied, 'Oh, no, you're not.'

A month later Shipman confirmed the news to King in his clinic without even bothering to elaborate. Jim King immediately moved to another GP, but it took him eight months to wean himself off morphine.

King also suspects that Fred Shipman killed his 80-year-old mother Elizabeth, who died suddenly in the hospital in 1994 after a visit from the GP. "The hospital rang to say she was having heart palpitations, but by the time we got there she was dead. There was no post mortem."

Jim King added: "I can never forgive him. What blows my mind is that all this could have been stopped. I want my mum and dad back. My life has been destroyed, and I want it back."

Undertaker Debbie Bambroffe had spent all her life in Hyde and even went to school with Fred Shipman's son Christopher. Part of her job was to visit local GPs, so she often talked to Primrose Shipman about Christopher's progress as an engineer when she went into her husband's surgery.

Her entire family was on Fred Shipman's books. But by the start of 1998, Debbie felt a growing sense of unease about Shipman, who'd earlier convinced her father that the high number of deaths was of no importance. "We would go to the home of the deceased, and it had got to the point where we could tell by the scenario that greeted us whether that person had been a patient of Dr. Shipman. It just didn't add up."

Then Debbie began comparing Shipman's death rate with those of the three other clinics in Hyde. His numbers were significantly higher. At first she convinced herself that more people were dying at home because Shipman didn't like to send people to a hospital to die. "It was easier to think that than to contemplate that he was killing these women off."

Debbie Bambroffe noticed that many of the deaths handled by Fred Shipman were elderly women, but they had not been ill just before they died. There were no pills at their bedside, no oxygen tanks, no district nurse notes. They often had not been in bed; often they were dressed and sitting up in a chair with a cup of tea at their side.

Debbie Bambroffe knew that what she suspected could wreck Shipman's career and, if she was wrong, it also could destroy hers. She had no real proof, just a gut instinct. Then, one evening in the early weeks of 1998, Shipman rang Debbie to ask her to attend the death of a woman who lived alone. "The woman had died suddenly, alone, and yet the coroner was not involved. And I found myself wondering how come Dr. Shipman had the key to the house?"

Debbie mentioned her fears to another GP, Dr. Susan Booth, as she visited the undertaker's chapel of rest to countersign a cremation certificate for the victim.

"Here I am again to do one of Fred's," said Dr. Booth on seeing Debbie Bambroffe.

"I think you're coming here too often. His death rates are very high, and they're nearly all women," responded Debbie.

Dr. Booth promised to mention it to her colleagues.

Another Hyde GP also harbored deep suspicions about the activities of Fred Shipman. Dr. Linda Reynolds was already haunted by the memory of another GP, Dr. Soe Myint, who had sexually assaulted his patients. For years, she'd known of his attacks on women patients, who went to her for treatment to get away from him. She'd tried to persuade them to tell the police, even offering to go with them, but they'd refused until Dr. Myint finally came to court and was imprisoned in 1997.

"I swore, 'Never again,' " she later said, shuddering at the recollection. "And this time it was more serious. Those other women could do something, but Dr. Shipman's patients couldn't. He had killed them."

Fred Shipman's one-man practice was just across the street from the Brook Surgery, where GPs were often asked to countersign cremation forms after Shipman's patients died. These forms always had to be signed by doctors in another practice as a matter of procedure. That other doctor was also obliged by law to ask about the patients' medical history and view the body.

Dr. Booth mentioned her suspicions and struck a chord with Dr. Reynolds, who'd already noticed the number of cremation certificates Shipman had asked her to countersign. Virtually always, it seemed, they were for elderly women.

Across the street at his practice, Fred Shipman—first alerted by Paul Massey's initial approach a few months earlier—was trying to avoid suspicion by rotating his requests for death certificate co-signatures between the Brook practice's five GPs. But nothing could hide the fact that his one-man surgery had completed forty-one certificates in 1997 compared with Brook's fourteen.

Dr. Reynolds then alerted the South Manchester coroner, Dr. John Pollard, who immediately called in Greater Manchester Police. A detective inspector, acting as an agent for Dr. Pollard, began looking into the claims about Shipman. Dr. Reynolds later insisted that she specifically told the police that she suspected Shipman of killing his patients. Yet a combination of oversight and Shipman's cover-up conspired to limit the evidence at the police's disposal at that time. In any case, who could believe that a doctor would commit mass murder on such a vast scale?

But for the moment, Dr. Reynolds was relieved by Dr. Pollard's receptive attitude. "Afterwards I felt very encouraged, because he was taking me seriously." Dr. Pollard also gave Dr. Reynolds a personal promise of complete confidentiality. He told her, "As far as I am concerned, if nothing comes of this, we have never spoken."

A detective was dispatched to interview Dr. Reynolds at her surgery that same day. Dr. Reynolds told the investigator she'd concluded that Shipman was a killer by examining his patients' death rate. She also gave the detective the Brook group's cremation records book going back to 1993.

Dr. Reynolds then told the officer that the bodies of two of Shipman's most recent victims still lay at Massey's funeral parlor. But when she suggested that he ask for a post mortem on them, the detective insisted he did not have enough evidence to order the examination.

She also warned him that Fred Shipman seemed to have been tipped off about inquiries into his activities.

The detective insisted that was highly unlikely, and he left Dr Reynolds's surgery saying he'd investigate the claims very thoroughly. But that officer had no back-up team, no incident room. Just a bunch of complicated figures that could have simply meant that death rates had gone up for a certain period.

Dr. Reynolds later recalled how she felt powerless to do anything more, but remained convinced that Shipman was a murderer. "I felt quite bad. I had accused another doctor—albeit old-fashioned, but concerned for the community—of killing his patients. I was dragging this man's reputation through the mud."

Shortly after that, two more cremation forms arrived at the Brook Surgery. Dr. Reynolds noted them, but then left for an extended vacation in America with her husband and children. Ironically, those two deaths seemed to be genuinely terminally ill patients. Dr. Reynolds even hoped that Shipman had stopped the killing because of the investigation that was under way.

"I was convinced he knew," Dr. Reynolds later explained. "I hoped that, because he had this shot across his bows, he had got the message and stopped. It was the best hope I had in the circumstances."

Hyde taxi driver John Shaw was already convinced of Shipman's guilt. He later recalled: "I knew for at least a year that something was wrong with Shipman. I kept losing my customers and it was always him who was the doctor. At first I thought he was unlucky or incompetent, then I realized it was something more sinister. I felt guilty, like an accomplice. I could have saved them. But I couldn't tell anyone. Who would have believed me?"

Manchester police investigated these initial claims by visiting Manchester's Registrar of Births, Marriages and Deaths. They were asked to provide details of those Shipman patients who had died over the previous six months. There had been thirty deaths but only nineteen death certificates were provided—eleven others were completely overlooked due to a clerical error.

Investigators even asked Dr. Alan Banks, 49, a medical advisor to the authority who paid Shipman's salary, to examine the files of fourteen Shipman patients who died. He told detectives he could find nothing wrong with the deaths. Fred Shipman was slipping through the net.

Fred Shipman was never directly contacted by police investigators. Detectives believed they had "insufficient" evidence to win any legal argument to search his premises. The clinic's death rate statistics were not even available at that time.

After six weeks of probing, the force informed South Manchester Coroner Dr. Pollard that they had drawn a blank and did not believe that Fred Shipman was a killer. The investigation was dropped.

Detective Chief Inspector Mike Williams later admitted: "Dr. Shipman quite successfully covered his tracks. As soon as we started interviewing doctors, it became public. We didn't have that sort of enormous piece of information which would justify us making that step and putting a slur on his character."

The force's Assistant Chief Constable Vincent Sweeney later insisted: "Relatives of Dr. Shipman were not interviewed, because approaching them about the paperwork would have been tantamount to accusing Dr. Shipman of wrongdoing, and would have breached the confidentiality of the inquiry. The system of justice in this country requires police officers to clarify facts and establish whether there is evidence to support accusations."

Yet a simple check on Fred Shipman's criminal record would have shown his conviction for that drug offense back in 1976. The police later insisted that even this would have been an insufficient basis on which to interview the doctor.

But the fact remains that they failed to make that check in the first place.

Fred Shipman's addiction to killing was far from over.

*   *   *

In the middle of the police inquiry—on February 9, 1998—
Jacqueline Gee, the daughter of Fred Shipman's elderly patient Pamela Hillier, called her mother at 4:30 P.M. There
was no reply. Mrs. Gee then phoned her mother's neighbors,
Mr. and Mrs. Ellwood, and asked them to check on Pamela.
Mr. Ellwood found Mrs. Hillier lying on her back on the
bedroom floor at the foot of the bed. A packet of tablets lay
on the bed. Mr. Ellwood and his wife tried to resuscitate
Mrs. Hillier and called an ambulance.

When paramedic Stephen Morris arrived, he peformed a
cardiopulmonary resuscitation and even used a defibrillator.
But Mrs. Hillier was already dead, although her body was
still without rigor mortis, which indicated that death had
occurred very recently. Fred Shipman telephoned the house
in the middle of all this. He asked Mr. Morris about the
details and promised to get to the house as quickly as possible.

Mrs. Gee then arrived, followed by Shipman, whom Mr.
Ellwood overheard telling the paramedics that it was not
necessary to call out the police as had been suggested. That
was when Mrs. Gee and her husband asked about a post
mortem. Shipman said there was no point, and added, "Let's
put it down to a stroke."

Shipman later insisted he'd left Mrs. Hillier alive after a
home visit on the day she died. He said that Pamela Hillier's
blood pressure was "high and very worrying," so he told
her to increase the dose of drugs. Then he left her Stalybridge Road town house.

Shipman claimed he'd called to see the 68-year-old
widow because she'd tripped over a carpet and fallen down.
He said she'd told him she had felt restless and tired on two
previous occasions on January 6 and February 5. After her
death he returned to his clinic and entered those incidents
into his computerized medical records, also forging blood-
pressure readings taken by practice nurse Gillian Morgan.
But Shipman made his first serious mistake by entering the

dates as January 5 and February 6 "because five comes before six."

It proved a costly error.

Just after the police dropped their inquiries, Fred Shipman
was visited at his practice by an elderly patient named
Maureen Ward. Practice receptionist Carol Chapman later
explained: "Dr. Shipman came out with her after her appointment and told us she was going on a cruise."

"I joked, 'I'll carry your bags for you.' She was fine. We
had a little conversation and a few pleasantries."

The following day, Fred Shipman informed the warden
at Mrs. Ward's sheltered housing complex at Ogden Court,
on Frank Street in Hyde, that he'd come to give Mrs. Ward
a letter about a hospital referral and found her dead. Shipman later changed his story by telling Carol Chapman that
he'd called at Mrs. Ward's apartment after seeing an ambulance outside her home. Mrs. Chapman later noticed Shipman telling other receptionists that he'd gone to give Mrs.
Ward a letter. Fred Shipman was breaking his cardinal rule
by forgetting his own lies.

As Mrs. Chapman later recalled: "Dr. Shipman came
back into the surgery in the afternoon and said Mrs. Ward
had died. I said, 'Which? Maureen?.'

"He said yes. I was very shocked and a little bit angry,
I think, probably a little snappy. I said she was in here yesterday and she was fine."

Christine Simpson—the warder at the complex where
Mrs. Ward lived—was also shocked to hear that Mrs. Ward
had died, as she'd seemed so well earlier that day. Shipman
even asked her to go with him to Mrs. Ward's first-floor flat
after he'd found her dead. "I was very, very surprised, very
shocked," Simpson later said. "I said I couldn't believe it.
He said to me, 'Well, she did have a brain tumor, you
know.' I said I didn't know, I had no idea, I was very surprised."

Other neighbors were equally stunned by the news. Mary
France and Mrs. Ward had been excited by the prospect of

going on a cruise together, and they'd arranged to have a cup of tea on the very day Mrs. Ward died. "I put the kettle on," Mary France said, "but she never came round."

There was also a chilling link between the death of Mrs. Ward and five other alleged Shipman victims: They all lived at Ogden Court, just a few hundred yards from Shipman's clinic on Market Street. Resident Alice Prestwick, aged 69, was the first one to go. She died in October 1988, followed by 81-year-old John Charlton twelve months later. Alice Kennedy, 88, died in January 1995, and then 87-year-old Muriel Ward died in October of that year. Gladys Saunders died in June 1996 and James King, 83, on Christmas Eve 1997.

Another of Fred Shipman's patients—Winifred Mellor—felt as if she had a new lease on life in May 1998. As her Catholic parish priest, Father Denis Maher explained: "We'd organized a trip to the Holy Land, and Winifred was the first person to put her name down for that trip. She was like a child looking forward to Christmas. She even said to me, 'All my life I've wanted to go to the Holy Land, and now I am going.'"

Shipman had even helped nurse Mrs. Mellor's husband before he died in 1989. Then 73-year-old Mrs. Mellor went to Fred Shipman's surgery complaining that she felt weary and unwell. The GP diagnosed pneumonia and pleurisy, prescribed antibiotics and told her to go home. Several hours later she was found dead at her flat on Corona Avenue in Hyde. Some hours afterwards, Shipman knocked on the door of one of Mrs. Mellor's neighbors and claimed he could see Mrs. Mellor through the front window and thought she was dead.

Shipman and the neighbor then managed to get into the house, where they found Mrs. Mellor dead in her chair. Shipman used the phone in the house to call Mrs. Mellor's daughter.

The first thing he said was: "Did you realize that your mother had been suffering from back pains?"

Her daughter had no idea. Shipman then admitted he'd been to see Mrs. Mellor earlier that afternoon and she'd needed hospital treatment. Mrs. Mellor's daughter offered to come to the house.

"Oh, there's no need for that," replied Shipman. "There's no point in sending her to hospital."

It was only then that it dawned on Mrs. Mellor's daughter that her mother might be dead.

"D'you mean my mother's dead?" she asked.

"Now you understand," responded the GP.

As Mrs. Mellor's daughter said later: "He'd made me guess that my mother was dead."

Father Denis Maher hadn't liked Fred Shipman since the moment they'd first met. He found the GP "insensitive and unsympathetic" following the death of Bianka Pomfret. Now he had a similar reaction to the way Shipman had handled Mrs. Mellor.

He never forgot how he'd been comforting Mrs. Mellor's family and had just given the last rites when Shipman "breezed into her home ignoring us completely." But then, death was normal for Fred Shipman. He'd long since dropped any emotional response to the subject.

In June 1998 Fred Shipman was called to the Commercial Street home of Mrs. Joan Melia after Derek Steele, one of her neighbors and closest friends, found her dead in a chair. Steele immediately noticed that the doctor seemed "nonchalant" about the death. Shipman left Mrs. Melia's apartment within minutes, saying he would issue a death certificate citing pneumonia as the cause. He insisted there was no need for a post mortem.

Derek Steele was heartbroken by the loss of his close friend. "We were companions and buddies. She had no close family and we spent a lot of time together. She walked everywhere and hardly ever visited her GP," recalled Mr Steele.

"Shipman seemed very blasé, nonchalant. I said, 'It's Joan.' Then he said, 'The tablets haven't had time to take effect.' He didn't do anything. He never touched her. I was quite surprised. Then he said to me, 'You'll have no problem with a death certificate. I'll make one out, and you can tell the undertaker to get in touch with me.' "

Fred Shipman later wrote in Mrs. Melia's medical notes that she'd been to the surgery and he'd diagnosed a chest infection and prescribed antibiotics. He clearly implied she'd had nothing more than a mild infection. So why didn't Shipman insist on a post mortem when she'd died suddenly the next day?

It was only when Mrs. Melia's body was later exhumed that toxicology tests showed she had died from morphine poisoning. Mrs. Melia's niece Jean Pinder remembered her aunt as always being a very fit lady, so she confronted Dr. Shipman shortly after her aunt died. Shipman immediately responded by insisting that Mrs. Melia had been in very poor health. "She died from pneumonia aggravated by emphysema," he told her.

"Did you tell Auntie Joan how ill she was?" she asked.

"I told her to go to bed," replied the GP.

"If she was so ill, why didn't you contact the hospital?"

"I'm afraid it was just one of those things. She could have just as easily died on the way to hospital."

On June 18, 1998, Joan Melia was buried at St. Mary's Parish Church, Newton, Hyde.

16

The Shipman home at 15 Roe Cross Green continued to resemble a garbage dump, with clothes, books and plates scattered across the floor, dirty dishes shoulder-high in the sink, the carpets thick with grime. One villager who went inside the house described it thus: "It was squalid. The sort of place where you would wipe your feet on the way out. I think the doctor was trying to grow penicillin in his grill pan. It turned my stomach."

The reason for the foul and dirty state of the Shipmans' house can almost certainly be traced to a deep-seated rebellion against the life both Fred and Primrose were leading. In many ways, Primrose had clearly given up on certain aspects of their life together. She knew her husband was secretive. She may even have picked up a clue or two about the murders. But, if she did, she would never have felt the confidence to confront him about them.

Primrose couldn't help but be painfully aware of her husband's obsession with his work, the long hours he put in, the contempt in which he held almost everyone else. It wasn't helped by the fact that the Shipmans lived in a state of semi-isolation, cut off from both their respective families. Primrose must have suspected that something was wrong, but couldn't work out what it was. At first she may have thought Fred had another woman, but she would have soon dismissed that idea, as her husband simply wasn't that sort of man. But, given the doubts she must have felt about their lives together, it's not surprising that she could no longer be bothered to even run the home along reasonably orga-

nized lines. Primrose was gradually becoming yet another
of Fred Shipman's victims.

At Shipman's clinic, the staff whispered amongst themselves that Fred was something of a tyrant at home who
made impossible demands on his family.

"Nobody eats until I get home," he would bark down the
telephone at Primrose most afternoons. Primrose and the
children would be waiting stiffly at the dinner table staring
at their plates until the patriarch marched through the door,
sometimes as late as 10 P.M. Primrose's stubborn devotion
to her husband was remarkable.

Despite all this, the bond between Fred and Primrose remained as strong as ever. It was always them against the
world, so they had to stick together.

"This lady's gone," was one of Fred Shipman's favorite remarks when he was closing the eyelid of a victim. Another
phrase, usually as he was pronouncing a patient dead who
was in her own bed or armchair, was, "That's a nice way
to go." So different from the convulsive tears, the desolation
and final exhaustion of his own mother's tragic death.

Most of Fred Shipman's victims died within minutes of
being injected by a lethal dose of drugs. Injecting the drug
into a vein instantly led to a slowness of breath and loss of
consciousness before breathing would stop altogether. Diamorphine—the clinical name for heroin—and morphine
were commonly used as painkillers. But there was always a
danger that they could suppress breathing, particularly if injected into a person who was not ill. And by injecting into
a vein rather than a muscle, Shipman could provoke rapid
death. Diamorphine is twice as strong as morphine. Just 30
mg is enough to kill a human being.

Fred Shipman was lost in a kind of maze of death. The
early killings had been carefully carried out; the women
were primed for murder, and there were no clues left behind.
Shipman had so enjoyed the quiet, peaceful thrill of a kill.
He had no regrets. It had been as deliberate as a fox stealing
a chicken.

But during the most recent killings, Shipman had become less calculated, and in the aftermath he had made particular errors. If he'd stuck to certain patients and continued to go about his job as usual, his chances of escaping detection would have remained high. However, Fred Shipman was running completely out of control. Killing had become necessary and he had already had one close shave with the prematurely halted police investigation. Shipman's addiction left him no time to run the rest of his life efficiently. For years he'd managed to hold it all together, but now it was starting to fall apart. Why?

The net was closing and he was getting sloppy. He was completely losing touch with reality. There had been warning signs like Jim King and that approach by funeral director Alan Massey. That first police investigation had been shelved, allowing him to carry on feeding his addiction to kill. But Fred Shipman knew in his heart that it would only be a matter of time before it would have to end.

Fred Shipman used a computer to keep most of the medical records in his practice. He knew that some patients could see computer entries during their consultations, so he also made handwritten records. Shipman wrote notes on buff-colored index cards when he made home visits, to detail particularly confidential information that he wanted to keep from them. Information about those home visits was also recorded on a standard form which was attached to the notes whenever he visited a patient. That information would then be transferred onto the computer when he got back to the surgery.

These forms were supposed to be filed away once the details had been entered into the computer. Years later investigators failed to locate many of them. The few that were found contained only the information noted by the receptionist at the time a visit was requested. Fred Shipman knew it was important to get rid of all written "evidence" of his lethal visits.

By this time Shipman's handwriting had virtually become

illegible, and he recorded few current details about patients. His own clinical management of their illnesses was equally disorganized. Information about prescriptions of drugs was usually brief and vague. The quantity of medicine was often not even mentioned, and the batch numbers of injected drugs were *never* recorded.

And when it came to "signing off" cremation forms, Fred Shipman was fond of using certain phrases and additional details about the circumstances of deaths. They included the following:

> — seen by self 11:30 neighbor saw patient at 13.00 found at 15.00 by self and neighbor
> — seen 2 hours before death with ct, atrial fibrillation & PND; found in chair by neighbor
> — own, seen at 15.00 found by relative about 16.00
> — saw patient at home, diagnosis made, arranged admission ambulance, patient dead when went back, all within 10 mins.

On the cremation forms Shipman made other comments in response to the question about persons present at death. Examples include:

> — no one, seen at 15.30 found at 16.00
> — no one other than self
> — no one seen by me 13.00 found by relative 14.30

Those cremation forms all featured the time and place of death, suddenness of death, and whether Shipman was present or had seen the patient shortly before death.

Around this time, Fred Shipman went to the Dutch city of Amsterdam for a weekend medical conference, and made a lasting impression on one female colleague. Dr. Amy Cumming explained: "He was a patronizing man—rather like a Dutch uncle. I'm a little older than him and yet he had this ability to make me feel small and inexperienced. We spent a weekend in Amsterdam for a conference. I had to keep reminding myself that I was older and more experienced than he was."

But Shipman's confidence put Dr. Cumming in a state of awe. She understood why so many of his patients were deceived by his veneer of compassion and authority. "He was very keen to explain to me all about the wonderful things he was doing in his practice. I was left thinking, 'How does he do it? He must have thirty-six hours in the day!'"

Dr. Cumming went on: "He talked a lot about the 'latest' methods, the 'latest' drugs and their benefits to his patients, how the drugs worked. It seemed to me he gave his patients a vast amount of time. I was filled with admiration. He was some kind of Super Doc."

And Fred Shipman never once behaved in an improper way toward Amy Cumming.

Back in Hyde, it certainly seemed at the time as if Fred Shipman's deathly secrets would never be uncovered. Not only had the police dropped their investigation into his activities, but the General Medical Council continued to sit on at least two disturbing psychiatric reports about Shipman that were produced after his 1976 drug conviction. They also hadn't been asked anything in relation to the complaints of three other incidents between 1985 and 1994. The GMC believed, in their own words, that "these did not suggest a fundamental problem." Yet those complaints definitely suggested a pattern of poor work performance sufficient enough to question Shipman's practice. The GMC later claimed: "Had Greater Manchester Police asked us if we had any information regarding Dr. Shipman, we would have cooperated with them fully."

Yet, since setting up his solo practice at the end of 1991, at least 100 of Shipman's patients had died under circumstances that would later lead investigators to conclude that Shipman killed them deliberately. Other clues to this extraordinary "death toll" came from the number of death certificates Shipman had been signing.

For most doctors the numbers remained pretty constant and low. Normally six to ten deaths per doctor per year occur in a community such as Hyde. In 1992—when Shipman first set up his solo practice—he issued just 7 certificates. In 1993 that number jumped to 28 before dropping to 16 in 1994. Then in 1995 it leapt up to 38, 42 in 1996, and 47 in 1997. In the first half of 1998 it was 24.

The 1997 figure of 47 was five times more than would be expected in a community such as Hyde.

The ease with which Fred Shipman was killing his patients threw the GP into a permanent state of over-anxiety. In some ways he hoped against hope that his latest victim would prove unkillable. But Shipman's addiction to death meant that his mind had become completely stagnant. If he'd become as deeply interested in something else, then perhaps this deadly obsession might have passed away. Shipman was as preoccupied with death as some people are with decorating their home or succeeding in their personal life. This state of purposelessness and boredom produced what philosopher Jean-Paul Sartre has described as "the vertigo of freedom."

Shipman suffered from severe bouts of insomnia as well. He lacked inner strength and felt he was at the mercy of the environment around him; everything that happened blew him off course. Depression, misery, boredom and nausea all bothered Fred Shipman in the second half of 1998.

That was why he needed the adrenaline rush that came with each killing. It was the only time when he became truly excited, happy, driven by a strong sense of purpose and expectancy. Then Shipman's mind became like a sledge-hammer, smashing through his dark and somber mood swings. Murder gave him a sense of being real, solid, god-like.

In Fred Shipman's mind there was little else to live for. What was the use of having all this power if he couldn't exert it? His mind was like a car engine, tearing itself to pieces because it was not properly connected to the chassis.

*   *   *

On June 9, 1998, Fred Shipman took blood samples from an elderly patient named Mrs. Kathleen Grundy, which he told her were part of a government health survey. A former mayoress of Hyde, Kathleen Grundy regularly told friends of her admiration for the GP. She'd even considered donating part of her own charity fund to his practice appeal before deciding it was an "inappropriate cause." Mrs. Grundy had been introduced to Shipman many years earlier when they both belonged to a local medical committee.

"She thought he was a good doctor," her friend Mary Clarke later explained. "She thought he was good for the practice and the people of Hyde. She admired his work. But then, all the people of Hyde thought highly of Dr. Shipman, not just Mrs. Grundy."

The morning Mrs. Grundy visited Fred Shipman's clinic she also agreed to "sign some papers" for Shipman which he said related to the blood test he'd just given her. Moments later, Fred Shipman called in his next, younger patient, Paul Spencer, and asked him to sign a document. The piece of paper was folded over so that Spencer could not tell what it was. He assumed it was a medical document.

"Dr. Shipman asked me if I wouldn't mind writing my name and address and putting my signature and occupation on the piece of paper," Spencer later recalled.

Spencer did notice the signature "K Grundy" on the far right-hand side, and put his own signature on the far left. "Then I was told, 'Thank you very much and you can leave the room,'" Spencer later explained. He noticed that the patient who followed him was then told to do the same thing. Spencer has always insisted he had no idea that the paperwork was Kathleen Grundy's will.

That same day Mrs. Grundy also met Linda Skelton, a part-time clerical assistant who knew Mrs. Grundy from the luncheon club both attended. Mrs. Grundy mentioned she'd been at the doctor's "to sign some papers." Mrs. Skelton later recalled: "She said there was nothing wrong with her, and there were people waiting, and she felt guilty because they were obviously people who were ill and waiting to see the doctor."

Back at his surgery, Fred Shipman was typing out the following on a standard last will and testament form he'd bought at his local stationery store: "I GIVE ALL MY ES-TATE, MONEY AND HOUSE TO MY DOCTOR. MY FAMILY ARE NOT IN NEED AND I WANT TO RE-WARD HIM FOR ALL THE CARE HE HAS GIVEN TO ME AND THE PEOPLE OF HYDE." Shipman left one fingerprint on the document, which was later to prove crucial in bringing him to justice.

The entire note had been written in the upper case, with missing letters where the typewriter had failed to keep up with his greedy fingers. Those who later saw the document described it as a "backhanded attempt at forgery."

Was Fred Shipman deliberately setting himself up for a fall? Was he trying to end his murderous reign by pointing the finger of suspicion right at himself? That will purported to leave the GP an estate worth £386,402, including Kathleen Grundy's home and a house she owned in Stockport.

When later asked by investigators if he knew anything about Mrs. Grundy's will, Shipman replied: "I have no knowledge of Mrs. Grundy's will. Is that the answer you were wanting?" Shipman later insisted that Mrs. Grundy had asked him to witness her will, but he'd requested that two patients do it instead. He even added chillingly: "Mrs. Grundy had used my pen, something I am never happy about people doing."

Kathleen Grundy's neighbor Audrey Adshead had lived next door to the former Hyde mayor for twenty years. In all that time Mrs. Grundy had only been in the hospital once. One day in June 1998 she saw Mrs. Grundy cutting bushes in her garden. They later chatted for over an hour, and Mrs. Grundy seemed very excited about a trip she was soon leaving for.

A few days later—on June 23—Kathleen Grundy visited another friend. She appeared fit and well, and as usual, talked with pride about her family. "She was very, very fond of her family," her friend later explained. "She never stopped talking about her grandsons and her daughter and her son-in-law. They were a very, very close, a very happy family."

Mrs. Grundy even mentioned that Dr. Shipman was due to call on her the next day to do some more blood tests. "She thought it was very good of him to visit her house to save her going to the surgery."

At 8:30 A.M. on June 24, 1998, Fred Shipman called at Mrs. Grundy's house. Shipman later claimed he left the house soon afterwards. Within minutes Mrs. Grundy's breathing slowed down to a rate of two to three breaths a minute. Within another few minutes it stopped altogether. She appeared to be asleep, but her lips, fingers and toes were turning a blue tinge. Her brain was no longer getting any oxygen. Shipman had injected a dose of morphine into Kathleen Grundy.

At 11:55 A.M. that day Mrs. Grundy was found dead by her friends John Green and Ronald Pickford, who'd come by when she failed to turn up to serve lunches at the local old people's club. They found the front door closed but not locked, and walked in to discover Mrs. Grundy's body, fully dressed as if she had been about to go out. They both knew that Mrs. Grundy was careful about security and had two mortice locks on her main door which she always locked, even if she was in the garden.

Shipman was immediately informed and contacted local police constable John Fitzgerald to explain that he'd visited Mrs. Grundy earlier that day, and she had complained of feeling unwell. "He said he'd liaised with the coroner's officer. As a result of the conversation he had with the coroner's officer, he was going to issue a death certificate claiming death from natural causes."

On June 25, 1998—the day after Mrs. Grundy's death—Shipman made four computer entries about her within six minutes of each other, even though they referred to visits made up to a year previously. He'd certified death as old age and would later make outrageous claims that she had been a heroin addict.

He planted three specific references to Mrs. Grundy's supposed drug addiction in her medical notes.

The first, dated October 12, 1996, remarked: *"Pupils small (?) constipated—query drug abuse—at her age (?) wait and see."*

Another, dated July 15, 1997, says: *"Had every (?) drug possible. Pupils small, dry mouth, possible drug abuse again (?). Denies taking any drugs other than for irritable bowel syndrome."*

The third, for November 26, 1997, notes: *"Denies everything. Still clinically nothing of note to confirm my suspicions."*

Fred Shipman seemed in a very good mood to his staff in the days following Mrs. Grundy's death. He even told one GP he knew in Hyde that he was planning to move to France to retire "very soon."

The law firm of Hamilton Ward received Fred Shipman's version of Kathleen Grundy's will in the post on June 24, 1998, the day she died. Kathleen Grundy's estate came to more than £380,000 ($530,000). The will was accompanied by a letter which Shipman wrote on the same typewriter he had used for the will. He dated it June 9 and signed it "K Grundy."

It said: *"Dear Sir, I enclose a copy of my will. I think it is clear in intent. I wish Dr Shipman to benefit by having my estate but if he dies or cannot accept it, then the estate goes to my daughter. I would like you to be the executor of the will. I intend to make an appointment to discuss this and my will in the near future."*

The staff at the offices of Hamilton Ward were puzzled: they had never acted for Mrs. Grundy. They filed the will and awaited developments. On June 30, they received a letter, without an address, dated June 28 and typed on the same make of typewriter as the earlier correspondence.

"Dear Sir, I regret to inform you that Mrs K Grundy of

79 Joel Lane, Hyde, died last week. I understand that she lodged a will with you, as I, a friend, typed it out for her. Her daughter is at the address and you can contact her there." It was signed *S* or *F Smith*.

Fred Shipman had ticked the "cremation" box on the will form. But Mrs. Grundy was not cremated: she was buried at Hyde chapel on July 1 after a funeral service attended by hundreds of friends. Shipman was not among them.

A couple weeks later, the staff at Hamilton Ward attorneys managed to contact Mrs. Grundy's daughter, Angela Woodruff, herself a lawyer living in Leamington Spa, Warwickshire, in the center of England. She was surprised to hear about the will, because she had one signed by her mother leaving the estate to her. When she saw it, she at once suspected it was a forgery. "The whole thing was just unbelievable," Mrs. Woodruff later recalled. "The thought of Mum signing a document so badly typed leaving everything to her doctor just didn't make any sense. It was inconceivable."

Mrs. Woodruff began her own inquiries, contacting the will's supposed witnesses and comparing the signatures. It took time to accept the "credibility gap" between what she expected of her mother's doctor and what she suspected him of. "For us to believe that the doctor had possibly forged a will, had possibly killed my mother, was a huge gap to cross," she later recalled.

On July 24, 1998, Mrs. Woodruff told police of her concerns and re-ignited a murder investigation that would become one of the biggest in British criminal history.

But why did Fred Shipman decide to try to make a financial profit from his killings? His first attempt at being left an estate had gone wrong when earlier victim Bianka Pomfret had changed her will at the last minute. Did Fred Shipman believe that Kathleen Grundy's estate might give him enough money to quit his job and get away from Hyde? Did Shipman believe the killings would stop if he inherited some money and ran away?

No doubt greed played a significant role in Shipman's

decision. Just a few days after killing Kathleen Grundy he took Primrose to a kitchen and bathroom store and told her to choose some new items for their run-down house. Shipman specified that he wanted to order a new fitted kitchen which included a double sink, waste disposal, oven, extractor fan and ten cupboards. He even told staff at the store: "I am coming into a large amount of money soon from a will, so money is no object."

17

Detectives were aware that Fred Shipman was unlikely to confess to his crimes, so they knew the case against him would have to be carefully constructed on a foundation of circumstantial and scientific evidence. In a unique move for the force, Detective Chief Inspector Mike Williams and Detective Superintendent Bernard Postles, an officer with twenty-seven years' experience, sought permission from Tameside coroner Dr. John Pollard to have the body of Kathleen Grundy exhumed from Hyde Cemetery for a postmortem examination on August 1, 1998.

The pathologist could not find any immediate cause for Mrs. Grundy's sudden death, so tissue samples were sent away for forensic examination—but they would not be back for some weeks.

Shipman's mystery informant told him that investigators were carrying out toxicology tests on Mrs. Grundy's body. He knew they would uncover evidence of morphine, so Shipman began busily smearing Mrs. Grundy's good name by adding even more written claims about her "drug addiction" to her computerized medical records.

Rumors eventually began circulating around Hyde about detectives looking into the activities of highly respected Dr. Fred Shipman. There was even talk of a body being exhumed. Throughout, Shipman was remarkably well informed about the police's progress. When one patient asked Shipman what was happening, the GP shrugged his shoulders and commented that it would be a while before the results were known, because the pathology labs were overloaded with work from the Omagh bombing in Northern Ireland that week. "I just hope they don't find a single trace of aspirin in her body," Shipman responded, with an insouciance that convinced his patient of the doctor's innocence. But who was keeping Fred Shipman so closely informed about the inquiry?

When another patient gave Shipman's loyal receptionist Carol Chapman a ride home and asked her what she thought about the police inquiries, she replied, albeit crudely, "It's a crock of shite."

On August 12, 1998, Fred Shipman spoke to district nurse Marion Gilchrist in what would later be described as "a rehearsal of his later police interviews." Shipman told the nurse how Mrs. Grundy had changed her will on the day of her death. He even admitted to Gilchrist: "I read thriller books, and I would have me guilty on the evidence." Then he broke down and wept, saying how unfair it was that he should become embroiled in a nasty row over a will. Then his voice lowered as he added with a burst of black humor: "The only thing I did wrong was not having her cremated. If I had had her cremated, I wouldn't be having all this trouble."

Two days later, the tests came back with confirmation that a huge dose of morphine had killed Kathleen Grundy. That discovery triggered a wide-ranging investigation into the sudden deaths of numerous other Shipman patients. Detectives immediately checked telephone and pager records for the clinic, the women's homes, and Greater Manchester Ambulance Service. They soon uncovered more trickery when they compared the records with Shipman's false claims that his victims had called him out, or that he had canceled ambulances, or that his surgery staff had paged him.

"That's when we first started realizing the enormity of it," senior investigator Bernard Postles later recalled. "My people at HQ reckoned that we had a tiger by the tail. My response to this was, 'We have got a pride of tigers by the tail.' It wasn't just the enormity of the deaths, but the enormity of what we were accusing somebody of, given their position in the community. What we did was constantly question each other, 'Have we got this wrong: are we missing something here? Are we dealing with something so out of character for a doctor that there is something wrong with us rather than him?' "

On August 14, 1998, investigators searched Fred Shipman's clinic as the GP and his still-loyal staff stood by. Shipman—still acting the complete innocent—handed detectives his typewriter. "I believe this is what you are looking for," he said with a hint of condescension. The officers thanked him and took it away for forensic examination. Fred Shipman later claimed that he lent Mrs. Grundy the typewriter (fingerprint experts eventually confirmed that there was no sign whatsoever of Mrs. Grundy's prints on the machine).

A thorough examination of Shipman's medical notes was also carried out. There were paper documents bound in the traditional buff-colored index cards. The passage Shipman had written claiming Mrs. Grundy was a drug addict immediately caught the attention of investigators. The entry for October 12, 1996, read: "*IBS* [irritable bowel syndrome] *again. Odd. Pupils small. Constipated. Query drug abuse? Query at her age? Query codeine? Wait and see.*" Two more entries, dated July 15 and November 26, 1997, suggested the same thing. That day police made an arrangement with Shipman for him to visit Ashton-under-Lyne Police Station on Tuesday, September 7. They were piling on the pressure, but were happy to let him "sweat it out" for a few weeks.

Some days later, Fred Shipman had a beer with his old friend Dr. David Walker, who later recalled: "He didn't seem to have any worries in the world, and he didn't seem concerned about what would happen. He was able to talk on all sorts of levels."

Walker and some of Shipman's other drinking pals had decided to take the GP out to "help him keep his spirits up." He explained: "We all thought he was innocent, it was all a terrible mistake and it would soon all be cleared up. We didn't discuss it much."

Fred Shipman briefly mentioned that he was due to visit the police the following Tuesday. "He said he'd sort it all out then." Walker and Shipman's other friends decided not to push the matter any further. Dr. Walker later recalled: "There was never a time when I didn't think he was anything but a decent guy. A dedicated doctor. He said he couldn't be doing with drug addicts and he wouldn't have them in his practice. He always seemed open. He talked about other things away from medicine, like his lad playing rugby. Most conversations were very normal. We enjoyed the real ale and the atmosphere. It was as simple as that."

Despite the obviously serious nature of the police's investigation, the GP was determined to continue his practice. The waiting room remained as hectic as ever. Patients queued beneath a huge array of good luck cards pinned to the wall. The receptionists had put them up with pride— there was no question of him being innocent. Most believed it was all a "terrible misunderstanding."

A siege mentality began to develop at the Market Street practice. Fred and Primrose now had his patients and staff on their side, versus the rest of the world. "He's a marvelous doctor, why don't you leave him alone?" was one of the most popular slants on the situation. All around the town, Fred Shipman's friends lined up to defend him. Shipman was overwhelmed by the support and decided to make some statements to certain, carefully chosen patients and associates. Lesley Pullford described how Shipman told her that he and the staff had a meeting and made plans for what to do with the money to be left by Mrs. Grundy should they get it. Shipman then said, "We will all have a week off each and on the anniversary of her death, give so much to old people's homes, and if anyone had a baby that day, give the money to a charity of their choice."

He also added that it would not be over quickly. "The next thing she is going to accuse me of *is forging her will*." Mrs. Pullford later claimed that she took this to be a reference to Mrs. Grundy's daughter. He broke down as he told Lesley Pulford how he'd like to scold Mrs. Grundy, if she came back from the dead: "If I could bring her back and sit her in that chair, I would say, 'Look at all the trouble it has caused. I was going to say I did not want the money, but, because of all this trouble, I will have it,' " he railed.

But when Shipman bumped into a medical colleague out on the streets of Hyde, he seemed in an altogether different frame of mind. Shipman's associate later recalled: "I saw him Wednesday afternoon and spent about two hours talking to him. It was a moving conversation. He was very distressed, and on a couple of occasions came close to tears. He actually told me about the Grundy will, and by the end I was utterly convinced this was a man who had, for whatever reason, been unjustly and wrongfully accused of trying to gain by ending a patient's life."

During those early days of the police investigation into Fred Shipman's activities, detectives were intrigued by the relationship between the GP and his wife. Primrose Shipman had long since happily settled for the role of doctor's wife, believing it gave her real status—something that had undoubtedly attracted her to Fred Shipman in the first place. But as she and her husband began to grow into their positions as pillars of the community, they'd become quite aloof from their neighbors. Primrose unintentionally gave the impression that they were invisible. "It was a baffling relationship," said one investigator.

Meanwhile, relatives of some of Fred Shipman's deceased patients were waking up to news of the Shipman investigation in the *Manchester Evening News*, which was the first newspaper to reveal the Shipman story to the world.

Bianka Pomfret's ex-husband Adrian contacted the police within hours of the first article appearing about Shipman. Many of his friends and relatives refused to believe that Fred Shipman was guilty of anything. "They said I had no right to condemn an innocent man," Mr. Pomfret later explained. "I told my mother-in-law Bianka was probably on the list, yet she sat there and said I should take people as I find them, and as far as she was concerned, he wasn't guilty until they found him so."

Adrian Pomfret became even more convinced of Fred Shipman's guilt when the police rang back and said that Shipman had claimed there were no witnesses who saw him at Bianka's house the day she died. "You'll have no problems with that, because he told me he was round there when I saw him later that night to view the body." The police also asked Mr. Pomfret if he knew that Shipman had been treating his former wife for angina for two years. "Straight away I remembered how he'd said she was going to dance on my grave because she was so healthy. There was no mention of angina."

Outside the Shipman home, an army of journalists were soon camped day and night. At one stage a local TV crew snatched some footage of Fred Shipman getting out of his car. He looked harassed and weary, but still managed to give off the air of a friendly country doctor. Was this really the man suspected of murdering numerous elderly patients? It was one of only two pieces of footage ever filmed of Shipman, and was sent around the world and used over and over.

Inside the Shipman home, the family spent most nights gathered around their only TV set watching the investigation unfold through the local and national news programs. One of youngest son Sam's friends who visited the Shipman house at the time later recalled: "Dr. Shipman would look at the screen, but not say a word. Nobody said anything, or even commented on it. It was as if it was nothing to do with the family. I don't think any of them believed it."

Similarly, many of the families of Shipman's victims still refused to believe he had killed their loved ones. "When this first broke about the will, it was like going into the surgery on Christmas Day where people festoon walls in Christmas cards," recalled Peter Wagstaff, son of Shipman victim Kathleen Wagstaff. "There were literally hundreds of cards from people wishing him well and hoping the matter would soon be sorted out. No one believed it."

Peter and Angela Wagstaff rallied behind their doctor.

"We sent a letter of support to him. We didn't believe anything. It was beyond the realms of belief that this well-respected GP could do anything like that."

But then Peter Wagstaff decided to check out for himself what the doctor had said about how his mother died. "I checked the phone bill from her home to see if she had phoned for Dr. Shipman, and also to see if Shipman phoned for the ambulance." Peter Wagstaff immediately noticed that no phone calls had been made that day, and contacted investigators.

Fred Shipman knew the police net was closing in on him, but he refused to believe that detectives would uncover the full extent of his crimes. He even bragged to one patient—whose mother later turned out to be yet another victim—that he'd be out of jail inside six years, maximum.

Margaret Williams had visited Shipman's surgery unaware that thirteen years earlier he had overseen the death of her mother May, 74. Mrs. Williams later recalled: "I said to him one day that I'd heard about the Mrs. Grundy case, and that everyone in the town supported him in his troubles.

"He replied, 'I've discussed it with my wife, and we think I'll get twelve years. I'll probably serve six, years and when I come out, I'll retire and we'll move away.'"

At 8:30 on September 7, 1998, Fred Shipman arrived with his attorney Ann Ball in her car at Ashton-under-Lyne Police Station. An old-fashioned blue police light embellished the modern structure, and there were a few sparse trees between the car park and the constant queue of traffic on Manchester Road. Shipman greeted *Manchester Evening News* photographer Chris Gleave with a shrug of the shoulders. As Gleave snapped shot after shot, his film whirring through his camera, the GP faced him up, stared intently and held out his hands, saying dryly, "Sure you got enough?"

Fred Shipman and Ann Ball then took a sudden detour away from the entrance to the police station after he told her he wasn't ready to go in. They took a twenty-minute walk through the terraced streets that ran behind the building. They walked past the local primary school where kids were playing in the yard. Then they moved alongside a builder's yard which was slowly grinding to life. There were also long rows of red-brick houses where families were rousing themselves for work.

MEN photographer Gleave and reporter Mikaela Sitford then appeared again alongside Shipman asking for a comment. Attorney Ann Ball was angry with the journalists: "He has nothing to say. Leave us alone." Shipman, hands jammed in his pockets, looked serious. He knew it would soon be over.

Finally, at 9 A.M., Shipman and his attorney walked into the police station. He was immediately arrested for the murder of 81-year-old former Mayoress Kathleen Grundy. Despite his bravado, Fred Shipman was mightily shocked by his arrest, especially when he was then handed over to be questioned by two junior officers, Detective Sergeant John Walker and Detective Constable Mark Denham.

Fred Shipman's first recorded response to detectives was, "You're stupid." Detective Chief Inspector Mike Williams, 50, later recalled: "I think we wrong-footed him. It was a deliberate ploy. I believe he felt he was important enough to warrant an officer of my ranking. It immediately showed in the inflection in his voice. I think he would have liked the chief constable to have interviewed him."

Detective Superintendent Bernard Postles also noticed that Fred Shipman seemed contemptuous of the low rank of the officers questioning him. "He tried to confuse them by saying, 'You don't understand medical matters. You are only plods,' " Postles later recalled. "He thought he had the upper hand because he had the superior intellect."

As Fred Shipman's fingers were pressed onto a moist, inky pad for his fingerprints, he joked with one investigator to be careful with his little finger, in which he suffered RSI. "Repetitive strain injury," he explained. Fred Shipman later claimed it was all a result of his busy hours at the computer keyboard.

Outside the modern low-rise police building, Primrose

and Sam waited patiently after showing up in the family's big red Renault, ready to take him home after "he'd helped police with their inquiries." Within half an hour they'd been advised to go home.

Shipman told Detective Sergeant Walker and Detective Constable Denham about the running of his surgery. When asked about his methods of record-keeping, he said: "I am a firm believer in the concept of general practice and computerization being held back by the underdeveloped finance and political decisions by the government. It doesn't stop me from computerizing my practice."

Ten miles away, police searched the Shipman family home in Gee Cross. They quickly found four 10 mg ampoules of diamorphine stored inside a box that also contained methotrimeprazine (Nozinan). Primrose and their two youngest sons David and Sam stood by as detectives systematically took apart the house. One investigator was astonished at how calm Primrose and the two boys reacted. "They were very helpful and quite pleasant, considering," one investigator later recalled. "One of the lads even showed us where to find things. He was a nice lad, very polite."

Investigators were appalled by how filthy the Shipman house was, with clothes strewn all over and food left lying around the kitchen. "It wasn't how you'd expect a doctor's house to be."

Detectives then discovered a collection of gold rings, necklaces, brooches and earrings in a cardboard box in the couple's bedroom. When asked who owned this jewelry box, Primrose replied, "Me." The detectives were surprised. As one later explained, "Her fingers were like Cumberland sausages; we couldn't believe she had ever worn such tiny rings."

The jewelry was all photographed and put into a catalogue for relatives of Shipman's victims to later examine. Few families had even noticed trinkets had gone missing when their loved ones were found dead. The police search team also found boxes and carrier bags in the garage, each stuffed with old medical records and labeled with the word "dead" in red letters. Shipman had chosen to keep some of his old records, instead of handing them over to the West Pennine Health Authority for storage.

However, as per his work contract, he was expected to keep them safe, obviously for confidentiality reasons. The 150 records stuffed haphazardly into boxes and bags were testament to his lax attitude—and some were testament to his murderous habits.

Investigators even employed a nurse from Merseyside, who spread all of Shipman's records on her kitchen table, deciphered the doctor's typical scrawl and tried to put events into chronological order. Another expert, Dr. John Grenville, was also called onto the team to examine the notes. He noticed how Shipman recorded that he'd left patient Ivy Lomas—apparently dying of a heart attack in his treatment room—while he attended the colds and sniffles of three other patients, and he did not even bother sending another victim, Joan Melia, to a hospital as "she would probably have died on the way there."

Back at Ashton-under-Lyne Police Station, Fred Shipman admitted to investigators that he didn't maintain a controlled drugs register. He said he was aware of the regulations, but since his arrest in 1976 he had made it his policy not to keep controlled drugs, and therefore did not need a register. Shipman also claimed that on the few occasions that controlled drugs were urgently required, he would write out a prescription on the patient's name and collect it immediately from a pharmacy.

In fact, Shipman had collected unused controlled drugs following the deaths of patients. He insisted he had destroyed these drugs, but detectives suspected he was lying from the onset. The discovery of ampoules of diamorphine in the Shipman family home was the proof they needed. Many of Shipman's prescriptions for diamorphine were for potentially lethal doses of 30 mg.

Shipman said he'd only administered part of the doses and discarded the remainder. Shipman admitted he knew it was an offense under the Misuse of Drugs Act to fail to make a record of the administration of a controlled drug to a patient.

Fred Shipman couldn't wait to show detectives his entries in Kathleen Grundy's medical records, because he believed they would immediately clear him of any involvement in her death. But what Shipman did not know was that Mrs. Grundy couldn't have had an appointment with him on October 12, 1997—as he'd stated in his records—because she'd been with her daughter on that day.

And Shipman's reference in his computerized records to Mrs. Grundy's alleged drug addiction problem occurred on a day when—according to his credit card transactions— Shipman was 200 miles away in the city of York buying one of his beloved tortoiseshell pens.

At that interview, Fred Shipman continued with his medical jargon and even objected to the investigators' interviewing technique. In an adjoining room, DS Postles and DCI Williams felt sorry for the interviewing officers, who were coping well considering Shipman's offhand attitude. "Shipman was extremely difficult to deal with in that first interview," DCI Williams recalled. "It was a minefield for the officers, who had to establish why Kathleen Grundy had morphine in her body, and understand medical issues. He set out to belittle the officers: 'I'm the intelligent one here.' He saw it as a competition, a challenge between him and us."

Fred Shipman continued to insist to detectives that Kathleen Grundy was a drug addict. "I have my suspicions that she was abusing narcotics over a period of a year or so. She may have given herself, accidentally, an overdose."

Shipman also told detectives he was "astonished" to find that he was the sole beneficiary of Mrs. Grundy's will. The GP insisted that he did not inject her with any drug prior to her death, and even pointed to comments on her medical records backing his claims about her drug addiction. Asked to explain why the will was typed on his typewriter, Shipman claimed that Mrs. Grundy had borrowed it several times.

But Fred Shipman's arrogance was about to lead to his downfall. Investigators had also taken Shipman's hard disk from his computer, which held all the patients' records. This was to prove the most damning evidence of all. Shipman was proud of his computerized system, and even referred to his practice appeal fund, which had raised £19,000 in six years thanks to the efforts and generosity of his devoted patients. Unknown to Shipman, investigators had already established that he'd tampered with the computers to make his victims look more ill than they really were.

One of the most classic examples of Shipman's fraudulent use of his computer was victim Maureen Ward, whose medical records showed all the signs of a woman with a brain tumor. Shipman noted on December 17, 1997, that she was suffering "*headache, it comes and goes, dull, nauseous, legs not steady, retina of eye is OK, eyesight is normal.*" But investigators soon established that the file on Mrs. Ward was not created until February 18, 1998, at 2:49 P.M.—forty-five minutes before he found her dead.

DCI Williams later spelled it out: "Maureen Ward was found by Dr. Shipman at 3:30 P.M. He was in surgery at 2:45 P.M. making that entry. Two minutes later there's an entry for the day before, suggesting secondary cancer of the brain. Two minutes after that, one for December 17. He was creating a history, so that having a look at it would show a tendency to the cause of death. He had done the dirty deed. He had called on her, went back to his computer, then went back to 'find' the body."

During that first interview, officers also concluded that Fred Shipman was a pathetic figure in many ways. "He was like a child who'd done something naughty and couldn't wait for someone to find out. He had to go back and make sure she was found."

Investigators would soon establish that it was the same with three other victims—Pamela Hillier, Winnie Mellor and Bianka Pomfret. Out of a list of more than 3,000 patients there was no way Shipman could remember blood pressure counts months after the supposed consultation.

Besides the murder of Mrs. Grundy, Shipman was charged with attempted theft by deception, and with three counts of forgery. He was held in custody that night in Ashton Police Station cells and appeared in front of Tameside Magistrates' Court the next morning.

At last investigators appeared to have their man.

18

The town of Hyde found itself even further under siege from journalists within hours of Fred Shipman's arrest. At Shipman's practice, Primrose manned the reception desk and patiently explained to callers that her husband would be returning to work as soon as possible. There seemed to be absolutely no question in her mind that her husband would be home soon.

Vast banner headlines in numerous national newspapers proclaimed Shipman's role as, allegedly, one of the country's most prolific serial killers. But none of this did anything to dampen the support of thousands of his Hyde "parishioners," many of whom claimed the newspapers were lying.

Friends, family and associates still refused to believe that Shipman was guilty, and referred inquiries to Primrose, who'd rapidly become extremely adept at refusing to comment and glaring angrily at any journalist who dared to call at the family home. Shipman's son Sam insisted to friends that his father would never be found guilty.

But a few days after Fred Shipman's arrest, neighbors noted that Sam descended into what appeared to be a deeply confused state—although there was no suggestion that he even considered his father's guilt a possibility. For many months afterwards he barely acknowledged anyone in the street. "He just seemed to be in a dreamworld. His face was blank. He was clearly in a state of shock," one neighbor later recalled. On one occasion the teenager was even harassed in the street by a group of reporters.

The rest of the family's confidence in Fred Shipman's innocence apparently never wavered. The Shipman offspring insisted to friends that their father was the victim of a ghastly mistake and would soon be released. They even claimed that the family still expected to take possession of Mrs. Grundy's house on Joel Lane. All this clearly suggested that Shipman had discussed the old lady's estate in some detail with his family.

In Nottingham, Fred Shipman's estranged family also faced the full onslaught of the fourth estate on their doorstep. All inquiries were greeted with a polite refusal to talk. In Wetherby, friends closed ranks around Primrose's elderly mother Enid Oxtoby and her disabled daughter Mary. But despite everything, Primrose remained out of contact with her family.

When one of the main whistle-blowers, Dr. Linda Reynolds, returned to work after her long vacation in the US, she was greeted by a chorus at her clinic. "Have you heard? They've arrested Fred!"

Dr. Reynolds was shocked. "I thought to myself, 'So there was something wrong. I was right,' " she later recalled. "I finally felt exonerated."

Coroner Dr. John Pollard later praised Dr. Reynolds. "She was extremely brave in coming forward. We had to treat her report in a careful and subtle way because she really was laying her reputation on the line by saying something was wrong. If it hadn't been, she would have looked extremely foolish. She had put her career in jeopardy by speaking out, but she was only doing what she thought was right."

Undertaker Debbie Bambroffe was also on vacation in Spain when the news of Shipman's arrest broke. She later recalled: "We saw it on television, and instantly there was a sickening feeling in the pit of my stomach."

But amongst Shipman friends and associates there was still much loyalty. Dr. David Walker and Shipman's other drinking friends even agreed to offer to stand bail for the GP, because they were so convinced of his innocence. "I just didn't believe he could do such a thing," recalled Dr. Walker.

Fred Shipman's own GP, Dr. Wally Ashworth, immediately offered £20,000 toward Shipman's bail. "What can I say? That is how sure I was" of his innocence, he later told a journalist.

Brian Holden, of the Rochdale Canal Society members, was just as shocked to hear about Shipman's arrest. "I thought it was somebody else at first. The photos of him looked so different from the man I knew. He had aged so much and had a beard, and I had a job (was hard-pressed) to remember because he was known as 'Fred' or 'Dr. Shipman.' I only worked it out because of the frequency with which his name was mentioned. Then journalists started calling me up. I told one person I knew him and soon everyone was asking me about him." Mr. Holden, a teacher for forty years, then added: "People who thought of me as nothing more than a respectable teacher of Latin and Greek suddenly all wanted to know what I thought of Dr. Shipman."

On September 21, Mrs. Joan Melia's coffin was raised from the earth of St. Mary's graveyard in nearby Newton. The following day, the body of Mrs. Winifred Mellor was exhumed from Highfield Cemetery in Bredbury. A week later, police supervised the removal of Bianka Pomfret from Hyde Cemetery. Traces of morphine and diamorphine were found in all their bodies.

In the late afternoon of October 5, 1998, Detective Constable Marie Snityhski, 34, and Detective Sergeant Mark Wareing confronted Fred Shipman—supported by his solicitor, Anne Ball—across a table in Ashton-under-Lyne Police Station for his second interview. DS Wareing first confronted Shipman about how he'd altered his computerized medical records for 73-year-old Winifred Mellor to create a false history of heart disease. Detective Wareing asked the doctor if he had anything to say, and Shipman replied, "Nothing."

Wareing then told Shipman he believed that Shipman had gone to Mrs. Mellor's house in Hyde on May 11, 1998, with the express intention of killing her. Wareing said: "You attended at 3 P.M. and that's when you murdered this lady. So much was your rush that you went back to the surgery and started altering this lady's computerized medical records. We can prove that only minutes after 3 P.M. you were fabricating this false medical history."

Shipman responded, "There's no answer."

Then the officer replied: "There's a very clear answer. You attended that house, you rolled up her sleeve and injected her with morphine, killing her, and that's what you were trying to cover up."

Shipman replied, "No."

The mood of the interview suddenly changed. Fred Shipman had been caught completely unaware. Questions had been put to him that he couldn't have anticipated, questions that he could not answer or fend off with his customary arrogance.

Detective Sergeant Wareing decided to move in for the kill, so to speak: "I am showing you—I'll put it in the middle of the room, because your solicitor [attorney] can examine it as well, then. It's an exhibit, JFA42, and it's an insertion behind your computer. There's a ghost image, and it records what's placed in when and what's removed . . ."

Fred Shipman did not respond. His solicitor, a medical expert—"white coat crime" she calls it—picked up the document, examined it, passed it to the doctor. He examined it.

That document showed Mrs. Mellor's record from August 1, 1997, a woman complaining of chest pains, accompanied by a doctor's note; "*?? angina*," was actually typed into the computer three minutes and thirty-nine seconds after the doctor had left Mrs. Mellor's house following her death on May 11, 1998.

Detective Wareing then told Shipman, "I'll ask you again, Doctor. Where's that information come from?"

Listening in on an audio link were two senior police officers, Detective Superintendent Bernard Postles and Detective Chief Inspector Mark Williams. They had worked many weeks for such a moment.

"I've no recollection of me putting that on the machine," is all Shipman could say as he was pressed again and again. He struggled to maintain his composure.

"I still have no recollection of entering that onto the computer . . . again, in the same manner as I've explained the other one, I cannot remember putting that on the computer. I'm well aware that that's how an audit trail works . . . there's no argument about that . . . you say, you're stating the obvious, that doesn't need an answer."

When interviewed by the two investigators about possible victim Irene Berry, Shipman was confronted with evidence that he'd faked medical records.

> POLICE: Let me just remind you the date of this lady's death 11 May 98. After three o'clock that afternoon, you endorsed the computer with the date of the first of October 97 referring to prior chest pains.
> SHIPMAN: I have no recollection of me putting that on the machine.
> POLICE: It's your pass code. It's your name.

Shipman then paused and took a long, deep breath.

> SHIPMAN: That doesn't alter the fact that I can't remember doing it.
> POLICE: You attended the house and you murdered this lady, and you went back to the surgery and started altering this lady's records. You tell me why you needed to do that?
> SHIPMAN: There is no answer.

Fred Shipman had run out of answers, except to point out that the clock on his computer was not set for summer time and it would be off by one hour.

Then attorney Ann Ball ended it by asking for a consultation with her client. Left alone with her, Shipman fell to his knees and broke out in uncontrollable sobs, tears streaming down his face. He was unable to go back to continue the interview that day.

As DCI Williams later explained: "They led him nicely up a particular path. Suddenly he's less arrogant; it takes more time for him to answer. He was floundering; he didn't know a counter-argument. We'd put the pin in the balloon." Williams and DS Postles later listened to the tapes of that interview over and over again. DCI Williams recalled: "There's a crucial moment where he knows the game is up. I thought he was going to cough it."

The DCI added: "It is difficult enough in any interview, but that's what we are trained to do. In these circumstances they had a more difficult job because of the way he reacted to them and treated them. They were extremely skillful. They were under extraordinary pressure, but they coped extremely well and did a damn good job."

DS Postles never forgot that satisfying moment as he sat in the adjoining room: "He considered he had won. 'I'm up to it, let's get the boxing gloves on.' The officers led him along. You get to the point where he can see it coming, when you listen to the tapes."

Britain's sensational national tabloid newspapers soon reflected the shock felt across the nation about the alleged activities of Fred Shipman.

IS GP BRITAIN'S BIGGEST EVER SERIAL KILLER? asked the *Daily Express*.

Fred Shipman was formally suspended from his job several weeks after his arrest, but because he was only suspended and not disqualified, the health authority was obliged to pay Shipman his salary. That would continue until the day of his conviction, unless, of course, he was acquitted.

Shipman could even still call himself *doctor* for the time being, said a spokesman for the General Medical Council, whose motto is "Protecting patients, guiding doctors." It also emerged that almost £20,000 for medical equipment to be bought by the surgery appeal fund, whose donors included some of Shipman's own victims, had gone straight into the

GP's own bank account. This even included more than £200 ($300) donated in lieu of flowers being sent to victim Kathleen Wagstaff's funeral.

Detectives tried to turn their attention toward Primrose Shipman and her possible role in her husband's crimes. Primrose had become an even more ungainly, plump figure with lank gray hair and eyes that had long since lost their sparkle. Having worked part-time at the surgery and shared the home where Fred Shipman stashed many of the drugs he used to kill patients, she might well have enlightened investigators in regard to many aspects of her husband's behavior. But as one officer later explained: "She wouldn't even come to the police station. Her lawyer said she would only be questioned if she were arrested, but we simply had no reason to do that."

In Hyde, a small, loyal core of friends and family tried to protect Primrose—and they all remained convinced of the GP's innocence. Neighbors even offered to help with household chores and one couple continually collected groceries for her and her children. Others came by the house to comfort the family and offer support. Primrose told friends that she was determined to continue her life as normally as possible.

Through the large window at the front of the house, Primrose could be seen tidying up the living room. Some in the community even began to believe that perhaps Primrose had been secretly instrumental in her husband's arrest, and that some kind of a deal had been struck with prosecutors and police, but this had always been steadfastly denied.

For many women, the spectacular downfall of their beloved husband would have been too much to bear. But Primrose was made of stronger stuff; she'd been with him long enough for his superior attitude to rub off on her, giving her the strength to confront the staring eyes of the people of Hyde. Local taxi driver Michael Kitchen, whose 70-year-old mother was one of Fred Shipman's victims, noted: "After Shipman was charged, it was disturbing to see Primrose wandering around Hyde."

In her local supermarket, one staff member refused to

serve Primrose. The clerk later said she felt physically sick that someone could stay with a man after he had been charged with so many horrible crimes. But Primrose ignored all the stares; she and Fred were still invincible, and she still believed that everything would be cleared up and Fred would be released from police custody. Primrose—who, throughout life, had been prepared to plow her own lonely furrow—was unbending. She heard the tongues wagging behind her back. Family friends later said that Primrose was "aware of and prepared for" the life of scrutiny and stigma that lay ahead.

Over at St. George's Church in Hyde, some were even saying prayers for the family, along with the relatives of those who'd been murdered by Shipman. Curate Dr. John Harries said: "We pray for the family of Dr. Shipman—Primrose, Christopher, David, Sarah and Sam—who are also victims of this betrayal, and who have suffered so greatly in the last few months."

In mid-October, Fred Shipman was taken under escort from jail to Ashton-under-Lyne Police Station. Guards later recalled that he was in an increasingly distressed and emotional state. He refused to comment when asked about ten other suspected victims. A doctor then declared him unfit to be interviewed any further by waiting detectives. The police were never allowed to interview Shipman again.

He was then taken across the road to Tameside Magistrates' Court, where he was accused of murdering Mrs. Melia, Mrs. Mellor and Mrs. Pomfret. As the charges were put to him, Fred Shipman visibly shook his head from side to side and said nothing. He sobbed quietly as he was remanded into custody and two security guards had to help him from the court.

The police had no doubt of Fred Shipman's guilt, but remained baffled about his motives. The only time he'd tried to gain from death turned out to be his undoing. Revenge and/or a sexual motive did not seem part of the equation. Senior investigator Bernard Postles concluded: "It appears he just got the compulsion to kill. We looked at greed, we looked at revenge. We examined the possibility that the victims were all women draining his drug fund. But although some of them made visits to him, this was not the case. Rage? Anger? He wasn't annoyed with these people. The clue to the motive is his attitude that he is superior, and wanted to control situations."

And there, possibly, lies the key to unlock Fred Shipman's sick and twisted mind. He seemed fixated at a specific level of self-esteem, which meant that his major preoccupation was the idea of intellectual and creative eminence within his own small world. He frequently treated Primrose and his family in a despotic manner, and expected total, unquestioned obedience, becoming furious at the least sign of resistance. Fred Shipman had an absolute obsession with being right. He rarely indulged in self-criticism, and his killings appeared to be a form of self-indulgence.

This may have provided him with the power. Even when he was proven wrong he'd evade the issue by flying into an even deeper rage at some invented affront to his dignity. Shipman's attitude was that if Primrose truly respected him, then she would not tell him if he was in the wrong. If she dared to, then he would consider that to be the ultimate insult. If Primrose had ever left him, he would probably have gone to pieces; maybe become an alcoholic, or perhaps even killed himself. Her submission to his demands formed the basis of his self-respect: her desertion would have pulled away his psychological foundations.

Yet Shipman's immediate circle—his wife and children— provided him with a much-needed psychological vitamin even if they had to put up with a certain level of resentment from Shipman. It often took the form of outrageous bullying—even when, in many ways, Shipman needed his family more than they needed him. He was a truly complex character.

Following Fred Shipman's minor collapse after his interview and court appearance, the GP was prescribed numerous tranquilizers. He quickly regained his iron will to survive and even tried to take control of his circumstances. Initially, Shipman had been remanded to Walton Prison, in Liverpool, fifty miles to the west of Hyde, because there was much concern that if he was incarcerated at Manchester's notorious Strangeways Prison, there was a high chance he would find himself facing relatives of some of his victims amongst the inmates and staff.

During his brief spell in Walton Prison, Fred Shipman shared a cell with Brian Ratford, then on remand for a drunk-driving charge. The GP informed his cellmate about different ways to kill someone.

But within weeks, Shipman was moved to Strangeways Prison after continual requests from his attorneys. They felt that Walton Prison was too far for Primrose and the children to travel to visit the jailed GP. Shipman was more concerned with seeing his family than any threat from inmates or staff.

Her Majesty's Prison Strangeways is a grim, fortress-like red-brick building that was constructed more than 100 years ago. It is a depressing institution where inmates have, over the years, mounted regular rooftop demonstrations to protest the appalling conditions. Cells line long landings, under a steepled roof which echoes with the noise of men trudging up and down the steel stairway.

Once he'd settled inside Strangeways, Fred Shipman took to prison life "like a natural." Father Denis Maher, the priest from St. Paul's Church, who'd lost three of his parishioners to the alleged mass killer, was appalled when he heard how Shipman was "strolling around the place as if he owned it."

One of the first people outside his family to visit Fred Shipman was Michael Taylor, who'd earlier met Shipman through the Small Practices Association.

"Fred tended to be somewhat grumpy at times," recalled Michael Taylor. "He could offend people, but he was also very prepared to help. I think it's fair to say that we respected him, and those of us who have been to his practice recognized that it was of high quality. He was very energetic, very meticulous."

Michael Taylor regarded Fred Shipman as a genuine friend, but later acknowledged that it was "a friendship based on acquaintanceship and mutual respect, the need for information and the need to learn together. He was not the sort of man I would seek out for a couple of [drinks]."

Within seconds of meeting Shipman in Strangeways, Taylor later recalled, the GP was telling him in no uncertain terms that the allegations against him were false. "He said it was very upsetting and disconcerting. He mentioned how he'd been on his way back from the post office when a patient crossed the road to see him and support him. He had just burst into tears."

Fred Shipman showed no regret for his alleged crimes because in his mind he had done no wrong. But in letters to other friends soon after his arrest, Shipman did admit that "even Primrose has started asking me about the deaths."

Fred Shipman's ability to adapt to prison life didn't surprise those who knew him well. He'd crawled back up from numerous setbacks during his life. In the corridors, cells and recreation wings at Strangeways he was going about his manipulative business in the only way he knew. He told fellow inmate Derrick Ismiel: "My work was faultless. I prided myself on my experience in caring for people who were terminally ill. How dare they question my professionalism? People knew me by my work. How can they actually accuse me of this?"

Fred Shipman still felt himself to be unquestionable and unassailable. The compassionate, kindly veneer which he'd so carefully perfected for elderly and needy patients was, to a certain extent, discarded. Beneath it seemed to lurk a bleak, callous, calculating man convinced of his own infallibility, determined to continue controlling everything around him, and confident that he possessed the intellect to fool them all.

Inside Strangeways, Shipman could barely hide his contempt for most other inmates—with the exception of Derrick Ismiel. In a chilling, monotone voice he told Ismiel one day, soon after his transfer to Strangeways: "They're never going to find me guilty. I'll show them all. This whole system is full of lies. They should have all died—and died like flies."

Shipman made a point of counseling inmates whom no one else would speak to. Prisoner Aaron Nicholls, who set fire to his 12-year-old girlfriend, Lauren Carhart, was one of his favorite "patients." Shipman defended his own actions by saying: "We're all in here for something." Shipman believed that by helping people such as Nicholls he was creating a position for himself within the prison hierarchy. Shipman's penchant for looking after certain fellow cons helped him gain a reputation as a combination of Florence Nightingale and Hannibal Lecter. Just as he did with his patients in the outside world, Shipman was successfully keeping people at a safe, admiring distance.

Inmate Tony Fleming shared a cell with Shipman at Strangeways and later claimed that the GP saved his life when Fleming tried to hang himself. His gasps woke the serial-killing doctor, who shouted to the wardens for help. Shipman then held Fleming up while the wardens cut him down. Afterwards, Shipman joked with the deeply depressed Fleming: "Next time, use someone else's shoelaces. Mine are ruined."

"If he'd really enjoyed killing, like they say, then he would have just left me hanging there. He's a good bloke," Fleming said after his release.

Shipman regularly played Monopoly and Scrabble in prison with inmates and staff members. But he clearly hated losing. "He was a cheating sod," recalled Tony Fleming. "If we bought property [for Monopoly] we put the money in the middle of the board, then he would slip it in his bank. We used to have a laugh about it. He was determined to beat me, and I didn't want to spoil his moment of glory."

Across Britain and the world, news of the serial killer doctor was hitting the front pages on almost a daily basis: On October 12, 1998, the London tabloid *Daily Mail* ran a headline screaming: MURDER CASE GP: MORE BODIES EXHUMED.

ACCUSED DOCTOR: POLICE PROBING 77 DEATHS hit the newsstands two days later. The article—also in the *Mail*—breathlessly exclaimed: "The deaths of 77 patients of a GP accused of four murders are now being investigated by detectives, it can be revealed."

Some of Britain's more serious broadsheet newspapers were rather more conservative with their accounts of Shipman's alleged activities: DOCTOR FACES INQUIRY OVER 20 DEATHS said *The Daily Telegraph*. But they all featured Shipman on their front pages.

On October 30, Shipman appeared at Liverpool Crown Court for what was described as a brief "plea and direction hearing" which would set an initial date for the start of the GP's trial. So far he'd been charged with the murders of Kathleen Grundy, Bianka Pomfret, Joan Melia, Winifred Mellor, Ivy Lomas and charity worker Marie Quinn.

In the first week of November 1998, three more victims were exhumed from their final resting places at Hyde Cemetery. Irene Turner, who'd died at the age of 67 in 1996, was the first one. She was followed twenty-four hours later by Alice Kitchen, who'd died in 1994 at age 70. Then, in the early hours of the following day, the remains of Jean Lilley were removed. She'd died only the previous year at the age of 58.

By mid-November 1998 the community of Hyde was stunned to hear the police publicly admit for the first time that they might have to dig up as many as twenty bodies as part of their ongoing investigation. Investigators had initially been hoping that nine exhumations might be sufficient for their case, although they still faced the problem of appeasing anxious relatives who'd reported suspicions about the deaths of their loved ones. Besides the nine bodies so far exhumed, detectives wanted to recover the remains of another alleged victim from her final resting place in Malta, but the family was completely opposed to the plan.

19

Fred Shipman, Category A prisoner—considered a danger to staff and other inmates—was kept under close observation because of genuine fears that he might commit suicide. Any inmate has the potential to harm himself; the noise, the smell, the attitudes of other prisoners and the endless indignities that come with the loss of liberty are particularly shocking for first-time prisoners. Every fifteen minutes, twenty-four hours a day, a warder would flip open the spyhole to his cell door. Random searches were also carried out to make sure Shipman had no potential weapons.

In the back of all the guards' minds was Britain's last notorious serial killer, Fred West, who killed himself while in prison in Birmingham awaiting trial. Down the hall from Shipman in Strangeways, a man accused of killing five elderly women hanged himself in his cell. Stephen Akinmurele, a 21-year-old with a hatred of old people, had had a history of violence and mental illness.

Another of Fred Shipman's Strangeways cellmates was 34-year-old heating engineer Peter Hall, who, after bludgeoning his girlfriend, Brazilian-born Celeste Bates to death, used her car to collect her seventeen-month-old son from daycare and battered him to death with a pick handle. Then he collected her eight-year-old son from school and killed him the same way, leaving a callous note for Bates's ex-husband that said, "You are welcome to your family back." Hall was racked with remorse and self-pity, while Fred Shipman was behaving as if he were the victim of a gross miscarriage of justice. Shipman even described Hall in a letter to one associate as "a decent cellmate." Hall eventually went to trial in March 1999 and was given three life sentences.

Fred Shipman tried to reply to every "reasonable" letter he received while awaiting trial. Even when old classmate Dr. Michael Heath sent him a letter pointing out that they had gone to school together, Shipman sent back a brief, polite note. Shipman apologized for not remembering Heath from school, and explained that he had "enough on" without digging up old memories. The note, signed "Fred," concluded: "I've learnt never to look back, as you always end up disappointed."

But the note gave away a few clues to Fred Shipman's state of mind as he awaited trial. Handwriting expert Patricia Leeson concluded that the writer—whose identity she did not know—was emotionally "locked in," and could be driven to amoral behavior by his "loss of integrity." Fred Shipman was in fact bored out of his brains in prison. His mind needed continual stimulation because he found it deeply stressful being the center of so much attention. He would give anything to keep a low profile, but the crimes he was charged with guaranteed that they would never happen again.

Graphologist Leeson explained: "This attitude could lead to him being overtaken professionally by people of lower intelligence, but with more confidence, causing an irritating sense of under-achievement. His writing shows that he tends to put off decisions and fails to follow through unless the task is important to him personally.

"His low self-image, which brings feelings of insecurity and anticipation of rejection, makes coping with problems difficult, and it is likely he would try to avoid taking final responsibility for his actions. He has been brought up to consider it incorrect to display emotions, and to maintain the stiff upper lip at all costs."

Now in prison for the first time in his life, Fred Shipman's emotions were under lock and key, and his excellent powers of communication simply covered his inner withdrawal. The charges he faced brought him a bizarre combination of respect and hatred from both inmates and staff. Shipman became quick to see slights and take offense. But in another sense, life in prison allowed Shipman to reveal a little more of his true self. Everyone knew what he was accused of, so he didn't have to put on the façade of being a friendly, harmless GP.

There was a strangely childish side to Fred Shipman following his arrest. At one stage he wrote in jokey terms about the armed police from the Tactical Support Group who transported him between prison and court. "We had a lovely drive at greater than the speed limit, lights on, flashing blue lights, the lot," he wrote. But he also described feeling "very, very lonely" when he sat in the dock at remand hearings. He wrote: "You get the dry mouth, fast heart rate and sweating."

In the early hours of Monday, December 7, 1998, police exhumed the grave of widow Sarah Ashworth, who was known as "Sally," and had died at 75 at her home on Bowlacre Road in Hyde, on April 17, 1993. Detectives were privately predicting that the number of unexplained deaths linked to Shipman might soon top the 100 mark.

A few hours after the exhumation, Fred Shipman was back in court. The GP seemed to have aged five years in a matter of months. He was flanked by four security guards while standing, shoulders hunched, in the dock of the magistrates' court at Ashton-under-Lyne in Greater Manchester. Dressed in a red sweater and blue open-necked shirt, he spoke only once to confirm his name before three more murder charges were put before him. Loyal wife Primrose looked across at her troubled husband from the public gallery and smiled in his direction. As Shipman was led away, he looked down at the ground, a broken figure.

On Wednesday, December 9, 1998, police investigators exhumed another body—widow Elizabeth Mellor—from Hyde Cemetery. Mrs. Mellor had been 75 when she died on November 30, 1994. A post-mortem examination was immediately carried out by a Home Office pathologist. Mrs. Mellor was the ninth corpse to be removed from Hyde Cemetery.

Tissue samples were sent to the Forensic Science Laboratory at Chorley, Lancashire. The result of the standard screening tests showed positive for morphine, but, just to be absolutely certain, hair samples were sent to Hans Sachs, at the University of Munich. Professor Sachs also found that morphine had been administered close to the time of death.

On Thursday, January 7, 1999, Fred Shipman was sent for trial on two further counts of murder involving the deaths of Ivy Lomas and Marie Quinn. Once again, Primrose was faithfully in attendance. This time Shipman appeared calm and collected at the two-minute hearing. Flanked by three guards, he spoke clearly when questioned.

During prison visits, Fred Shipman continued to insist to Primrose and his children that he was completely innocent. But he'd spent so much time lying, that it's entirely possible he believed his own fabrications. Shipman's self-image had faded rapidly since his incarceration, however, and he had physically deteriorated as well. He was like someone who was partly deaf: he'd gotten used to never hearing sounds below a certain level, to never dealing with certain issues.

Shipman longed for an earthquake of feeling to shake him out of his indifference. The truth was, he could only be shaken out of it by the prospect of another kill. Obeying the same rules as everyone else had long since ceased to satisfy Fred Shipman. He'd crossed the borderline between thought and action long ago. But now that he was incarcerated, there was little chance of him ever killing again.

There seems little doubt that Primrose Shipman sensed her husband's inner feelings. In one letter she wrote to him in the early part of 1999, she referred to how she was writing sitting at the family dining table while the rain poured down outside. She compared his pain of incarceration to her own pain at his absence, and consoled him by mentioning the one-hour-a-day visiting time they were allowed. Primrose still appeared to be very much under his power and influence.

While awaiting trial, Fred Shipman wrote a series of letters to his local Member of Parliament (MP), Tom Pendry, and a number of fellow GPs. He said he was worried about the standard of treatment being offered to his patients during his enforced absence. The letters reinforced the GP's complete self-denial of his alleged crimes.

In one letter from Strangeways Prison, Inmate CJ 8198 told Pendry that his clinic was likely to be closed down. He complained that the locum seeing his patients had been given a restricted list of drugs to use, and even claimed that few of his patients had ever suffered any side effects from his treatment.

In a number of letters to one former medical colleague, Charles Douglas, Shipman further confirmed his complete and utter state of self-denial. As Dr. Douglas later explained: "Time and time he has said it and it has made it difficult for me to write back. There's nothing I can point to as showing who he really was. This wasn't someone who had just had a bad day. This is somebody who apparently committed some horrendous crimes to a level that is quite staggering. Totally out of the norm. There is nothing that I have seen which would explain it."

On Monday, February 22, 1999, Fred Shipman was charged with murdering seven more female patients—bringing the total to fifteen. He even managed to flash a smile to Primrose as he was led from Tameside Magistrates' Court following a four-minute appearance. Smartly dressed in a jersey and white shirt, and with neatly trimmed hair and beard, Shipman replied clearly with "I do" when he was asked by the magistrate if he understood the new charges. He seemed in a better, brighter mood than during previous court appearances.

Primrose smiled reassuringly at her husband from the back of the court. Six of the seven new charges referred to cremations, not burials, as with the previous eight.

They were: college lecturer Maureen Ward, 57, of Ogden Court, Hyde, who died on February 18, 1998; Marie West, 81, of Knott Fold, Gee Cross, who died on March 6, 1995, and was well known in Hyde, where she owned and ran a dress shop; Muriel Grimshaw, 76, from Berkeley Crescent, Hyde, who'd died on July 14, 1997, and was the widow of retired office clerk Harold Grimshaw; Norah Nuttall, 65, from Gee Cross, who died on January 26, 1998; Lizzie Adams, 77, from Hyde, who died on February 28, 1997. Kathleen Wagstaff, 81, who was from Gee Cross, and died on December 9, 1997; and Pamela Hillier, 68, from Hyde, who died on February 9, 1998. All apart from Muriel Grimshaw had been cremated.

Father Denis Maher had been present during five of the exhumations, including those whose families he'd comforted when they originally died. "At four in the morning, when I was standing at the graveside of those who were being exhumed, he [Shipman] should have been made to stand beside me while their bodies were literally dragged out of their graves. Perhaps then he would begin to realize the enormity of the hurt that he had caused the people of Hyde."

Yet despite condemning Fred Shipman for his crimes, Father Maher stressed that he would forgive the GP, adding that he "would love to visit him in prison." But he made a point of saying that before that could happen, Shipman would have to face up to the crimes he had committed and admit them openly. Few expected him to do so.

Inside Strangeways, Fred Shipman insisted that staff and inmates call him "Doctor." He was considered such a well-behaved prisoner that he was even picked out to welcome visiting VIPs while awaiting trial. The Queen of England's daughter Princess Anne shook hands with the suspected serial killer and chatted with him while touring the tough prison as royal patron of the Butler Trust, a prison welfare organization. The Princess later commented that she had found Fred Shipman to be polite and well-spoken, and many who were present believed that Anne was intrigued to meet the alleged mass killer. Shipman was irritated because he wasn't allowed to tell the Princess about conditions inside Strangeways. After she left the jail, Shipman bragged about his royal connection and then openly insulted Anne's looks, telling one inmate, "It was nice to meet a normal woman again. Pity she looks like a horse."

Fred Shipman had become the equivalent of a one-man freak show at a circus. Everyone from inmates to officers wanted to take a look at the killer GP. He was the only prisoner in his cell block without photos of topless women on his walls. He preferred pictures of his beloved family and steam trains. Shipman saw himself as intellectually superior to the day-to-day riff-raff of prison life. His attitude got him banned from the prison quiz nights because he knew all the answers and always won. But it was Fred Shipman's penchant for holding unofficial medical sessions that raised the most eyebrows. One ex-inmate explained: "He held [a clinic] in his cell on Saturday and even some of the prison officers went to him for a diagnosis."

He'd give them precise instructions as to which medication to ask for when they saw the prison doctors. He also gave them his expert opinion on medical evidence being used in other inmates' cases, and even helped some of them write letters.

Shipman continued corresponding with old colleagues and friends out of the blue. The central theme of most letters was, naturally, his innocence, and he maintained that he was the victim of an appalling mistake. But there were other, very down-to-earth references in his letters. In one he talked about bookmakers William Hill offering odds of 9/5 on for a guilty verdict, 15/1 not guilty. He'd also adjusted his own assessment of his chances of ever being freed as "possibly ten per cent. Perhaps all the jury will be dead from the neck up" he wrote in a letter, "but that is unlikely." Was Shipman at last coming to terms with his fate?

Even Shipman's use of tranquilizers gave him an excuse

to show some dark humor in one letter. "Me, I keep taking the tablets," he wrote. He also described prison routine as very ordered: "go there, come here, do this, do that."

Shipman spent much of his time in jail preparing for his court case. He claimed the only evidence the police had was that he practiced as he always had; he believed he was guilty only of being a good doctor. He also claimed the police were withholding evidence from his attorneys. Eventually, Shipman was given a single cell in Strangeways because of the mountain of paperwork he had to deal with in connection with his trial. He eventually amassed a stack of folders ten feet high, covered in stickers with notes for his lawyers.

Primrose continued to write regularly to her husband. In one letter she even referred to his alleged victims and conceded: *"Well I am very sorry for them as you happen to be my husband and I love you very much and am not thinking of leaving you. Funny what sets me off. I need all my friends and supporters but that has given me thought. I wonder if other women have looked at it that way."*

In another letter—on March 2, 1999—Primrose, not exactly a scholar of the English language, wrote: *"My dearest Fred. Only 216 days to go* [until the trial], *good idea, keep my maths going. I have done everything this morning when I should have done the paper work, sorted the clean sock* [sic], *made bed . . ."*

And so Primrose droned on. It was almost as if she was trying to avoid the most important issue. She even described how she'd listened to a radio program about secrets of a long marriage on the popular British show, *Woman's Hour.*

In the middle of 1999, Shipman wrote to one friend and claimed he was supporting Primrose. "She is being affected by the length of time it is all taking. I'm now comforting her on visits," he revealed.

Sarah, Christopher, David and Sam seemed to the outside world to be standing by their mother. But behind the scenes, conflict must have arisen as they began to come to terms with the fact that their father might be a mass murderer. Primrose would have faced divided loyalties; whether to

continue her unswerving support for her husband or begin
to concede to the children. At that time psychiatrist Ian Stephen predicted: "She will go along with what her husband
tells her. If it's 'I did not do it; I was set up,' she will feel
obliged to go along with that."

Did some of the children start questioning why Primrose
did not recognize her husband's criminal behavior sooner?
However, it is perfectly plausible that she had no idea of
her husband's murderous activities. "Serial killers can act
much like the children's cartoon character Mr. Benn," explained Stephen. "They have that ability to go through a
door and become someone else. Shipman was probably able
to make a clean split between his activities at work and his
home life."

Inside Strangeways, Shipman was proclaimed "too
clever" to take daily classes with the rest of the inmates.
Instead, he became an assistant to the teachers who taught
English and art to the prisoners from 9:30 to 11:30 each
morning. He also regularly continued to challenge the wardens to games of Scrabble. But most of the time he was
bored, and obliged to carry out menial jailhouse tasks such
as breakfast duty and mopping out his cell.

Shipman was locked up between lunch and dinner, but
this was usually broken by Primrose's daily visit at 2 P.M.
sharp. After dinner—at around 6:30 P.M.—he'd find himself
locked up in his cell for the night. That was when he'd write
letters, surrounded by those photos of his family: Primrose
and Sarah on a trip to Buckingham Palace; young Sam in
his school uniform. They reminded Fred Shipman of the life
he'd left behind. It was the normal fragment of his twisted
world which had kept him sane through his "killing years."

While awaiting trial, Fred Shipman continued to claim to
other inmates that he wouldn't get a long sentence even if
he was convicted. "He made it all sound like he'd been
doing his patients a favor," one inmate later recalled.

Shipman's legal team even tried to get his murder trial
abandoned during the pre-trial hearings. Instead, they requested three separate trials: one for the murder of the last

victim, Kathleen Grundy; one for the women who were buried; and one for those who were cremated. But Judge Mr. Justice Forbes threw out the request and also turned down their application that the trial should be heard in London, because, they had argued, he could not have a fair trial anywhere in the north of England due to the intense media coverage.

Meanwhile the ever-loyal Primrose bought a modest second-hand red Metro car after her Ford Sierra had been crashed by joyriders. The Shipmans' daughter Sarah then moved to a new home within a mile of the prison, and his sons Christopher, David and Sam continued to be regular visitors to Strangeways.

One of Primrose's few friends in the months following her husband's arrest was Shipman's practice manager John Gilmore, who'd been sacked from a previous NHS position years earlier for gross malpractice. (Gilmore later claimed that he had been unfairly dismissed, and his legal action against the Health Authority was settled out of court.) He spent many evenings at Primrose's home comforting her and listening to her confusion over the charges facing Fred Shipman, one of his oldest friends.

Fred Shipman's more distant relatives were naturally shocked by his arrest. His Uncle Reg Shipman back in Nottingham said: "I'm glad his dad isn't alive to see this. He was a good man, a good father. They were a well-brought-up family. I just don't know why this has happened."

Old school friend Alan Goddard was watching the TV news with his wife when he saw some slow-motion footage of Fred Shipman being led away in handcuffs. "I didn't recognize his picture, but he looked a lot like his dad," Goddard recalled with a shudder. "I can't believe it's true."

Another childhood friend, John Soar, was convinced that Fred was mentally ill: "I feel sorry for him and his family, as well as the victims. Such a waste of talent. If I was asked why Fred Shipman would be in the newspapers at 53, I would say because he was an exemplary GP doing something for his community, not this."

Former classmate Terry Swinn agreed: "You need strength of character to become a doctor, put in the graft. I liked him. I'm perplexed, as everyone else is." Another classmate, Bob Studholme, put it, bizarrely, in sporting terms. "He has rather let the side down," he said, referring to the infamy Shipman had brought to High Pavement Grammar School. Studholme believed that Shipman's problems began when he struggled to get the grades he needed for entrance into medical school, especially after his mother died. Then there was that shotgun wedding to Primrose when he was still a student. Studholme also said it was significant that his old classmate stopped playing any sports the moment he met Primrose. "I was very shocked to hear that. He'd been so keen on rugby."

Studholme added: "Fred needed to work hard to get qualifications, and he would take everything seriously. He would have been equally serious about that marriage and about his children. His focus was taken away from sport, concentrating on family and being qualified. If I saw him now, I would say, 'Hi, Fred, how are you?' Then I would ask him about it man to man—'What the bloody hell have you done?' "

Studholme continued with his Shipman theory: "Doctors have to have a degree of detachment. Life is full of people who die; you can't win them all. We have to respect that aspect. We all have a bill to pay in life. It's not malice that led to Fred's actions, there's a kink that allowed that, perhaps overwork. People setting him up, going to him when things go wrong. All of us are only one inch from this. Women with small children under threat are capable of killing. The Germans have a saying: 'Let the pig out.' It means letting off steam, getting rid of frustration. Like he did on the rugby pitch [field]. Maybe that was it. He didn't permit himself to let go; now he has in the worst possible way."

Over at Lord Derby Road—where the family first settled when they arrived in Hyde—neighbors refused to speak ill of the Shipmans. There were still many who simply could not believe Shipman was a mass murderer.

There was intense speculation about Shipman's eventual

trial. Killers often change their pleas to guilty at the last minute once confronted with the enormity of their actions. Then the main argument in court would concern their sanity at the time they committed the crimes. But Fred Shipman made it clear that he was going to plead not guilty. He planned to make the most of his court appearance and drag the case out for as long as possible. He insisted to his lawyers that he would give evidence himself—and he'd be proclaiming his innocence to his last breath.

Shipman even wrote from prison to his old friend and GP Dr. Wally Ashworth protesting that he had had nothing to do with the deaths. Dr. Ashworth later recalled: "He never doubted he would be acquitted. I do feel rather guilty that I haven't visited him in prison and probably never will. Despite everything, he was remarkably attentive to me when I was ill, and I owe him a debt for that."

Fred Shipman's incarceration continued to confuse the entire community.

20

In the early summer of 1999, psychiatrist Dr. Richard Badcock interviewed Fred Shipman in Strangeways Prison on behalf of prosecutors. Shipman continued to deny committing the murders, leaving few clues as to his motive. Dr. Badcock later claimed that Shipman was a "classic" necrophiliac: a man obsessed not with having sex with the dead, but with the act of inducing death, and controlling and observing the moment when life leaves the body.

Shipman was meticulous at positioning his victims before he injected them. He enjoyed waiting with them while they died, and was excited at being present when his handiwork was discovered by others. He also relished having evaded capture for so long, and he gained an extra buzz of excitement from those he murdered inside his own clinic. He even enjoyed breaking the news to his victims' relatives.

Dr. Badcock believes that Shipman's necrophiliac tendencies were triggered by the death of his mother. Killing others made perfect sense to Shipman's twisted logic. Shipman's perceived arrogance and his fascination with state-of-the-art computers were manifestations of his need for control, whether that be of people or machines.

Deep inside, Fred Shipman was nothing more than a shell of a person, continually having to re-invent himself for the outside world. Sooner or later his obsession with control forced him to make others do things according to his will. A form of sadism had taken over Shipman's mind. At work he frequently humiliated people in such a way that they knew they were being demeaned. Inflicting pain or torture on his victims and seeing them take it was part of his addiction. It was the only way Fred Shipman could see himself in control.

Fred Shipman had become like a country with only an atomic bomb as a defense policy; a person with the ultimate control, but little else. Shipman's own special brand of necrophilia was a psychological disorder rather than an illness. But it was undoubtedly a disorder which transcended the conventional disciplines of medicine.

There was also one apparent link to Shipman's sexuality; he regarded the real act of sex as messy and difficult and to be avoided. Sex was one of the few times when he lost control of his surroundings. That's one reason he grew to prefer the huge intellectual buzz of murder. It became the power base replacement for real sex.

Fred Shipman's relationship with Primrose remained an enigma. He still retained total control over her, both mentally and physically, yet he held her accountable for everything that either went wrong for him or displeased him. He was not an easy husband, by any means.

Despite languishing in Strangeways, Fred Shipman was awarded a 7.3 percent pay raise. The increase consisted of 3.5 percent for all GPs in the UK and a further 3.8 percent in backdated pay. In addition to his wages, Shipman also had a contributory National Health Service pension scheme to which his employers paid £3,000 ($4,500) a year, and he contributed £4,500 ($6,000). Shipman instructed Primrose to cash in two financial policies believed to be held at a Manchester-based investment company. The policies were thought to be worth at least £30,000 ($50,000).

Behind the scenes, Fred Shipman's vast legal costs were to be paid jointly by the Medical Defense Union and legal aid. They were expected to reach several hundred thousand dollars once the trial was completed.

During the summer of 1999, Dr. Linda Reynolds—one of the GPs most responsible for bringing Shipman to justice—was diagnosed with terminal cancer. Her husband Nigel and children Caroline, 21, and William, 18, were

naturally devastated. She wasn't even certain she would live
long enough to see Shipman brought to trial. "I just hope I
live to see the conclusion of all this," she said stoically.
"And I hope he stays in prison for the rest of his life."

But even in her eleventh hour of life she was able to
maintain her sense of humor about the Shipman case: "I had
a 90-year-old patient who joked, 'You are a terrible doctor;
if I had Dr. Shipman, I would not have all this pain now.' "

Dr. Reynolds could not have been more different from
Fred Shipman. "I loved my job; being part of the community; looking after generations of the same family; the intellectual stimulation of making a diagnosis; just being able
to help people, be kind to them," she said sadly. "I would
have liked ten more years to look after the people of Hyde—
I was just getting started with them."

Amazingly, morphine, diamorphine and various other drugs
seized from Fred Shipman's home in September 1998 lay
untouched in an exhibits bag without a contents label for
nearly a year at the headquarters of the Greater Manchester
Police. It was only re-discovered when Detective Constable
Dave O'Brien was sorting out exhibits to be returned or
destroyed in August 1999.

During police interrogation, Shipman had insisted that he
did not keep any drugs, or even have a register to do so.
The police had been incredibly inefficient in failing to cor-
rectly log the bag when it was originally found in the house.
The drugs in question had been reported by Fred Shipman
as being destroyed in 1995 in his surgery. Investigators had
come dangerously close to losing a vital piece of evidence.

Meanwhile, thirty grief counselors were standing by to
help the friends and relatives of Fred Shipman's victims to
cope with the surge of graphic publicity expected when the
GP's trial started at Preston Crown Court late in 1999. The
local health authority also set up a confidential helpline for
any concerned relatives of possible Shipman victims. Since
the murder inquiry had started, almost 200 people had been

referred by police for support and more than seventy had
contacted the helpline.

The town of Preston, forty miles from Hyde, was chosen to
host the Shipman trial because police and attorneys believed
it would be virtually impossible to find an impartial jury any
nearer to the scene of the GP's alleged crimes. In many
ways, Preston was very similar in size and influence to
Hyde, with its prosperity built on the thriving cotton industry of the Industrial Revolution.

The Crown Court at Preston was known as "the Old Bailey of the North" in reference to the most famous court in
Britain—the Old Bailey in London, where many of the most
famous criminals of all time have been tried. It was set
amongst grandiose Victorian buildings with a statue of Justice, blind and carrying scales, just like the one that topped
the London version. The current Preston Crown Court was
opened in 1904 and consisted of two courtrooms with eight
cells. A third court was added in 1965. The entire building
was renovated in 1995 at a cost of £1.2 million ($1.8 mil-
lion). The Crown Court was used to being at the center of
the world's press attention; six years earlier, two 10-year-
old schoolboys were jailed for the murder of 2-year-old tod-
dler James Bulger, who was kidnapped from a Liverpool
shopping mall in 1993.

Fred Shipman's trial was due to be heard in Court One,
which is decorated in bright green tiles and rich oak pan-
eling with ornate cornicing. A stained-glass center to the
curved ceiling allows daylight to pour into the courtroom.
Hanging from the walls are portraits of past chairmen of the
Lancashire Quarter Sessions. Across the hall Number Two
Court was transformed into a media center to cope with the
vast number of journalists expected to visit from across the
globe. There was even an audiolink allowing the overflow
of reporters who could not get seats in the actual court to
follow the proceedings.

Thirty-eight press seats were allocated on a first-come,
first-served basis. Britain's numerous national newspapers,

TV and radio news organizations were first on the starting line. Extra power points for laptops were installed in Court Two and another room was set aside for court artists, as no cameras would be allowed to record the proceedings.

Outside the courthouse, Harris Street—named after a nineteenth-century philanthropist—was to be closed off between the court and the Harris Library from three days before the trial commenced until the day after the end of the proceedings. The only vehicles allowed in were the television and radio broadcast vans, which left a trail of thick black cables behind them, leading to electricity outlets in the library.

Chief prosecutor in the Shipman trial was Richard Henriques, who'd also prosecuted the James Bulger case. Henriques, 55, was leader of the Northern Circuit of barristers, which made him the most senior and respected lawyer in the northwest of England. He came from a long line of attorneys; his Madeira-born father had been a celebrated divorce lawyer. Henriques earned in excess of £500,000 a year ($750,000). Both he and his junior attorney, Peter Wright QC, were based in nearby Manchester.

Fred Shipman's attorney, Nicola Davies QC, 46, specialized in medical cases. Born in South Wales, she read law at Birmingham University and had been involved in several previous high-profile cases. Slim, fair-haired, and always immaculately dressed, Nicola Davies was particularly adept at dissecting expert evidence.

The judge at the trial was 61-year-old Thayne Forbes, who had been the presiding judge of the Northern Circuit for two and a half years by the time the Shipman case came to court. Of Scottish descent, he was born on the Isle of Wight in the south of England and educated at the very exclusive (and expensive) Winchester private school. He gained his law degree from London University. Forbes had a reputation for being scrupulously fair and meticulous: none of his trials had ever been successfully appealed against. His owlish, patient and occasionally amused expression often diffused some awkward courtroom battles.

Thus the scene was set for the trial of one of the most cold-blooded killers in British criminal history.

At 8:50 A.M. on October 4, 1999, Fred Shipman was driven into the back yard of Preston Crown Court in a prison van. Primrose and sons David and Sam had arrived in a nearby parking lot and were walking up the steps into the court, shielded by a burly six-foot "family friend" when the boys found themselves having to protect Primrose from reporters surging toward them.

Before Fred Shipman walked in that morning, a sense of expectation gripped the courtroom; but then the GP shuffled into view: a small man, with a neatly trimmed beard and a large bald patch, wearing a gray suit, dark tie and white shirt. His clothes hung off his shoulders and his thinning hair was combed forward. He'd lost at least twenty-five pounds, shrinking from a thirty-six- to a thirty-two-inch waist. He was 53 years old, but looked as if he was about to hit his seventies. Shipman immediately peered at the jury through his shiny round gold-rimmed glasses.

The trial was opened and immediately adjourned after only fifteen minutes for legal arguments. Just across the court in the public gallery, Primrose, Sam and David, plus several friends, sat and watched the proceedings. Primrose, in a maroon-and-green—checked jacket, looked as matronly as usual.

Dozens of camera crews, photographers and journalists from across the world were present. Three documentary teams were covering the case, along with at least a dozen TV news crews. Special arrangements had also been made to seat the relatives of some of Shipman's victims.

The following day, world events such as a horrific earthquake in Turkey ensured that the uneventful first day of the Fred Shipman trial did not make the front page of many newspapers. Court officials predicted that the trial would not properly get started until a jury was sworn in the following Monday. Prosecutor Richard Henriques had already warned the judge that his opening evidence would take at least three days to deliver.

Shipman faced sixteen charges, fifteen of murder and one of forging Mrs. Grundy's will. The fifteen women were: Kathleen Grundy, Joan Melia, Winifred Mellor, Bianka Pomfret, Marie Quinn, Ivy Lomas, Irene Turner, Jean Lilley, Muriel Grimshaw, Marie West, Kathleen Wagstaff, Pamela Hillier, Norah Nuttall, Elizabeth Adams and Maureen Ward.

Outside the court a small crowd appeared each morning before opening time at 10:30 A.M. to watch the "stars" of the case. Many in the crowd were local women eager to examine Primrose, the wife of the so-called "monster." Heavy-set Primrose was usually flanked by at least one of her loyal children escorting her to take her place in her pre-designated spot in the public gallery. Often she was greeted by a chorus of " 'Morning, Primrose" as the regulars gathered. Primrose returned the greeting with a friendly enough expression before being ushered inside to her specially reserved seat.

Primrose sat every day at her place in the front of the public gallery with her hands clasped in her lap. Occasionally she exchanged pleasantries with people around her, but mostly kept to herself. She even handed out chocolates to those sitting beside her in court. Primrose referred all press inquiries about the case to the Medical Defense Union, but happily chatted to people at the court kiosk where she bought regular coffees.

She did not go out of her way to avoid journalists in the court's lobby. "She seemed completely at ease. There was always a look of friendly defiance on her face," said one person who attended the trial.

Bianka Pomfret's ex-husband Adrian found Primrose's attitude very disturbing: "I used to see Primrose on the TV, but on the day I was in court, Primrose was walking down the corridor. She was laughing and joking. It was like she was enjoying a day out."

At the end of each day, Primrose and her brood were often pursued to a nearby multi-story parking lot by pho-

tographers and TV cameras, but they never once reacted
angrily to the onslaught of flashguns—not even when two
youths shouted obscenities from the crowd gathered on the
courtroom steps. But the beginning of the trial was so low-
key that even the dozen or so police crash barriers seemed
a gross overreaction. Inside the courtroom, officials didn't
need to use the "Public Gallery Full" sign during those first
few days of the trial.

Over the following five days a panel of sixty potential
jurors were warned by attorneys that the trial could last five
months, and then asked if there was any reason why they
could not serve for that long. More than twenty immediately
put their hands up. The judge excused a single mother, a
woman who regularly suffered from bronchitis in the winter
and a man who'd planned a fortieth wedding anniversary
holiday. Others, like a man who was planning a trip to Dis-
neyland, were denied permission to leave. On Monday, October 11, 1998, seven men and five women, ranging in age
from their mid-twenties to their late fifties, were sworn in.

In his opening statement to the jury, prosecutor Henriques referred to how Shipman had "exercised the ultimate
power of controlling life and death, and repeated it so often
that he must have found the drama of taking life to his
taste."

In the dock, Fred Shipman cut a modest, slightly chaotic
figure as he struggled with a vast pile of papers on his lap,
making copious notes to pass to his lawyers. Eventually, a
table was installed in the dock to allow him to spread out
the mountain of paperwork. Overall, the prosecution case
was scheduled to last twenty-five days and be punctuated
by two breaks of a few days each. But the presentation of
evidence was not without a few laughs: prosecutor Henriques brought smiles to the jurors' faces when he asked
pathologist Dr. John Rutherford to explain his medical evidence more simply by saying, "Can you put that in lay-
man's terms, bearing in mind that we are in Preston, not a
city?" There was consternation in the local press: was the

prosecutor suggesting that the people of Preston were not as clever as those who lived in cities?

On October 12, 1999, Fred Shipman's so-called joke as his victim Ivy Lomas lay dead in front of him earned front-page banner headlines in the *Manchester Evening News*—much to the horror of many of the respectable middle-class inhabitants of Hyde. The newspaper splashed its coverage with a headline: GP's 'JOKE AS VICTIM LAY DEAD.' The paper devoted three entire pages to what was only the second full day of Shipman's trial. Not surprisingly, every copy in Hyde was sold out within minutes of hitting the streets.

Preston Crown Court then heard how lawyers received the will from one of Shipman's last victims, Mrs. Kathleen Grundy. Brian Burgess told the court he became suspicious after taking a phone call from a distressed man informing him that Mrs. Grundy had only just died. Burgess said that his firm, Hamilton Ward, usually insisted on first meeting people who asked them to be executors of their will. Experts testified that the portable typewriter seized from Fred Shipman's home was almost certainly the one used to write the documents. Michael Allen, a forensic document examiner for sixteen years, told the court: "My opinion is that these two questioned signatures on the items were not written by K. Grundy. Rather, they are poor, crude forgeries of her signature written by some other person."

Asked if it was possible to determine the real author of the signatures, he replied: "No." Allen also explained to the court how forgers covered up their natural style, which made them impossible to identify. Asked by prosecutor Richard Henriques whether a signature may be genuine, but different from usual because of old age, Mr. Allen replied no. He conceded that old age could have an effect on handwriting, but would not fundamentally alter its style. He also said the signature featured on a cover letter to the will was a forgery.

Another expert named Andrew Watson told the court that Dr. Shipman had impressed a fingerprint from his left little finger in the bottom left-hand corner of the will.

Then the court heard how Fred Shipman had made an

entry in Kathleen Grundy's medical records on the day after
she died. But the doctor had dated his remarks one year
earlier. Detective Sergeant John Ashley of the Greater Manchester Police computer examination unit told the court how
he had come across an entry dated June 23, 1997 stating:
*"Term: malaise symptom. Comments: nothing definite, just
feels tired, nothing specific. Blood fresh from morning . . .
old? Anything at all? Depressed although always happy.
Lives on own, socially active."*

Sergeant Ashley said that the record had actually been
created on June 25, 1998. The court then heard how six
computers were networked together at the three-story clinic
on Market Street. The password for the system used by all
the staff was Fred Shipman's initials, HFS. Sergeant Ashley
took a copy of the hard disk on which patients' records were
kept and examined those of Mrs. Grundy. A 365-day,
twenty-four-hour clock recorded when all notes were actually made.

Mrs. Grundy's records included an entry concerning wax
in her ear, stating: *"comments: So little leave alone."* It was
dated June 23, 1998—the day before she died—and was
created that day.

Throughout all this, Primrose watched her husband from
the public gallery with the couple's only daughter and eldest
child, Sarah. When she tried to catch Fred Shipman's eye,
he turned away.

The court also heard from patient Claire Hutchinson,
whom Shipman persuaded to "witness" Mrs. Grundy's signature on a piece of paper in Shipman's surgery on June 9,
1998. The court was told how Shipman even admitted to
nurse Marion Gilchrist that he should have had Mrs. Grundy
cremated to "save all this trouble."

Then the court heard how the son and daughter of one
of Shipman's victims had been left hurt and confused by
Shipman's explanations for their "very fit" mother's sudden
and unexpected death. Pamela Hillier's two adult children
said they finally accepted the GP's diagnosis of natural
causes even though he had "been going round in circles."

Shipman had even warned the family that a post mortem could prove a very unpleasant thing for their mother's body to go through.

On Monday, November 8, a local tramp took refuge from the cold in the public gallery, having somehow slipped through the security dragnet. Twice during evidence he drifted off to sleep, snoring off the contents of a beer can he'd left on the court steps. The first time he was awoken, he muttered the word "Murderer" loud enough for those in the gallery to hear, including Primrose.

Eventually the tramp screamed "Murderer!" even louder, and everyone in the court turned toward him—except Fred Shipman. The judge and jury left the court while security guards tried to cajole the bum to leave. He refused to budge, gripping the side of his seat. Then he was dramatically man-handled out of the courtroom, shouting "Fuckin' murderer!" as he went.

The following day a bomb scare closed the court. As ushers escorted the jury to a nearby hotel, the Liverpool bomb squad arrived and police helicopters dramatically hovered overhead. Three hours later the search was completed. There were no bombs, but at least everyone got half a day off, as it was a Friday, and the judge decided to adjourn proceedings for the weekend.

One of the most moving pieces of testimony came from Ann Brown, daughter of victim Muriel Grimshaw, after she'd given evidence about the last days of her mother's life. She talked about the death of her first husband, Raymond Jones, in November 1993. She described to the court how he died in the early morning and how Fred Shipman attended soon afterwards, and took away two or three boxes of diamorphine. The court went quiet as the notion crossed everyone's minds that Ann Brown's mother might have been killed with diamorphine stockpiled after the death of her own husband.

Father Denis Maher also gave evidence in court about his encounters with Shipman. He later claimed that the GP had tried to "eyeball" him during the hearing. "He avoided all eye contact when he pushed past me inside the court earlier in the day. But once I was in the witness box, he stared at me. I was quite afraid. It was as if he was daring me to talk about him, deliberately looking straight at me. I could see him looking straight through me. It was chilling. I'll never forget the look on his face."

The court also heard how Fred Shipman prescribed heroin for patients who were already dead. Additonally, the GP wrote heroin prescriptions for a further eighteen people, who either did not receive it, or only received part of it.

That, according to prosecutors, was how Shipman stockpiled the drug. Thousands of milligrams of heroin remained unaccounted for. One patient, 72-year-old James Arrandale, was prescribed 1,000 mg of heroin over two days in July 1995. Shipman took away unused ampoules of the drug after Mr. Arrandale's death, saying that he would dispose of them. But when police later raided Shipman's home, they found four ampoules from that batch.

In court, Primrose was having a profound and disturbing effect on many of the relatives of Shipman's victims assembled near her in the public gallery. "She'd blotted it out, but many of the family members in the public gallery were quite wound up about the fact that she appeared to be smiling all the time," Bianka Pomfret's ex-husband Adrian recalled. "When I looked across, I could see she was in a heck of a state, but mentally gone overboard. She was shaking her head and everything."

Primrose Shipman remained a long way from accepting that her husband was a mass murderer.

21

Just after noon on Thursday, November 25, 1999, Fred Shipman rose hesitatingly to his feet, turned to his right, and shuffled past the jury and into the witness box. The whole courtroom held its breath as the GP accused of mass murder prepared to make his debut.

He took the short walk from the dock to the witness box escorted by a prison officer, and rather than swearing an oath on the Bible, affirmed to tell the truth.

"My full name is Harold Frederick Shipman," he said. His voice was strong and confident to begin with, but soon fell away. Shipman even apologized as his voice faltered, saying it was because of tablets he was taking. Primrose watched intently from the public gallery.

Shipman looked frail and nervous. His gray suit hung loosely on his hunched shoulders, and he wore a white shirt with a gray striped tie. He spoke in low, husky tones and was frequently asked by the judge to speak more clearly.

The court then heard how in 1992 he left the Hyde practice he'd shared with six other doctors and set up his own one-man operation. Asked why, he responded: "It was at the time of fundholding. The other doctors were not as committed."

The light through the stained-glass ceiling caught the gold rim of his glasses as he looked up at the jurors. They all looked straight back. Fred Shipman's earthy Nottingham accent was betrayed by his pronunciation of words such as "blood" and "past" and "once a month." Yet at the start of that first day in the witness box he tried to sound reasonably positive. He clearly wanted the jury to know what sort of doctor he was. His pride was unmistakable when he disclosed that he didn't have much time for word processors, adding: "I'm one of the few doctors in the area who still hand-writes letters."

Note the present tense. Fred Shipman used it through much of his evidence. He talked of "my practice" as though he had left it only the previous day and would soon be back behind his desk.

Shipman took a transfixed court audience through his weekly work routine. His hands tapped out the rhythm of his words on the rail of the witness box when he needed help to get them out. He said Monday was the day he did most of his administration before afternoon surgery. Friday was reserved for minor operations, "removing warts, or ingrown toenails," he said. "Nothing glamorous."

Then a smile began breaking across his face more often. He talked about making home visits, and how, if he had time on his way back, "I might pop in and have a word with the wife."

"The wife" remained seated at the back of the court, listening avidly to every word. Occasionally she fingered her wedding ring. Across the oak-paneled court, the couple's eyes seldom met. Next to Primrose that day was 20-year-old son David.

It wasn't until more than two hours after Shipman entered the witness box that the name of any of his alleged victims was mentioned in court. Kathleen Grundy was the first. Fred Shipman maintained that she was a drug addict. Her daughter Angela Woodruff stopped taking notes and fixed the doctor with a stare as he gave his evidence.

Speaking in a hoarse voice, Shipman said he believed that 81-year-old Mrs. Grundy had simply died of old age, although he repeated that she'd shown symptoms of drug use. Shipman said: "Abuse of drugs in the elderly is becoming more recognized. I began to suspect that she was actually abusing a drug. It had to be something like codeine, pethidine or perhaps morphine."

Shipman then referred to the day in June 1998 when Mrs. Grundy asked him to witness her signature on what he claimed were "some papers." He went on: "I jokingly said to her that if it was a will and she was going to give me some money, then I couldn't do it. There was a moment of pause when I realized it was something like that."

Shipman admitted then asking two other patients in his waiting room to sign the papers. Asked if he thought he would be beneficiary of her will, he said: "I thought the patients' fund would benefit by one or two hundred pounds, I didn't want to get entangled." Shipman said it was the same day he noticed that Mrs. Grundy appeared to be suffering a decline in her health. He added: "She used to be very bright, very talkative, with enormous enthusiasm. But on that evening, I thought she looked old, not well, going downhill."

Shipman then told the court that two weeks later he'd visited Grundy's home to perform some blood tests. He added: "Her face was more wrinkled than normal and she appeared slow in her movements." The court heard how later that same day a friend found Mrs. Grundy dead in her living room. Shipman wrote on her death certificate that the cause was old age.

Then the jury finally heard the question they were being asked to consider: "Did you murder Kathleen Grundy?"

"No," Dr. Shipman replied firmly, "I did not."

Sometimes Fred Shipman muttered silently into his close-cropped beard and shook his bird-like head in irritation. But as his evidence progressed he became curiously more detached, as though he felt the worst was over. Every few moments he'd take off his gold-rimmed glasses, wipe them methodically with a handkerchief, hold them aloft, then peer closely through narrowed eyes as though searching out the slightest smears.

During the lunchtime break, Primrose smiled and nodded amicably to familiar court reporters and officials in the outside hallway and café. But once back in her designated spot in the public gallery, her face returned to an emotionless

mask and her eyes fixed on her husband. It was almost as
if she was keeping an eye on him, making sure he didn't
say anything which might implicate her. Shipman rarely
glanced up at her.

That afternoon, Fred Shipman's testimony brought lines
around the block for the forty available public gallery seats.
A gaggle of women also sat on the steps outside Court One,
eating cookies, sharing cans of soda and waiting to replace
anyone who might decide to leave the proceedings early.

Meanwhile, Fred Shipman eventually regained a little of
his confidence; he frowned when his attorney shared a joke
with the judge, making it crystal clear that in his opinion it
was no laughing matter. As Fred Shipman left the court
building at the end of his first day of giving evidence, a film
crew from *Sky TV* network, Britain's Murdoch affiliate,
grabbed footage of him being led to the prison truck that
would take him back to Strangeways jail. He looked shattered, like a man with the weight of the world on his shoulders.

Those who attended court during Shipman's testimony were
struck by the utter normality of his appearance and verbal
delivery to the court. Many spectators who'd attended reli-
giously since the start of the trial claimed to have "medical
backgrounds," and were enthralled by the Shipman case.
Some, such as David McGrady, admitted being engrossed
in the ghoulish aspects. "It's disturbing, but fascinating," he
admitted to one curious reporter. He even conceded that it
made him nervous about visiting his own GP. Other members of the public who attended even included a handful of
loyal patients from Fred Shipman's practice.

The next day, Shipman's only admission was that he did
backdate his computer records. He claimed that was because
he had to bring his files in line with when the patient said
they had first noticed the symptoms. Then Shipman gave
the jury a glance of his finest bedside manner when he
talked about one alleged victim's medication. "I'm sure you
all know people who, when they have an angina attack, put

a tablet under their tongue—this is a souped-up version. Aspirin, as you are all aware, has had lots of publicity, and I expect everyone knows that it is what we give to make the blood less sticky."

Fred Shipman then referred back to Bianka Pomfret and told the court: "She told me she was having chest pains and had some pain to other parts of the body including the left arm. I told her I thought the diagnosis was angina, lack of oxygen getting into the heart, and I said we needed further investigation." He said he advised Mrs. Pomfret to see a cardiologist, and left her to think it over.

When asked by his defense attorney Nicola Davies if he had given Mrs. Pomfret a dose of morphine or diamorphine, he said: "No, I did not." And when asked if he'd murdered her, he replied, "No, I did not."

Shipman regularly looked down to refer to two large files in front of him. Primrose and 20-year-old David sat in the public gallery just a few feet away. Shipman told the court how Mrs. Pomfret had just returned from seeing her family in Germany, and that her state of health was quite good, but she had relapsed after a couple of weeks back in Hyde. Shipman said: "She felt tired, listless, had no energy and even after a sleep she felt she should sleep longer."

Shipman insisted that he changed her medication onto a less strong drug in order to reduce the side effects which were causing her tiredness. Shipman then explained how, less than four hours later, he received a call reporting that Mrs. Pomfret had collapsed at home. "I believed she had a heart attack because of the history she had given me earlier in the day regarding chest pains." He repeated that he did not give Mrs. Pomfret either morphine or diamorphine.

Asked why he'd recorded coronary thrombosis as a contributory cause of death, Dr. Shipman replied: "I was told Mrs. Pomfret was found sat on a settee with a cold mug of tea or coffee by her side, and a burned-out cigarette either in her hand or in an ashtray. It seemed obvious she had made no attempt to get to the phone or kitchen, or anything. Whatever happened was fairly rapid."

On Monday, November 29, 1999, Shipman admitted in court that he should have called an ambulance for alleged victim Ivy Lomas when she collapsed at his surgery. Shipman told the jury: "In hindsight, it may have been better to have called for an ambulance immediately." Shipman described how Mrs. Lomas was a regular visitor to his surgery, often complaining of chest pains and depression. He said she "looked gray and sweaty" at her appointment. He took her to the treatment room to be tested on the EKG machine, but as she climbed onto the bed, she collapsed. Shipman admitted that he did not call his receptionist, Carol Chapman, for help because there were three other patients in the waiting room. He tried to resuscitate Mrs. Lomas on his own because, being fully trained in first aid, he believed he knew what to do. Shipman said he could carry out first aid "better than the average person." But after fifteen minutes, he claimed, he found that his efforts had completely failed.

Shipman then told the court he decided that Mrs. Lomas had died of a heart attack because she smoked and had a family history of heart disease. He even admitted that he dealt with three more patients while Mrs. Lomas lay dead in the treatment room. Shipman said he treated them in order to get them out of the surgery swiftly. The prosecution alleged that Shipman had administered a fatal dose of morphine or diamorphine to Mrs. Lomas while she was in the treatment room.

Fred Shipman then admitted to Preston Crown Court that he let one patient die in front of his eyes because he thought it better "to let nature take its course." The GP told the jury how he was called to the home of widow Marie Quinn, 67, and found her lying on the kitchen floor. Although he could feel a pulse, she was not breathing and felt "floppy."

Earlier, Mrs. Quinn had called the surgery and said she was paralyzed down one side, and would leave the door open for him to visit. Shipman said he diagnosed a stroke, but decided to do nothing rather than reviving the widow and condemning her to life in a nursing home.

Asked to explain this decision by his lawyer Nicola Davies, he said: "I'm sure GPs all over the country get the same problem. They have to decide whether to attempt resuscitation or let nature take its course. Whatever happened to Marie Quinn was on a major scale. She was deeply unconscious. I made the decision that I would not attempt resuscitation. I would review the situation in a couple of minutes' time. If she was starting to improve, I would get her to hospital, but two minutes later there were no signs of life. She was dead."

Shipman then added: "Patients who survive often have loss of personality, loss of use of the body, and often end up in a nursing home. Mrs. Quinn was an independent, likable person, and to go from that to being dependent on someone she did not know was something I couldn't envisage her doing."

That day the jury also heard about Irene Turner, also 67, who was found dead on July 11, 1996, within minutes of Shipman leaving her house. Then there was victim Jean Lilley, who Shipman claimed he left alive, but needing hospital treatment, on the day she died. Shipman described Mrs. Lilley—who suffered from angina, high cholesterol and a serious lung condition—as a "courageous patient."

On December 1, Shipman broke down weeping in the witness box as he answered questions about the death of Kathleen Wagstaff. He said she had collapsed and died in front of him in her home. She had earlier called him, complaining of chest pains. When he examined her, he informed her that she should go to the hospital.

Shipman explained: "I looked around for the phone and looked at Mrs. Wagstaff, who was sat in the chair with her mouth open. I asked her if she was okay, but there was no response. I shook her, but she was floppy. She had a coronary."

He said he tried to resuscitate Mrs. Wagstaff, but failed. Shipman then told the court that he drove to a nearby school where he knew her daughter-in-law Angela worked.

He said: "I explained that her mother had died. I should have made it clear it was her mother-in-law. I thought I had done so, but she became extremely distressed and drove to her mother's house."

He said he was "more upset than her relatives," and sank into his seat weeping, his head in his hands. His breakdown came just before the lunch adjournment. After regaining his composure, he said that his distress over the 81-year-old's death was to blame for the error he made on her cremation certificate, which had said a neighbor was present when she died.

Asked by Nicola Davies why he had made the mistake, Shipman replied: "I was quite upset. I don't think I was quite clear in my own mind when I completed this document. This was one of the few times I was possibly more upset than the relatives."

Then, as his legal team looked up at him, Shipman sank back into his chair, put his head in his hands and began sobbing again. He continued crying for at least two minutes, his head barely visible above the sides of the oak-paneled witness box at Preston Crown Court. He even wiped his eyes with tissues handed to him by an usher.

Then Nicola Davies asked the judge, Mr. Justice Forbes, for an early lunchtime adjournment so her client could regain his composure. As the jurors left the courtroom three minutes earlier than scheduled, Shipman walked the ten paces back into the dock and then on to the stairway leading to the cells. The entire scene was witnessed by Primrose, who fidgeted nervously, but showed no other signs of emotion or concern for her husband.

That afternoon Fred Shipman told the court his account of what happened to patient Winifred Mellor, 73, when she visited his surgery in May 1998 without an appointment, complaining of chest pains. Shipman explained: "I said it sounded like angina, and talked to her about what we should do." He said he asked her to return to the surgery later in the day to arrange an appointment with a cardiologist. When she failed to get in touch, he decided to visit her house, which was on his way home.

After knocking on the door and getting no reply, he said

he looked in the window and saw her sitting motionless in a chair. A next-door neighbor who had a spare key to the house let Shipman in, and he certified that Mrs. Mellor was dead. He recalled to the court: "With the history she had given me earlier in the afternoon, I considered that the likely cause of death was that she had had a heart attack."

Once again, Fred Shipman was asked if he had administered any morphine or diamorphine to Mrs. Mellor. He replied firmly: "No."

Then Shipman was again asked if he had murdered any of his patients.

"Did you murder Bianka Pomfret on December 10, 1997?" asked Nicola Davies.

"No, I did not," he replied.

"Did you murder Winifred Mellor on May 11, 1998?" Davies continued.

"No, I did not," responded Shipman, looking straight ahead.

"Did you murder Joan Melia on twelfth June, 1998?" asked Miss Davies.

"No, I did not," answered the GP.

22

Fred Shipman looked surprised when Nicola Davies sat down at the end of his testimony to her. He'd been expecting her questioning to go on beyond the outline of the deaths. He was so upset that when prosecutor Henriques stood up to start his cross-examination, Shipman broke down, telling the judge he was unwell. He was given a fifteen-minute break, but he still looked uncomfortable when he returned to the witness box.

For the following seven days, prosecutor Henriques picked over every aspect of Shipman's evidence, constantly highlighting inconsistencies in the GP's records of the deaths, and the uncanny similarities between many deaths. Shipman admitted "a bad habit" of prescribing very large amounts of morphine for patients in need of it, claiming that he had no idea what had subsequently happened to the drugs. He insisted that the morphine found at his house was "an oversight."

While speaking to the court about the death of Ivy Lomas, prosecutor Henriques came back at Shipman like a shot when discussing the doctor's claims.

"If this lady died at 4:10 P.M., she must have been administered, or administered to herself, diamorphine between 4 and 4:10 P.M., mustn't she?"

With a sigh in his voice, Shipman replied wearily: "You could put the evidence that way and, yes, I would agree."

But Shipman said he had no knowledge of where the drug came from.

Then Henriques's tone became much sterner. "Dr. Shipman," he said, "there is no sensible explanation, is there?"

A long pause followed before Shipman replied pedantically: "Was that a statement or a question?"

Clearly irritated, Henriques snapped back: "You know very well it was a question." Then, for good measure, he repeated it.

Shipman admitted: "I don't know of any explanation."

"Save except for your guilt," replied Henriques quick as a flash.

Just as fast, Shipman volleyed back: "That's what you're saying, and I disagree with it strongly. I didn't administer anything to this lady, and I had no idea how she got it in her body."

Once again Henriques suggested there was no explanation—other than Fred Shipman's guilt. Again the GP denied it. "I can think of no explanation at all. I'm not guilty of administering anything to this lady."

Henriques then changed tack and condemned Shipman for leaving a dead patient while he attended to three others at his clinic.

"To leave a deceased person without any attempt to contact next of kin is a disgrace," he said tersely.

"In your opinion," the GP responded sharply.

But the prosecutor would not let go. "It's unprofessional to leave someone for dead in the back room."

Shipman insisted to the court that there was no "terrible rush," considering the patient was dead.

And so the duel continued.

Henriques, in his black robes, with large black-framed glasses, was a tall, formidable figure who tended to lean over the podium during his delivery to the courtroom. Henriques even put it to Shipman that he'd treated the other patients on that day because he was waiting for Ivy to die. If she was dead, then there'd be no need for an ambulance to be called, and she wouldn't be seen by another doctor, who might have discovered the morphine in her system.

But perhaps the most dramatic moment of the day came when Henriques asked Shipman: "Have you any sadness?"

The GP's face was completely expressionless. Silence enveloped the courtroom. You could have heard a pin drop. Eventually he answered: "I'm not quite sure what you are asking me."

"Did you have any sadness?" boomed Henriques at the top of his voice.

In a flat voice, devoid of emotion, Shipman replied calmly: "You're always sad when a patient dies."

As the court recessed that day, Fred Shipman was led from the witness box, staring resolutely at the ground, wringing his hands as he went.

The following morning, Primrose appeared in her usual seat in court, but this time she had younger son Sam, 17, alongside her. He wore a handsome dark suit, and during breaks in proceedings could be found talking and joking on his mobile phone in the corridor. Sam's favorite drink was *Orange Tango*, and one time he was heard commenting to the ladies at the snack bar that he was always having trouble staying awake in the courtroom.

The following day, Thursday, Shipman and Henriques continued their face-off while discussing the death of Kathleen Wagstaff.

"It is an unhappy coincidence," the prosecutor told the court, referring to the fact that it was December 9, 1999—two years to the day since 81-year-old Mrs. Wagstaff had died.

"Have you any disturbance that we should deal with this on the second anniversary of this event?" asked the prosecutor. "No," Shipman replied. Mrs. Wagstaff's relatives watched from the gallery. Her sons Peter and John, both well dressed, sat with Peter's blonde wife Angela and listened intently as Henriques questioned Shipman: "You had no reason whatsoever in the world to visit Mrs. Wagstaff, did you?"

Shipman replied: "Mrs. Wagstaff rang the surgery, I answered the phone and she complained of chest pains."

But then the prosecutor produced phone bills that proved there was no call from Mrs. Wagstaff's house to Shipman's surgery. There was also no written surgery record.

"I'm going to suggest you made up a phone call from Mrs. Wagstaff to your surgery," Henriques said.

But according to Shipman, he and his patient went inside and sat down, and she told him she had been having chest pains. Shortly afterwards she collapsed.

Shipman explained: "The situation was, she clinically had a coronary."

Yet, Henriques pointed out to the court, the doctor failed to call for an ambulance, just as he failed to make any record of his examination of her.

Henriques added: "It is a fact, isn't it, that not once in any of the fifteen cases did you yourself—as opposed to the surgery or a relation—summon an ambulance?"

"That's correct," replied Shipman coldly.

Then Henriques asked: "Do you accept any blame or responsibility for the death of Laura Kathleen Wagstaff?"

"No, I don't," replied Shipman without any hesitation.

And that is how the hearing proceeded as Henriques took the court through case histories of the dead women. Shipman in turn explained why he was not guilty.

But in some cases, particularly that of Ivy Lomas, the GP offered no real explanation of her death. He even admitted that, despite writing "heart disease" on her death certificate, she must have died from morphine poisoning. He agreed the morphine level was so high that death would have occurred within five minutes.

Shipman told Preston Crown Court that he should have had a post mortem for his alleged victim Muriel Grimshaw—because it would have prevented him being accused of murder. He said he had discussed Mrs. Grimshaw's death with her daughter Anne Brown, and they'd decided a post mortem was not required. "In hindsight, I would have had it done, but at the time I didn't think it was necessary," he said.

Shipman repeated to the court that he thought victim Kathleen Grundy had a drug habit—and she knew of his suspicions. He denied smearing her good name by placing his claims on her medical records after he realized that police had carried out toxicology tests on her body that uncovered evidence of morphine.

Shipman claimed that Mrs. Grundy must have taken the morphine between his visit on the morning of her death and when her body was found. Prosecutor Henriques then asked: "So she might have got into her motor car and driven to some drug dealers and obtained diamorphine, and then gone home and administered herself?"

The GP replied: "I don't think it is my role to ascertain where she was getting diamorphine from, if she was taking it."

But Shipman did admit to the court that there were no signs that Mrs. Grundy had taken drugs on the day she died. Then prosecutor Henriques questioned Shipman about his conversation with district nurse Marion Gilchrist, in which he said he would have found himself guilty on the evidence, before his arrest and before the toxicology results were known.

Shipman insisted to the court that this was his own special brand of black humor. He explained: "I was being under suspicion. I could see my name as a GP would vanish and you could see from the police side there was reasonable evidence that I had killed Mrs. Grundy."

He later added: "The police told me they were looking into her death and possibly forging the will. I didn't raise any objection of the fact it was typed on my typewriter. I knew the police would go very hard and very enthusiastically to get me. And that explains the comment. It was black humor so I could survive the next two weeks until they arrested me."

Then Henriques asked Shipman: "Do you know of anybody who would wish you to have Mrs. Grundy's estate?"

Shipman responded: "I couldn't think of anybody, unless Mrs. Grundy took it into her head that's what she wanted to do."

The prosecutor hit back: "Are you suggesting Mrs. Grundy forged her own will?"

Shipman said: "That's not true. It was a rhetorical question and a rhetorical answer."

On December 7, 1999, Shipman even claimed in court that he was not surprised when four of his victims had "suddenly" revealed secret medical problems that he subsequently blamed for their deaths. Henriques asked Shipman: "They gave you medical histories of which you were previously unaware? In three cases on the day they died, and in the case of Miss Ward, the day before?"

Shipman replied: "I was given those histories, yes."

Then Henriques steamed in: "Does it happen with any regularity that patients see you and say, 'I have a medical history I have not previously disclosed to you?' "

Shipman simply replied: "No."

The following day Fred Shipman was accused in court of telling his receptionist a lie as victim Ivy Lomas lay dead in his surgery. The jury heard that he claimed he'd been delayed because of a "technical problem," when in fact she had just died in the treatment room. Shipman was asked by Richard Henriques: "You told her a bare-faced lie?"

Shipman admitted it "wasn't the truth," but said he was worried about other patients hearing.

Shipman also agreed that if Mrs. Lomas had died at 4:10 P.M. she must have been administered morphine between 4 P.M. and 4:10 P.M. The GP also testified that he did not leave her side, nor did he administer the drug himself, but he had no explanation to offer.

The next case brought to light was that of 81-year-old Marie West, whom Shipman watched die, completely unaware that a neighbor was in the kitchen all the time. Prosecutor Henriques identified those minutes as the so-called "silent period" when Shipman waited for the drug to take effect on Mrs. West.

Shipman hit back from the witness box: "No, it was not." He claimed he was surprised to find neighbor Marion Hadfield in the kitchen. He told her he was looking for a telephone to call relatives.

Prosecutor Henriques insisted to the court: "What had

happened was, you had been caught out by Mrs. Hadfield's presence, and there you were, trapped, Mrs. West barely dead. You were taken by surprise, coming up with the best explanation you could. That is the real truth."

Shipman replied, "No." But he did agree that he made no attempt to resuscitate Mrs. West.

"The simple reason was, this lady was beyond resuscitation because she had had a massive amount of diamorphine," Henriques told the court.

But Shipman insisted: "There is no doubt in my mind that the lady had a sudden lethal stroke."

"Or a sudden lethal stroke of diamorphine," Henriques hit back.

When questioned about resuscitation, Shipman told the court that he did not attempt to revive the woman, nor did he call 999 (the UK version of 911), because she was already dead. He told Henriques that "the effort put into resuscitating her would not have given good results."

The prosecutor then asked: "Have you not heard of people's lives being saved by resuscitation?"

The GP answered: "Yes, I have done it myself."

Henriques hit back: "The lady was beyond defibrillation and resuscitation because she had a massive dose of morphine."

"No, she had not," insisted Shipman.

Later, prosecutor Henriques told Shipman in front of the jury: "Not once in all these cases did you call an ambulance . . . Not once did you admit any patient to hospital . . . Not once did you permit a post mortem . . . The simple explanation for all the evidence in this case is your guilt."

On Wednesday, December 22—with all the evidence heard—the judge wished the jury a merry Christmas and a pleasant holiday, telling them that he would see them again on January 5, 2000.

In the middle of his trial, Shipman's former Strangeways cellmate Tony Fleming was surprised to receive some letters from the GP. In them he discussed his trial and how impressed he was by his attorney Ann Ball, "she of the steel-tipped heels and intimidating nature." Prisoner CJ8198 also seemed to be reveling in his notoriety. "I never thought court would be more interesting. Fascinated to see the QC's [attorneys] set out their wares with booby traps hidden. No applause which I feel would help the audience."

Cellmate Fleming—now back in the outside world—added: "I miss him. He'd sit there and listen to all my problems. He was very caring. He was also a very intelligent, very interesting bloke." Fleming's words had a familiar ring about them; they sounded like so many of Fred Shipman's patients.

23

When the court reconvened in the first week of the new millennium, Prosecutor Henriques addressed the jury with his closing speech. Speaking calmly and incisively, he reminded them that they had heard the evidence of more than 120 prosecution witnesses. He spoke about how Shipman had abused the trust of his victims and their families. "They trusted him to care for them, their relatives trusted him to tell the truth about the circumstances in which the patients died and the community trusted him to complete records with honesty and integrity."

He continued: "As they grieved, this determined man deployed any and every device to ensure that no post mortem took place. He would overbear, belittle, bamboozle and disadvantage relatives until they accepted the doctor's words that they should not 'put their mother through it.' "

Fred Shipman, wearing his all-too-familiar charcoal gray suit, white shirt, and a striped green-and-red tie, listened to the prosecutor while writing notes on a legal pad. But most of the marks were doodles: he sketched a Christmas tree, a lectern with a heavy book on it and what appeared to be a church window behind it. He also drew in a grid of squares, which he filled with crosses and dashes, as if he was playing a game of his own creation with himself, making the marks frantically and repetitively. Shipman appeared even more slouched in his chair, and every so often his bony shoulders heaved and he sighed out loud. Ann Ball frequently glanced at him, as if she was genuinely unsure he would survive the day.

Prosecutor Richard Henriques told the court that Fred Shipman had betrayed the trust of his patients with a "trail of murder," then lied to save himself. Henriques said the only alternative to believing that Shipman was guilty was to imagine a serial killer following the doctor.

Henriques ended his summing-up to the jury by repeating Fred Shipman's own description of his situation, as given to the practice nurse before his arrest: "I read thrillers, and I would have me guilty on the evidence."

Defense attorney Nicola Davies then began her argument by saying: "A doctor's primary objective is to care for his patients. A doctor's training is directed at that one aim. Doctors are expected to care for their patients, not kill them."

She said that by the time of his arrest, Shipman's patient list was 3,100, much bigger than the national average. "No patient had to register with Dr. Shipman, but the fact that so many did must be something upon which inferences can be drawn. It is not unreasonable inference that patients who followed him were satisfied with the care he provided."

Defender Davies insisted that in all professions, including medicine, individuals carried out their duties with their own "idiosyncrasies." She argued that Shipman's Market Street practice had a spirit and ethos where every member of the staff, including Shipman, would carry out tasks to help one another.

Nicola Davies reminded the jury that Shipman also called on patients when not required to do so, to see how they were. "In the context of this case, the way the prosecution put it, that has taken on a sinister inference. But the fact is, doctors do cold-call, and have every right to cold-call. It's part of their duty to care."

Davies painted a portrait of a dedicated doctor who frequently went beyond the call of duty. Keeping records was not his specialty, she said, because he was "more interested in the patients than the paperwork." She told the court: "It is alleged this doctor failed to care for his patients, and killed them. Such an allegation requires a high degree of proof, and detailed analysis of the evidence. There is no clear and cogent truth of what substance was administered in what quantity or in what form. The prosecution have also manifestly failed even to raise the question of motive. They claim there was a power complex behind the doctor's actions. It is said he enjoyed all this killing. But where is the evidence?"

She then accused prosecutors of failing to find a true motive for the killings, dismissing the "power complex" argument as amateur psychological theory. She described the stockpiling of morphine by the GP as "a red herring." With regard to the forged Grundy will, Davies said the crude attempt could not have originated with Fred Shipman. "Are these the letters the sort a devious, clever and cunning man would write?" she asked, before also claiming that the scientific evidence from the bodies was "inherently unreliable" and that the prosecution case "stands and falls" on that evidence.

Nicola Davies said that Shipman had sought to spare families the unpleasantness of a post mortem, but this too had been turned against him. "Dr. Shipman can't be the only doctor practicing in this country who could wish, and properly wish, to spare the relatives this grief. On the scale of things, what is more important: that his patients were cared for, or that immaculate records were being kept?"

On January 7, 2000, three months of evidence ended with defender Davies claiming that the scientific evidence against the family doctor was also "unreliable." Miss Davies also suggested that the youngest victim, 49-year-old Bianka Pomfret, had suicidal thoughts just two days before her death. In a final plea to the jury, she said: "We come back to this. Before the court is a doctor faced with fifteen counts of murder and one of forgery. In respect of these fifteen counts, they are wholly reliant on the base findings of toxicology, and that toxicology is based on scientific evidence. It is our submission that scientific evidence is unsafe and unreliable. It is our submission to you that, because of the inherently unreliable nature of that scientific evidence, the very basis of the Crown's case has to go. And in the absence of such scientific evidence, the inference to be drawn from it relating to the behavior of the doctor, relied upon by the Crown, also fails. With it fails the entirety of the prosecution case."

Judge Forbes's summary began on Monday, January 10. He described it as "tragic and deeply disturbing case."

"The allegations could not be more serious: a doctor accused of murdering fifteen of his patients. Inevitably in the course of this case you will have heard evidence that will have caused anger, disgust, profound dismay and deep sympathy. They must not be allowed to cloud your judgment. You must consider the facts dispassionately."

The judge urged the jurors to "be fair" as they decided their verdict. He asked them to put aside any strong feelings and emotions aroused by this case. He told them that they had to make allowances for the strain of giving evidence in court. "You must, of course, apply the same fair standards to the evidence given by Dr. Shipman. Do not hold it against him that he came to give evidence to you from the dock. Make every possible allowance for the strain Dr. Shipman must have been under giving his evidence. It cannot be easy giving evidence in circumstances in which you face charges as serious as [these]."

Justice Forbes continued: "It is Dr. Shipman's case that he did not forge Mrs. Grundy's will, and did not administer morphine or diamorphine, whether by injection of otherwise, to any of the alleged victims."

Friday, January 14 passed without anyone mentioning the fact that it was Fred Shipman's fifty-fourth birthday.

On Monday, January 24, 2000, the jury at Preston Crown Court finally retired to decide whether Fred Shipman was guilty. The jurors were sent out after an eight-minute address by Mr. Justice Forbes on the fifty-second day of the trial. The judge told the jury that they had to consider each of the cases separately. "These counts do not stand or fall together," he said. Forbes also told the jurors to consider their verdicts only on what they had heard and seen in the court. He reminded them that the burden of proof lay with the prosecution, and added: "Dr. Shipman does not have to prove anything."

Meanwhile Fred Shipman stood silently in the dock wearing a pale brown suit, white shirt and tie. In the public gallery Primrose and their eldest son Christopher, as well as relatives of some of the alleged victims, sat silently. After five hours of deliberation the jurors were sent home for the night. Primrose constantly looked reassuredly at Shipman while the jury was out. "Wifely support" was how she later described it.

While the jury was deliberating, the British Medical Association took the extraordinary step of circulating Shipman's previous convictions to members, so that they were prepared for media questions in the event of a guilty verdict. The e-mails included a question-and-answer document to make sure that the doctors were briefed. But by sending it out while the jury was still considering its verdicts, it constituted a serious risk to the cause of justice.

Forbes hauled lawyers acting for the organization, which represents doctors, into court to explain why details of Shipman's previous conviction had been passed over to its members before the trial was completed. By making public the information, the BMA had risked leaking the details to the trial jury—which would have made it impossible for them to reach unbiased verdicts. A re-trial would have been out of the question, because the case had attracted so much publicity that it would have been impossible to find a fresh, untainted jury.

Justice Forbes told BMA lawyers: "The outrage and horror that the public would necessarily have felt cannot possibly be exaggerated. This is such a serious matter, it would not be appropriate for me to accept the apology to bring the matter to an end."

But he decided not to abandon the trial.

On Friday, January 28, 2000, the jury at Preston Crown Court was sent out to consider its verdicts for a fifth consecutive day. It wasn't until the late afternoon of Monday, January 31—one week after they'd originally retired—that they returned. Everyone assembled in the courtroom expected them to be sent home for the night once again. Then a whisper went through the ranks that the jury had asked for another ten minutes.

Primrose, wearing a black suit, sat next to son Christopher, with David just behind her. Perhaps she'd decided on black because she knew the end was near.

At 4:33 P.M. the jury trooped back into the courtroom and the foreman announced in a clear, strong voice that all their verdicts were unanimous. The court was so quiet that even a pin dropping would have been heard.

"GUILTY . . . GUILTY . . . GUILTY . . ." Sixteen times.

Fred Shipman remained stock-still. A stony face giving nothing away. There was an audible sigh from Primrose as the first guilty verdict was returned, the first and only time she had publicly registered the enormity of her husband's crimes. But both Fred Shipman's sons lowered their eyes and shrank in their seats. David looked close to tears.

A jubilant cry of "Yes!" accompanied one of the later verdicts. A clenched-fist salute punched the air for another. The relatives of the victims were finally having their day in court.

Mr. Justice Forbes then told Fred Shipman: "Harold Frederick Shipman, stand up. You have finally been brought to justice by the verdict of this jury. I have no doubt whatsoever that these are true verdicts. The time has now come for me to pass sentence upon you for these wicked, wicked crimes. Each of your victims was your patient. You murdered each and every one of your victims by a calculated and cold-blooded perversion of your medical skills for your own evil and wicked purpose.

"You took advantage of and grossly abused their trust. You were, after all, each victim's doctor. I have little doubt each of your victims smiled and thanked you as she submitted to your deadly ministrations. None realized yours was not a healing touch. None knew in truth you had brought her death, death disguised as a caring attention of a good doctor. As your counsel rightly states, on each of the fifteen counts which I pass sentence upon you, the sentence is prescribed by law. However, I take the view that justice demands I pass in respect of each and every count of murder the sentence of life imprisonment. In the ordinary way, I would not do this in open court, but in your case, I am satisfied justice demands I make my views known at the conclusion of this trial."

After passing fifteen life sentences and a four-year sentence for the forgery, the judge then broke with the usual tradition of sending his recommendations about the length of the sentence to the Home Secretary in writing.

"I have formed the conclusion that the crimes you stand convicted of are so heinous that in your case, life must mean life. My recommendation will be that you spend the remainder of your days in prison."

Every word of the judge's withering criticism of Shipman was savored by the victims' survivors. When the court was told of Shipman's previous convictions for forging prescriptions, it provoked gasps from the public gallery.

Justice Forbes then removed his wig to address the relatives directly, paying unusual tribute to their stoicism and patience. Accompanied by muffled sobs from the public gallery, his own voice crackled as tears clearly welled up behind his glasses. "I am very aware this trial has been harrowing and painful for all of you. Many of you had to relive in public the shock and grief and sorrow resulting from the death of your loved one. I would like you to know how much I admire the courage and quiet dignity you have shown. Your evidence was at times immensely moving and touched the hearts of all who heard it. Each of you has made a significant contribution to the course of justice."

The judge also commended the investigating police officers, Detective Superintendent Bernard Postles and Detective Chief Inspector Mike Williams, for their work. "As far as I am aware, there has never been another case in this country which has required the investigation of so many murders by a single individual. This has been a deeply disturbing trial, and the significance cannot be understated. This has also been a historical trial."

Fred Shipman remained aloof to the last: the small man with steely gray eyes staring into the distance as the litany of his crimes was put before him. It seemed almost an inconvenience to Shipman that he should be made to listen as Mr. Justice Forbes, his voice sometimes faltering under the awful weight of his words, continued addressing the court.

Behind the dock, the relatives of the victims sobbed and held out their hands to each other. But Fred Shipman didn't bat an eyelid. After a few moments, he simply gazed distractedly at the mahogany carvings above the judge's chair.

As the judge finished speaking, there was a spontaneous, if unconventional, smattering of applause from the public gallery. Red-eyed but relieved, the relatives of the victims filed out of court, leaving Primrose and her family to be escorted away by security guards.

Primrose, with her helmet of graying hair, had been making copious notes earlier in the trial. But now her pen was stilled. The nervous hand-kneading that betrayed her anxiety had gone, too. She had no intention of leaving her husband, especially as his legal team was expected to mount an immediate appeal. She even shared Fred Shipman's optimism about the outcome of the trial; it emerged that she had ordered flowers to be sent to the family's house for his "welcome home" party.

After sentencing, Primrose had wanted to join her serial-killing husband immediately, but that was out of the question. She later said she was "devastated" by the verdicts. For twenty minutes she had to endure the agony of all eyes watching her as the court slowly emptied. Just then, a mobile phone went off in her handbag. The tune it played would have been familiar to most of Fred Shipman's victims. It also had a ghastly irony: "Jesu, Joy of Man's Desiring."

Primrose emerged briefly for photographs outside the court, but when she later answered the door to the family home she appeared tearful as she uttered, "No comment." Her son David, 20, also red-eyed, said: "There will be no comment now. No comment in the future. No comment at any time."

Throughout the trial, Primrose had made the journey to Preston Crown Court and visited Strangeways Prison virtually every day. Her unbowed loyalty was fascinating, and it perhaps held the key to much of Fred Shipman's behavior. Always modestly and plainly dressed, Primrose was unswerving in her duty to stand by her husband. But why? It must truly have been a remarkable marriage to withstand all the secrecy behind Fred Shipman. Perhaps he did confide in his wife. Maybe he told her the reasons behind his crimes. On the other hand, perhaps she simply refused to accept the truth. Shipman's bedside manner had worked miracles on his own wife. He was a godlike figure to Primrose, and nothing would ever change that.

The now slightly ungainly, plump and otherwise unremarkable wife with her gray hair cut in a convenient bob had taken the same seat in the public gallery each and every day. Barely a flicker of emotion was revealed by her throughout the fifty-three days of the trial. To many, she seemed to have battened down the hatches and done what she had always done best—kept the family together.

Few doubted that Fred and Primrose were as much in love after his arrest as throughout their thirty-four-year marriage. She seemed to revel in his brilliance, even as he had stood in the witness box blandly denying the heinous crimes he had committed.

What no one in the court that day could fail to miss was the unique and deeply moving mixture of grief and relief that swept over the faces of the victims' relatives. One by one in the public gallery, like a living map of Hyde, little clutches of people broke down in tears as the verdicts had been announced. They hugged each other for support—different families, but sharing the same burden. The sound of weeping continued on and off for more than half an hour.

It had been punctuated with muted shouts of delight as it became clear that Fred Shipman was not going to get away with murder.

But none of this highly charged emotion seemed to register with Fred Shipman. His witness box performance had been unimpressive. With the same lifeless, methodical manner that dominated his character as a doctor, Shipman tried to convince the jury that he was right, and everyone else was wrong. The jurors were mostly young, ordinary men and women, tasked with testing everything he said. He failed the test miserably. After the verdicts were announced, Shipman was taken downstairs to the bowels of the court, where he had his pick of the empty cells.

Within hours of his latest court appearance, tributes for some of Shipman's alleged victims were recorded in the local *Manchester Evening News*. A friend of Maureen Ward told how the widow was about to go on a Caribbean holiday. "She was a lovely woman, so kind and thoughtful. She would often pop into the neighbors' and ask them if they needed any shopping."

Retired secretary Pamela Hillier, who was a member of the Friends of Mottram Parish Church, would never be forgotten by Friends secretary Katherine Elwood. "She was a lovely, kind person. She would help anybody if they needed it."

Outside Preston Crown Court, victim Jean Lilley's family—Albert, Odette and Wayne—issued a statement saying: "Jean Lilley was a loving, caring wife and mother who dearly cared about her family and friends. She will always be loved and missed. Dr. Shipman may have taken her life from us, but he can never take our memories."

Liz Hunter, who saw Shipman leave the home of her friend, Jean Lilley, just minutes after he killed her, said she was still coming to terms with the verdicts. "At the moment I am still trying to take it all in. The biggest thing I keep asking myself is why I didn't go down to stay with her. Even if I had stayed with her and I had seen him give her something, I wouldn't have known what it was, I'm not a doctor. I do know that if she had thought she was dying, she would have asked me to stay with her. She didn't want to die alone—that was her biggest fear, to die alone. Technically she didn't, he was there. You want someone with you who cares about you—not someone who wants to kill you."

The family of victim Kathleen Wagstaff said: "We feel a sense of relief that this part of the nightmare is at an end, and justice has been done. To lose our mother in such circumstances leaves us with a feeling of deep sadness that we were so badly betrayed by someone in whom we had great trust."

And so the tributes went on. But they clearly hid the true feelings of an entire community who was so shell-shocked by the news that they still refused to believe their favorite GP capable of mass murder.

Immediately after Shipman's sentencing it was announced that he was likely to be charged with another twenty-three murders, and may have been responsible for hundreds of other deaths.

The Shipman case sent ripples of concern and indignation throughout Britain; The government's health secretary, Alan Milburn, made a statement in the House of Commons on the day of sentencing. He said: "Our sympathies lie with the very many families who have been victims of these dreadful crimes. As an individual, Harold Shipman betrayed the trust of his patients. He also betrayed the professionalism of our country's dedicated family doctors."

There was a public outcry when it was openly disclosed that Shipman had been drawing his £100,000 ($150,000) salary—taxpayers' money—right up until he was convicted of mass murder. His earnings as a GP had increased since his arrest in September 1988, because his own practice was having to offer more services, such as bereavement counseling for many of his victims' families, and extra nursing hours to support Shipman's stand-in, Dr. Haz Lloyd, at the Market Street clinic. In the weeks following his sentencing,

Shipman waited for a final check from his paymasters at the West Pennine Health Authority.

Despite the trial and subsequent conviction, Fred Shipman's practice only lost two hundred patients out of a total of more than two thousand. Yet many of the relatives of the GP's victims discovered they would only get derisory compensation payouts estimated to be no more than £10,000 ($15,000) under the Criminal Injuries Compensation Act. Alternatively, the victims' families were advised that they could try and sue Fred Shipman, if they could prove they suffered posttraumatic stress.

Within days it was announced that safeguards on family doctors would be tightened to prevent any similar cases in the future. Health Minister Alan Milburn announced that an inquiry would be launched which would also review the rules on death certificates and the procedures for allowing cremations and burials. Milburn also promised to close the loophole which allowed Shipman to draw his NHS salary for another month. He also was considering removing the doctor's pension rights.

There was astonishment amongst the general public that Shipman was still registered as a GP under the rules of the General Medical Council, despite being Britain's worst serial killer. It would be some weeks before he'd finally be struck off for good.

24

For thousands of Fred Shipman's patients, the truth was going to be extremely hard to swallow. They'd trusted him implicitly and had paid a dear price for it. At the presbytery of St. Paul's, Father Denis Maher's phone was still constantly ringing. He'd been there when his parishioners were bereaved. He'd been there when those same loved ones were exhumed for re-examination. And he'd been there in court giving testimony against Fred Shipman.

Now, following the trial, Father Maher was once more on hand to provide comfort and support to the families of the GP's victims. Father Maher knew only too well that the community of Hyde was still in shock. The outcome of Fred Shipman's trial hadn't really made it any easier for the families of his victims. So in the midst of the grief and confusion, many turned to Father Maher. "The question I was asked many times was: 'Is he evil? Can he be forgiven?' "

Father Maher explained: "What he did can be seen as intrinsically evil. He murdered people, but he also betrayed their trust. His patients would have opened the door with trust to him, let him in with a smile. He violated that very sacred trust. I believe we can forgive; if we refuse forgiveness, we perpetrate evil. If I refuse to forgive, I am making pain for myself. Forgiveness is for people who have done evil. You can condemn what has been done, but still forgive the person."

Father Maher was also chaplain to the local police, so he soon heard that the number of Shipman victims was expected to hit triple figures. He even acknowledged that Fred Shipman himself probably had no idea how many victims there were. Father Maher explained: "Who knows how many he may have killed? It could have been going on for a long, long time. As chaplain, I have seen the people engaged in the forensic work every week. They have been affected by it: they have never been involved in anything like this before."

Following the end of the Shipman trial, Father Maher gave numerous informal counseling sessions and even held a service at his own church for anyone who felt they might have been touched by Fred Shipman's evil work. Father Maher also appealed to many of his flock not to vent their anger at Fred Shipman's family. "I am aware what an ordeal it must be for his wife. His family are as much victims as anyone else. They must be going through a terrible time."

The Shipman trial verdict dominated the British newspapers in the days following his sentencing. Among a host of issues raised, much criticism was pointed in the direction of the medical authorities. The *Sun* wanted to know why Shipman was allowed to carry on practicing after spending six months in a drug addiction clinic. And why was his conviction for forging prescriptions glossed over?

Other newspapers agreed. As the London *Daily Mail* pointed out: "We shall never know exactly how many patients died as a result of that outrageously complacent decision." *The Daily Telegraph* cautioned against an overreaction by arguing that the worst outcome of the case would be if, whenever a patient died, suspicion fell upon his or her doctor.

But there was no getting away from the fact that Fred Shipman had destroyed, albeit temporarily, that vital bond of trust between doctor and patient.

Just after the end of the trial, the ex-husband of Shipman's special friend and victim Bianka Pomfret encountered Primrose Shipman. "She was at York Station taking photographs," explained Adrian Pomfret. "She looked totally undamaged and really happy. How could she look so unbothered about what had happened?"

*   *   *

The day after sentencing, the muffled bells of St. George rang for an hour and a half, and produced an eerie echo which carried right across Hyde. Many of Hyde's still-shocked residents filed into their parish church to remember Fred Shipman's victims. Emotions overflowed during the forty-minute Church of England service which featured hymns and prayers carefully chosen to try to console and conciliate a horrified community.

The 400-strong congregation included many of the detectives who had worked on the murder inquiry, plus Tameside's mayor, Frank Robinson. As schoolgirl Julia Mann sang "*Pie Jesu,*" a middle-aged man pulled out a handkerchief and dabbed at his eyes. One woman sobbed openly when five candles were lit in front of the altar by local people representing every generation of Hyde's community. But the most moving moment came when the Reverend John Harries told his flock: "We will never be the same as we were yesterday. Our innocence has been lost. Nothing anyone can say or do can take away the pain and hurt that we feel. For so long, many in our midst have been grieving, and wounds opened time and time again as we sat through the trial or heard the stories of others."

And still many in Hyde found it hard to believe that their respected GP was a serial killer. A few days after Shipman was sentenced, one of his patients called at his clinic. Dorothy Heywood, 69, was treated by Fred Shipman for more than twenty years. She said she was "in total shock." She added: "He was the best doctor I've ever been to. This is very hard to come to terms with."

Over at the Shipmans' home in Mottram, a policeman stood guard in the driveway. Behind drawn curtains the flickering of a television could be seen as Primrose and at least two of her children watched the countless news broadcasts about Fred Shipman's murderous activities.

Within forty-eight hours of his conviction, Shipman had penned yet another letter to Primrose. He still controlled the powerplay of the relationship and clearly continued to view himself as a towering intellect, a man whose judgment should never, ever be questioned. Primrose had stuck by him throughout everything. The couple had even brought up four fine, seemingly well-adjusted children in a wholly responsible manner.

However, in the aftermath of the trial, it seemed that the two youngest, Sam and David, were suffering from their father's conviction. The stress of his father's trial meant that David, 20, had to re-take his latest set of exams at Newcastle University, where he studied engineering. Sam had left school and was studying to be a nurseryman at an agricultural college near Preston. "He wanted to get as far away from medicine as he could," explained one school friend.

By the time of his father's arrest, oldest son Christopher had moved to Dartford, Kent, in the south of England, although he did remain in close contact with his family, and even traveled up to attend court on a number of occasions.

And despite his incarceration, Fred remained Primrose's Svengali figure. He seemed to have complete power over her, and she was apparently prepared to do anything for him. Many later speculated that that power was equal in strength to the way that the other notorious British serial killer of recent times—Fred West—had control over his wife, although there is certainly no indication at all that Primrose actually took part in any of her husband's crimes.

Primrose was a classic example of a less confident woman drawn in by a powerful man. By all accounts, Primrose could not manage her life on her own, and that's why she continued visiting Fred at every available opportunity. Of course, she knew something wasn't right, but she would hardly have been able to pursue it. Fred Shipman was a dominant character, full of his own self-importance. She didn't dare cross him. In any case, he would never have allowed that.

When it came to making contact again with her family, Primrose was evidently so consumed by feelings about the long-ago pregnancy "scandal" that she couldn't face up to her mother, even more than thirty years after that hastily arranged marriage. Primrose also hung onto her husband because, in some ways, she felt that she was not worthy of Fred Shipman or his attentions. He made her feel grateful for his existence.

There was a complete imbalance of power in their relationship, but it suited them both. She was submissive; Primrose's self-esteem had been at rock bottom for many years, and that was why the house remained in such a mess. She seemed to block out all the unpleasant thoughts and considerations. Primrose did not want to do or say anything that might jeopardize her relationship with her husband. The purpose of her life was to serve him—she had nothing else.

From Fred Shipman's point of view, he desperately needed Primrose to remain completely dependent on him. His partner had to continue to adore him and bow to his every whim.

Fred Shipman may have appeared outwardly calm as those life sentences were announced in court, but by the time he got back to Strangeways jail, he was in a state of complete and utter shock. One warder later recalled: "He totally went to pieces—whimpering, bleating, pining for the world he had forfeited."

Shipman sat and rocked back and forth, saying over and over again: "How can they do this to me, of all people? After all I have done? I am a great doctor, a caring man. This is an affront." There was no remorse. No consideration for those whose lives he took, or the families left behind. The previously charming, relaxed demeanor was replaced by a manic stare. Shipman shuffled along the corridors looking as if he lived in another world from everyone else. He spent increasing amounts of time in a plastic suit on a bare plastic mattress curled up like a baby. One ex-inmate who encountered Shipman in Strangeways later said: "I do not think he will last more than a year inside, now. I think he will top [kill] himself at the first opportunity he gets."

Fred Shipman found himself once again on twenty-four-hour round-the-clock suicide watch. But as the weeks passed, he gradually began adjusting to his fate. He wanted to maintain an element of control, even within the prison system. For jail was a world where the rules were clear-cut, where he was cleverer than many around him, and the sheer number of his victims accorded him a great deal of respect.

Primrose saw her husband for the first time since his sentencing on January 31, accompanied by David and Christopher. She arrived at Strangeways jail for a one-hour visit. Handsome David resembled his father at the same age in many startling ways, with his dark, Latin looks. Primrose, wearing a dark skirt and turquoise jacket, walked straight into the jail's reception area without having to go through the usual procedure of collecting a security pass from the visitor center. But she and both sons were thoroughly searched before being escorted through a maze of corridors to meet Shipman. The Shipmans were told that they'd initially be allowed to make four visits a month to see Fred before he was moved to another prison to serve out his sentence.

After the visit, Primrose maintained her traditional grim silence to the waiting reporters as the three family members climbed into her Metro. David and Chris looked stunned by the explosion of press cameras.

A few days after sentencing, Father Denis Maher had decided that the Shipman family deserved some mercy—despite Fred's horrendous crimes. He later recalled: "I felt a lot of sympathy for his family, especially his sons. I heard from many that they were nice kids, so I took it upon myself one night to go to their house and see them. I wasn't sure which house they lived in, but eventually I found the next-door house, and the couple in there asked me in and talked to me. They encouraged me, and told me where the Shipmans lived."

Father Maher went and knocked at the front door of the GP's home. "One of the sons answered it. I could see people milling about behind. The house was a complete mess." The priest heard the Shipmans' son go back inside and ask his

mother what he should do. "She said, 'Don't talk to him,' "
recalled Father Maher. "Then he came back, said they didn't
want to speak to me. That was it. I never even got in the
hallway. They shut the door firmly, but politely."

Fred Shipman's sentencing did not bring the families of his
victims any nearer to an emotional closure on the subject.
One Greater Manchester Police source admitted privately to
a local newspaper reporter: "Where will it all end? There
could be hundreds." And a relative of one suspected victim
said: "We feel like we are in a limbo. At one time we
thought our loved ones died a natural death, but now we
can never be absolutely sure."

Gradually, dozens of family members began to speak out
about their worst fears. James Ashton, 60, whose widowed
mother Dora died in Shipman's clinic in 1995, said: "Shipman told me it was a stroke. I didn't doubt him, and that is
what he put on the death certificate, but now we just don't
know what to believe."

Joe Kitchen, 42, endured the torment of seeing the body
of his mother Alice exhumed as part of the police investigation. He said: "Shipman has left a trail of lies and deceit
in his wake. He may have been handed fifteen life terms,
but the sentence is only just beginning for many people in
Hyde."

Spinster Joan Harding, an 82-year-old retired council
worker, was another patient who died in Shipman's clinic.
Close friend Winnie Richards said: "We mourned her once,
and I feel like I'm having to mourn her again." Marion
Higham, a retired wages clerk, died at her Hyde home in
1996. A neighbor said: "As soon as we realized what Shipman had been doing, we thought Marion had fallen victim
to him."

Widowed mother-of-two Josephine Hall died at the age
of 69. Daughter Josephine Allen said: "I wrestled with my
thoughts, and felt I had to go to the police. I wanted them
to say, 'No you're wrong,' but they didn't." Retired mill
worker Elsie Cheetham, 76, died in April 1997. Neighbor

Ken Houlsworth, 67, said: "She didn't deserve to have her life cut short."

Businesswoman Joan Dean—once an extra on the popular British TV soap, *Coronation Street*—died at her Hyde home in February 1988. *Coronation Street* actor John Savident, who plays butcher Fred Gee, was a close family friend, and read two Shakespeare poems at her funeral. Afterwards, Joan's son Brian found that an 18-carat Omega watch and a £5,000 engagement ring were missing.

Gladys Saunders, 82, died in June 1996. A friend said: "Dr. Shipman was there. A neighbor went out to get some milk from the shop and when she got back, Shipman said Gladys had gone." Widow Hilda Hibbert, 81, died in January 1996—just minutes after Shipman left her house. Granddaughter Jane said: "I'm ninety-five percent sure he murdered her."

Irene Heathcote, 76, died in 1996 after a visit from Shipman. Son-in-law Duncan McAlpine, 60, said: "My wife Susan feels Shipman should be hanged." Lively Edith Brady, 72, was found dead in 1996. Daughter Pam Turner said: "I just want to know why. I owe it to my mum." Other alleged victims included Marie Fernley, Edith Brock and Bertha Moss, who died in 1995; Valerie Cuthbert and Marjorie Waller who died in 1996; Lottie Bennison, who died in 1997; and Cissy Davies and Mabel Shawcross, who died in 1998.

Police knew only too well that there would be even more deaths to investigate eventually.

On February 18, 2000, families of twenty-three of Fred Shipman's alleged victims reacted angrily when told that the GP would not face any more murder charges. David Calvert-Smith, the director of England's Public Prosecution Service had decided that, after the mass of publicity given to the Shipman case, it would be impossible to give him a fair trial. Calvert-Smith told the families of his "reluctant" and highly unusual decision not to proceed in letters, delivered to the homes of the relatives by special courier early that morning.

Calvert-Smith said: "I have reluctantly concluded that there are insurmountable legal difficulties to further trials taking place." After giving his reasons, he added: "I hope my explanation is to some degree helpful to you and that you will in time be able to come to terms with your tragic loss."

Calvert-Smith had overruled detectives convinced of Shipman's guilt in the deaths of those patients. But police promised to continue their inquiries into many more cases involving Shipman. They still believed there was enough evidence for a second or even a third trial.

But Calvert-Smith insisted: "I have had to consider the effect of the enormous publicity upon any further trial of Harold Shipman on new charges, and he has already been sent to prison for the rest of his natural life. In reaching this decision, I have been acutely aware of the distress of relatives of the deceased and the understandable desire for some of them for a further public trial in a criminal court."

He claimed "a considerable majority" of the relatives of the alleged victims had accepted that a new trial could not take place, and added that further proceedings could delay or hamper the progress of a public inquiry into Shipman's activities. "Normally a decision to prosecute would automatically follow if there is enough evidence for a realistic prospect of conviction of murder," he said. "But this has been an exceptional and, I hope, unique case."

Calvert-Smith then said any decision about the deaths of Fred Shipman's other alleged victims would now be a matter for John Pollard, coroner in Tameside, Greater Manchester. "I am going to assess the whole Shipman situation fully," responded Pollard.

But many of the relatives of Shipman's numerous victims still wanted Shipman prosecuted: "I'm outraged that the Crown Prosecution Service is not going ahead," said Suzanne Bennison, whose grandmother Edith Brock died in November 1995. "If they think they can appease me by shoving a letter through my door and thinking I will go away quietly, they have chosen the wrong person." John Hibbert, son of Hilda Hibbert, who died at home in her armchair four years earlier, said: "Shipman has literally got away with murder."

The families of many of Fred Shipman's alleged victims also became angry about the British government's decision to hold an independent inquiry into his murders outside of the public view. Lead investigator Lord Laming promised that "care and sensitivity" would be used when relatives were asked to give evidence. He also said the inquiry would be swift and thorough, although the decision to hold it in private had been made because the terms of the National Health Service Act dictated that it had to be held behind closed doors.

Some weeks after the end of Fred Shipman's trial, moves were finally made to completely close down his one-man practice on Market Street in Hyde. Many felt that it served as a constant reminder to the relatives of victims, and any incoming new GP should be given an opportunity to make a clean start. The decision to move to new premises was endorsed by the Tameside and Glossop community health council. "We think it would be very unsettling for patients to be treated in premises where at least five women have died at the hands of their GP," said council Chairwoman Pauline Davenport.

But the local West Pennine area health authority did not expect any move for at least three months. "In the short term, the only realistic option is to keep the surgery open," said a spokesman.

Back in his prison cell, Fred Shipman continued to lobby the health authority about the poor standard of care being provided by the temporary doctor who had taken his place. Shipman clearly remained in a complete state of self-denial about his murderous habits.

25

Inside Manchester's Strangeways Prison, two members of the staff whose mothers may have been amongst Fred Shipman's numerous victims were sent home until the GP could be transferred following his conviction. Shipman was held in the healthcare unit while being carefully monitored by medical staff. A prison spokesman explained: "It is routine for newly convicted prisoners to be monitored in this way if there has been a long trial of this nature."

Warders still believed Shipman might try to commit suicide, and he was categorized as a high-risk inmate. Prisoners normally spend at least a month being assessed before being transferred to another high-security jail, but in Fred Shipman's case it was rushed through so that the two suspended prison officers could return to work as quickly as possible.

Because his victims were all elderly and predominately female, Shipman found himself isolated in a similar way to sex offenders. "There is little doubt that he would be targeted, because he was such a prolific murderer and his victims were someone's mum or grandparent," said one member of the prison staff.

Then Fred Shipman was transferred out of Strangeways to the high-security Frankland Prison in County Durham. He had asked to be transferred to Wakefield jail, in nearby West Yorkshire, because he thought Durham was too far for his family to travel to visit him. That request was turned down.

Frankland jail is the sort of place that gives the prison

service a respectable name. It's not the usual grim, gray collection of typically British Victorian buildings, even though it contains many of the nation's most deadly criminals. Furthermore, relations between staff and inmates are reasonable. But despite these relative amenities, there's little to smile about if you're facing up to the prospect of spending the rest of your life in prison.

Within weeks of Fred Shipman's incarceration in Frankland Prison, his family moved to be closer to him. They also wanted to escape the memories associated with their home in Mottram. Primrose informed a select group of friends that she was moving to Whitby, North Yorkshire, midway between Frankland and Wakefield Prisons, where Shipman still hoped to be transferred eventually.

A family friend explained at the time: "Primrose is standing by him. She used to see him almost daily when he was on remand at Strangeways, but now it's a lot harder. By moving, it also gets the family away from the house and all its bad memories."

Around the same time as Primrose was packing her bags, the *Sun* newspaper revealed that Fred Shipman's practice had been re-listed in the 2000–2001 South Manchester phone book, despite his conviction. It gave his name, the surgery's address and its phone numbers.

On February 10, 2000, Fred Shipman was finally struck off the medical register by the General Medical Council. He did not appear before the GMC's professional conduct committee in London and was not represented by attorneys. The hearing had been speeded up following Shipman's conviction. Committee chairman Rodney Yates said: "The committee are appalled by the evidence. It is abhorrent that Dr. Shipman cold-bloodedly murdered fifteen patients, using his medical skills. He greatly undermined the trust the public place in the medical profession, in particular their family doctors."

That same day Shipman made it clear through his lawyers that he still intended to appeal his convictions. His attorneys claimed that pre-trial publicity linking the GP to the murders of more than 100 people may have influenced the jury. Shipman was told that he had until the end of the month to file papers requesting an appeal against the sixteen convictions, which included the forgery of the Grundy will.

On Monday, March 6, 2000, one of the doctors who helped bring Fred Shipman to justice died of cancer. Dr. Linda Reynolds, only 49 years old, had put her career and health on the line by speaking out about her fears concerning Shipman. She'd noticed that the death rate amongst Shipman's patients was three times higher than at the Brook Surgery, where she worked, nearby. Dr. Reynolds died at her home in Stockport with her husband Nigel at her side. The couple had two children, Caroline, 22, and William, 18. Mr. Reynolds later explained: "What she did was against her nature, she was not interventionist. I have utter respect and admiration for my wife, and know what this cost her."

Coroner Mr. Pollard said: "I will never forget how brave she was to come forward and put her profession on the line. Dr. Reynolds was a very courageous and stoical person who acted in a very helpful and brave manner."

In April 2000, it was revealed that three of twenty-six alleged new victims had been exhumed during the original police inquiry, and inquests on those victims—Sarah Ashworth, Alice Kitchen and Elizabeth Mellor—were imminent. South Manchester coroner John Pollard even wrote to the then–Home Secretary Jack Straw seeking permission to open the inquests. Pollard stressed that, unlike in a criminal trial, an inquest would not seek to establish Shipman's guilt or innocence, but simply establish the facts. Pollard explained: "It is my intention to inform Dr. Shipman of the inquests and to notify him of his right to attend." That meant that Shipman could be called from his prison cell to give evidence. But he was highly unlikely to cooperate.

The following month, May 2000, police investigators revealed that their long-standing investigation into Shipman's activities now suggested he'd killed close to 200 people. Investigators already knew that Shipman's guilt could never be determined from cases dating before 1985, because itemized phone bills, medical records and cremation certificates on which detectives relied did not exist.

The Shipman case was now dwarfing Britain's other notorious murder investigations: Dennis Nilsen, who admitted killing sixteen gay men in London between 1978 and 1983; arsonist Bruce Lee, jailed in 1981 for murdering fifteen people by setting their houses ablaze; Yorkshire Ripper Peter Sutcliffe, who killed thirteen times; and Fred and Rose West, who murdered at least twelve young women. Even the world's most notorious serial killer, Andrei Chikatilo, stood accused of murdering a comparatively paltry fifty-two women and boys in the Soviet Union between 1978 and 1990.

Out of a moral obligation to the families, a team of twenty police officers continued the investigation, despite the fact that prosecutions were unlikely. "There was a need to find them some sort of closure," explained one investigator.

The fallout from the Shipman case continued for many months following the end of his trial. Dr. Alan Banks—medical advisor to the authority who paid Shipman's salary—was suspended from his job. He'd examined the files of fourteen Shipman patients during the first police investigation, but told detectives that he could find nothing wrong. After Shipman's trial, 49-year-old Dr. Banks was ordered to remain at home until further notice by his bosses at the West Pennine Health Authority.

Dr. Banks said: "I do not feel that I have done anything wrong, or behaved in anything but a professional manner. I have already talked things over with my legal people and I have no doubt about being completely vindicated when all the facts are known." Indeed, in August 2000, Dr. Banks was reinstated, based on the health authority's conclusion that Shipman's forgeries made it impossible to detect any wrongdoing.

Even Fred Shipman's small group of drinking pals in Mottram were now convinced that he was a mass killer. But despite their feelings about Shipman, his friend Dr. David Walker made a special effort to look after the GP's youngest son Sam. "He's a lovely lad, and he needed to be helped to pull through all this," added Dr. Walker.

Dr. Walker and his friends were convinced that Fred Shipman would probably kill himself. "I thought he might do it before the end of the trial. I still think he might. He'll need to be carefully watched," said Dr. Walker. Many in Hyde believed that the sooner Shipman died, the better.

Fred Shipman was soon making a lasting impression on other inmates and staff at Frankland Prison. Many quickly dubbed him "The Good Doctor," rather than regarding him as the evil, psychopathic genius portrayed in court during his trial. Fred Shipman had dispensed death and sympathy to hundreds of innocent old ladies in Hyde, and then set up his own practice within the red-brick walls of Frankland Prison.

Other lifers in Frankland believed that Shipman was more trustworthy than the prison doctor. "It's only injections he's a bit dodgy with, he can't get the drugs in here, so we're all safe. He told me he wouldn't trust the prison doctors to treat his cat—if he had one," one old bank robber later recalled. An inmate suffering chest pains went to see Shipman because prison doctors had not prescribed any treatment for him. Shipman diagnosed a cracked rib, and the man was immediately treated properly.

Fred Shipman soon overcame the fear and suspicion of an entire prison to gain the respect of his fellow inmates. As one recently released prisoner explained: "At first we thought he was a right nutter, but he's a cool guy. He's interested in us, and he's proved he's a decent fellow."

And yet, some inmates in Frankland found Shipman devoid of emotion and extremely arrogant. "He seemed to have no trace of emotion," explained one prisoner. "He never even mentioned the women he'd killed by name. The only person he talked about was Kathleen Grundy. The other women were just numbers."

Shipman—described at his trial as a fanatical control freak—clearly had excellent coping skills. "The only difference is that he can't knock any of us off without the [guards] noticing," added the former inmate, with tongue firmly in cheek. Shipman continued to insist to everyone inside Frankland that he was innocent of the murders connected to his name. "Most inmates say they're innocent, but the Doc, as we call him, is pretty convincing and, you know, if you look at the evidence against him, it does look flimsy," said one former inmate. Others might disagree.

But there were some disturbing side effects to Fred Shipman's incarceration. Warders at Frankland feared that Shipman—by now a frail 54 years old—was being pressurized by certain heavyweight inmates (including three notorious armed robbers) to give them a worse diagnosis so they could get lighter duties or go into the prison hospital. Eventually prison staff prevented Shipman—prisoner CJ8198—from treating his flock by putting him in permanent solitary confinement in the jail's hospital.

Meanwhile Primrose moved into the house she'd bought in nearby Whitby. She strolled casually up to the prison gates each week taking numerous calls on her mobile, which still played the haunting melody of the hymn "Jesu, Joy of Man's Desiring." Primrose usually arrived with sons David and Christopher for a one-hour visit. The couple's two other children, Sarah and Sam, also made regular appearances at Frankland.

Primrose—increasingly obese—tended to dress in long skirts and baggy sweaters and jackets. Her distinctively tatty ten-year-old Metro soon became a familiar sight to local journalists camped outside the prison. Reporters who tried to quote her found that she never uttered anything other than "No comment."

Primrose's first impression of Frankland was its starkness. Along with all visitors, she was obliged to book in at the entrance and then sit in reception to wait for her name to be called out. Then she had her photo taken, in keeping with prison rules. She was only allowed to take £10 in change into the prison, which could be used at the various vending machines inside the visitors' hall.

Then Primrose was escorted to another building where her fingerprints were taken, and her shoes, watch and cardigan were carefully examined for contraband. She then walked through an X-ray machine and was escorted to yet another building through more glass doors.

Then a dog sniffed her for drugs before she finally got into the visitors' hall. Shipman and other sensitive inmates, such as child molesters, were made to greet visitors in a separate room just off the main hall. Two members of the staff stood by at all times.

It's known as "the nonces' [child molesters'] area" to the rest of the prisoners. Fred Shipman—still refusing to concede his crimes—was categorized with the child offenders "for his own safety." Other inmates say to this day that Shipman is deeply offended to be classified with "the nonces." Undoubtedly prison authorities moved Shipman "to try and water down his influence amongst the other inmates," one guard later explained.

Primrose seemed determined not to miss one visit. In the visitors' room she could be seen hanging onto Fred's every word. Nothing—not even the prospect of him never being a free man—could deter her from her duty as the faithful wife. Shipman even told one inmate about how supportive his family was being: "I have talked to all of them. Primrose and my children are being very supportive, particularly Sam. They are standing by me, and they will get me through this. They are loyal because they know I am innocent."

Many of Shipman's family associates were seriously concerned about the health of Primrose. "She is losing the whole focus of her life," said one. Even Shipman confided to one Frankland prison officer: "Primrose is affected. I'm now comforting her on visits." Not even Fred Shipman's incarceration could prevent him from controlling his wife's life.

Shipman bitterly complained about being held in the hospital wing at Frankland. His cell had a clear plastic door to enable warders to continue to watch over him around the clock. One source said: "He has ranted and raved about being called a monster. He insists he is innocent and he will fight his conviction. It seems as if he has shut out all the killings from his mind."

Soon after arriving at Frankland Prison, Fred Shipman began suffering serious eyesight problems and made his only trip out of Frankland for treatment at the Sunderland Eye Infirmary. The visit—Shipman arrived handcuffed to two wardens at 10 A.M. one Monday morning—was shrouded in secrecy. It sparked criticism from other patients who claimed that Shipman "was being treated like a royal." Patients were ordered to stay inside rooms and banned from corridors while Shipman was in the hospital.

Back inside Frankland, Shipman received visits at least once a month from detectives still trying to urge him to cooperate with their inquiries into the hundreds of other deaths amongst his patients. When a video link was set up for Shipman to give evidence at one of the new inquests into yet another victim, it remained blank. He even refused three invitations by the coroner examining the death of one victim—Sarah Ashworth—to exercise his right to question witnesses.

By the middle of 2000, Shipman was translating Harry Potter books into Braille inside Frankland. It was a perfectly normal prison job, not dissimilar from making license plates in a US jail. Some British tabloid newspapers expressed horror that this so-called "monster" should have been given such a pleasant job. But then, not many prisoners would have the intelligence to translate into Braille. "Shipman started in the unit not long ago, and had to undergo training, but he's learned very quickly," one prison source explained. "He's really enjoying having something more interesting to do, and he's impressed by the fact it's Harry Potter."

Inside the healthcare center at Frankland, Shipman wasn't even awakened until 7:45 each morning. But he remained on a supervised suicide watch, because staff still feared he might try to kill himself. Officially, prison authorities stated that Shipman was shattered by his incarceration, but that's not the picture painted by other inmates—or even by the murdering medic himself.

In one outburst to prison officers and other inmates at Frankland, Shipman shouted: "I am not going to commit suicide, because I am going to fight to prove my innocence. I am not a monster. I have given injections to tens of thousands of patients in my thirty years, so it is ridiculous to suggest that I would start killing them at the end of my career."

But physically, Shipman had deteriorated since his incarceration. At one stage, he wrote his beloved Primrose a poem which referred to his despair and how he still loved his wife very much.

Primrose's reply was even more bizarre, talking about her "lust and passion," and how she was not certain if either of them had ever experienced such emotions together. Was Primrose's obedient mask slipping ever so slightly?

Yet Primrose continued facing up to humiliation in the only way she knew—by ignoring everyone else in the world apart from her beloved Fred. She knew only too well that if her father George were still alive, he would be telling her that the day she met Fred Shipman on that bus in Leeds was the start of her inevitable downfall.

Shipman told one friend in a letter that a fellow inmate had advised him to treat jail like a foreign country. He wrote: "You go along with the local customs and it will not impinge on you too much. The problem is getting to know the customs."

Many recognized that he was heavily reliant on visits from his wife. One said: "He always made sure he looked his best for her, and would change into his own clothes before he went to the visiting hall."

By the time the police had concluded their secondary investigation on the Shipman case in May 2000, detectives believed he was responsible for an additional 192 deaths, even after many cases were dropped from the statistics because they were already suffering from terminal illnesses.

Over in Shipman's original killing ground of Todmorden, West Yorkshire, local newspaper reporter Pete Devine was undertaking his own investigation into suspicious deaths that had occurred when the GP practiced in the town. He identified most of the apparent victims through the deaths column of his own newspaper, the *Todmorden News and Advertiser*.

Those figures seemed to indicate an increase in the number of deaths in the area during Fred Shipman's "reign," with 401 deaths between March 1, 1974, and September 30, 1975. Fred Shipman had undoubtedly "honed his skills" as a mass murderer in Todmorden. Despite being a young, relatively inexperienced doctor, he'd signed twenty-two death certificates, considerably more than any of his colleagues during the sixteen months he worked in the town. And when Shipman departed, the death rate dropped. Local MP Chris McCafferty immediately called for a public inquiry into Shipman's activities in Todmorden.

Meanwhile, despite his claims that he would fight his conviction, Fred Shipman still had not filed a valid appeal. He'd submitted a request for an appeal to Preston Crown Court, but the document, believed to be a handwritten note by Shipman, was not in order. The killer GP had also parted company with his trial lawyer Ann Ball. Shipman struggled to find a new lawyer to represent him. He told friends and family that other attorneys he approached were coming up with excuses, and that he was considering conducting his own defense. The old, defiant Fred Shipman was never far from the surface.

26

In Frankland Prison, Fred Shipman came across another notorious British mass killer, Roy Archibald Hall. Hall—known in prison circles as "the Perfect Gentleman"—was allowed to stay in the healthcare wing while visiting a friend who was dying of cancer at the time.

"I found him very polite and lent him copies of *Country Life* magazine, and the staff seemed to like him," he later told this author. Shipman even said to Roy Hall that he was desperate to help his wife earn some money so she could survive in the outside world without him. Hall—who committed a series of brutal murders before being hunted down by the police in the 1960s—found the killer doctor fascinating "but very guarded."

After many hours of conversation, Roy Hall is convinced that the GP killed his patients to feel in control of them "as they passed under his control to death." Hall explained: "Fred seemed very cold within. He had few friends. In fact, I'd go as far as to say he was either a freak or insane."

Before Roy Hall left the hospital wing at Frankland, Fred Shipman struck up a conversation with him about writing his own book. Hall's memoirs, entitled *A Perfect Gentleman*, had just been published. Shipman even said he swore his fellow inmates to secrecy whenever they were released, because he wanted to "save up" his life story so that one day he could put pen to paper.

It was then announced that the story of Shipman's murderous reign in Hyde was to be made into a £1.5 million ($2.3 million) TV movie starring 62-year-old British TV actor James Bollam as the good doctor. The filmmakers insisted they would be concentrating on the police investigation into the killings.

Meanwhile Greater Manchester Police mounted an investigation to find out who was responsible for tipping Shipman off about their initial inquiries. They believed that Shipman initially avoided arrest thanks to his mystery informant keeping him one step ahead of investigators. If they discovered their identity, that person would face a charge of conspiracy to pervert the course of justice.

The crimes of Fred Shipman were forcing people across Britain to re-examine the behavior of their own GPs. One inquiry into the activities of a doctor was triggered after his wife called the television show *This Morning* to contribute to a discussion about Shipman's crimes. The caller claimed that her husband had deliberately given lethal doses of diamorphine to two female patients. One of the women was understood to have been given 15 milligrams of the drug and the other 20 milligrams. Both died within hours of the injections. The show—hosted by well-known British TV personalities Judy Finnigan and Richard Madeley—did not broadcast her call, which was made without her husband's knowledge. But her comments led the program makers to inform police.

It eventually emerged that the case had already been investigated by the General Medical Council, the British medical profession's regulatory body. The doctor was understood to live in South Yorkshire, near Shipman's old killing ground of Todmorden. At one time he had had more than 2,500 patients on his list, and had been allowed to continue to practice after 350 patients signed a petition supporting him. There was no doubting the shades of Shipman in the case. Police immediately contacted the local medical authorities seeking details of his past. The officer in charge of the case, Detective Chief Superintendent Mick Burdis of South Yorkshire Police said: "It is early regarding any inquiry. We have not received any formal allegations." But there was a feeling throughout Britain that there might be quite a few other potential "Doctor Shipmans" across the nation.

The fallout from Fred Shipman's murderous activities continued. A conflict broke out between the two most senior bodies of Britain's medical profession—the British Medical Association and the General Medical Council. The dispute was sparked by attempts to restore public confidence in doctors in the wake of Shipman's conviction.

A national opinion poll, commissioned by the BMA, reported that 89 percent of the public still regarded medicine as the most trustworthy of professions. But the GMC was completely contradicting this by working on a set of proposals for improving self-regulation of the profession.

In Todmorden, local reporter Pete Devine continued to dig up more and more suspicious deaths connected to Fred Shipman's stay in the area. On June 16, 2000, the situation reached a head when he hosted a meeting at a Todmorden hall to talk to worried relatives. Devine told them how his three-month investigation had uncovered some "worrying statistics."

Local politicians demanded that more than 100 mystery deaths that occurred during Fred Shipman's stay in the town should be re-examined.

Many wanted Shipman to end the uncertainty of countless relatives by making a full confession. But Fred Shipman still had no intention of admitting his crimes. "Under these circumstances, we may never know the full extent of his actions, but it is important that every lead is investigated," one local politician told the packed Todmorden hall.

A Todmorden patient who nearly died at the hands of Fred Shipman in 1974 came forward and revealed her close escape for the first time. Elaine Oswald was by now a professor at Tennessee University in the US. She revealed that Shipman had told her she had an allergic reaction to a painkiller after injecting her with what is now thought to have been diamorphine. She even admitted that she would like to face Shipman once more to ask him why he had tried to kill her. "I would love to meet him in person, face to face. I am consumed with wanting to know why he tried to kill me. Did I remind him of his dead mother? Was I wearing something which triggered this?"

Elaine Oswald pointed out that her young age at the time contradicted the assumption that he only killed older patients. "It makes me wonder how many others there have been. How did he manage to get away with killing so many? He obviously didn't start with older people, judging by what he did to me."

In June 2000, many of the families of Fred Shipman's victims went to the high court to try to force Health Secretary Alan Milburn to hold a long-awaited government inquiry in public. The families of victims also demanded to know why the GP had been allowed to go on killing for so long.

The British press even mounted a legal challenge to a ruling denying them access to the inquiry. Journalists and relatives of the victims wanted to know:

1. Why local GPs were allowed to stockpile a staggering 13,000 milligrams of diamorphine.
2. How Shipman had been allowed to continue practicing after his earlier drug convictions, an oversight that led to a killing spree which stunned the world.
3. Who was responsible for a series of devastating errors that allowed Shipman to go on wiping out innocent victims long after he should have been caught.

The government capitulated and announced that the inquiry would be held in public, although it would still be some time before it was opened.

It wasn't until six months after Fred Shipman's conviction that the first full-time doctor was appointed to step into Shipman's shoes. Dr. Amy Cumming, a GP for thirty years, bravely agreed to take on Fred Shipman's former patients at her premises in nearby Denton. Dr. Cumming explained, "It will be an uphill struggle, but I feel I have a responsibility to the people of Hyde. I find it amazing no other practice has applied to do the same."

Incredibly, almost a third of Shipman's patients still expressed a reluctance to move. Dr. Cumming knew Fred Shipman well, but was surprised by the patients' loyalty to the jailed doctor. She later recalled: "Like many, I believed he was innocent. I couldn't believe he would be capable of killing. But gradually, as the evidence in his trial came out, it became obvious. The number of people dying in his surgery was extraordinary, as were his methods of disposal [of the bodies]."

Dr. Cummings added: "If a doctor works in an isolated environment, nobody questions his or her work. People come in to do audits, but they tend to trust what you, the doctor, say—partly because it's so hard to cross-check the facts."

But Dr. Cummings did encounter some patients who were not so keen on Fred Shipman. "I had a young woman in my clinic the other day who did one day's work with Shipman when she was a teenager. Someone died in the surgery that very day. She was traumatized. It put her off being a doctor for life," explained Dr. Cumming. "Several of Shipman's former patients have told me they feel glad to be alive.

"They say: 'I'm lucky to have got away.' Coming bruisingly close to death has made many of his patients anxious at the thought of seeing a new doctor. One or two have said: 'I think my aunt/mother/sister was helped on her way by Shipman, but I won't take it up with the police, as I don't want to re-open old wounds.' "

In the middle of August 2000, coroner Dr. John Pollard ruled that Mrs. Sarah Ashworth had been unlawfully killed, but he was prevented by law from specifically naming Fred Shipman as her murderer. Pollard told the court that there were striking similarities between Mrs. Ashworth's sudden death and those of the fifteen other women Shipman was earlier convicted of killing. He also said it would be "an affront to common sense" to seek to explain them as mere coincidence.

Weeks later, Coroner Pollard was re-assessing his verdict on yet another of Shipman's alleged victims. He labeled the death of 78-year-old Nellie Mullen as an unlawful killing after hearing how she'd died during a visit by Shipman to her bungalow in Lanegate, Hyde, on May 2, 1993. The GP had recorded on her cremation certificate that she died two hours *after* a witness said he had found Mrs. Mullen dead. Shipman had also told Mrs. Mullen's niece, Patricia Rooke, that her aunt had died even later in the day, while he waited for an ambulance.

The inquest also heard that Shipman's notes gave the cause of death as coronary thrombosis, yet this was incompatible with the state in which her body was found. Specialist GP Dr. John Grenville said he would have expected such a patient to have suffered pain and distress and be lying down when she died. But yet again, one of Shipman's patients had been found sitting upright in her chair, dressed to go out and with a peaceful expression on her face. It backed the suggestion that all Shipman really wanted to do was ensure that his patients died a "happy death."

As Dr. Grenville later stated: "None of it rings true. It's like throwing six lots of sixes on a dice. It may happen once, but if it happens twice, you suspect the dice is loaded. If it happens 192 times, you can bet your life it's loaded."

Experts trying to analyze Fred Shipman's murderous ways were now privately admitting that there could be close to 400 victims. They concluded that Britain's worst-ever serial killer mainly went about his business in the afternoon. For reasons still only known to himself, Fred Shipman appeared to prefer administering lethal injections after a light lunch prepared by the ever-loyal Primrose.

This macabre twist was one of the most baffling, but inescapable, conclusions from an official report published in January 2001. The report—commissioned by the Department of Health—struggled to put a definitive figure on the total number of Shipman victims, and did not have the detail that would be expected of the public inquiry. Report chairman Professor Richard Baker of Leicester University said there were 236 deaths among patients that were directly suspicious, but added that the true death toll could be as high as 345. His analysis showed that more than half the patients who died under Shipman's supervision were recorded by the GP as dying of heart failure or old age. They may all have been murdered.

Liam Donaldson, Britain's Chief Medical Officer, said it was "inexplicable" that Shipman could have murdered for so long without being caught. He said part of the Baker report portrayed a cycle of "death in the afternoon" with 55 percent of Shipman's patients dying between 1 P.M. and 7 P.M.—most of them between 2 P.M. and 4:30 P.M.—compared with 25 percent of other GPs.

Families of some of Shipman's numerous victims met with Professor Baker when he briefed them at Dukinfield Town Hall, near Hyde. There was criticism that Shipman himself did not give evidence to the Baker inquiry. Some believed that the doctor would have agreed to help the inquiry but was never asked. British Members of Parliament were particularly interested in how Shipman had managed to obtain such large quantities of controlled drugs.

The Baker Report itself concluded the following:
— Shipman issued an excess of 297 death certificates.
— There were 236 more deaths in the homes of Shipman patients than would be expected.
— Highest death rates were among female patients aged between 64 and 75 years of age, but also among older men.
— There were excess deaths from the beginning of Shipman's career, but they did not occur every year.
— Shipman was more likely, and relatives and caretakers were less likely, to be present when patients died.

The report concluded: "There is convincing evidence that the observed numbers of deaths among Shipman's patients was in excess of what would have been expected."

A total of 166 deaths were described as "highly suspicious" and 43 were described as "moderately suspicious."

Professor Baker explained: "I am conscious that these findings are going to be distressing to the families of the victims of Shipman, but I hope that understanding the facts will be useful in coming to terms with what has happened."

Baker said he felt rage about the way Shipman had "abused the trust of the people who depended on him completely."

A newspaper headline on the same day summed it all up: DOCTOR SHIPMAN 'MURDERED 265' OF HIS PATIENTS. Now the only doubt about the figures being released was whether or not they would continue to rise.

Health Minister John Hutton promised that a public tribunal following the Baker Report would look carefully at the issue of controlled drugs. Hutton even promised a closed-circuit TV link to Hyde Town Hall so that residents could keep in touch with the hearings.

However, no actual date was given for the inquiry, although it was announced that the chairman, High Court Judge Dame Janet Smith, would be based in offices next to Manchester's Piccadilly Station; and Manchester Town Hall would be used for the witness hearings.

But many still believed it was all a matter of too much too late.

27

Fred Shipman spent his fifty-fifth birthday—January 14, 2001—behind bars at Frankland Prison. With police inquiries continuing, he found himself still regularly receiving visits from investigators armed with the obligatory tape-recorder, hoping he'd decide to capitulate and face up to the enormity of his crimes. But Shipman said nothing each time and referred them to his lawyer.

Much of Shipman's time by now was occupied with writing letters to his family and a select band of friends who had remained in contact with him since his trial. On the surface his mood never seemed to alter. He was often seen holding Primrose's hand in the visiting room, whispering instructions to her. One prison visitor later explained: "She seemed to listen avidly to his every word. She just kept nodding her head in agreement. She didn't seem to say much back to him."

Shipman continued claiming that he was planning to write a book, but since that would involve confessing to, or at the very least explaining the crimes, it seemed unlikely he would ever really put pen to paper. (Repeated written requests to Fred Shipman to cooperate with this author have gone unanswered.)

Greater Manchester Police then announced that they'd opened investigations into the deaths of sixty-two other patients. This was in addition to the 192 cases they had already examined.

Not surprisingly, many of Britain's sensationalist tabloids soon got word of the ever-rising toll. The London Evening

Standard claimed: SHIPMAN'S DEATH TOLL COULD BE AS HIGH AS 345.

In Manchester, police drew up a list of thirteen "characteristics" describing Fred Shipman's so-called technique that might help worried relatives conclude whether their loved ones could be amongst his numerous victims.

They were:

1. She was of a certain age.
2. She was a widow or living alone.
3. She died in the afternoon.
4. She died at home.
5. She complained of minor ailments before her death.
6. She saw Shipman on the day of her death.
7. Shipman asserted he had telephoned for an ambulance.
8. Her door was open or "on the latch."
9. Her body was found upright in a chair or on a settee.
10. The victim looked peaceful or appeared to be asleep.
11. She died wearing normal day clothes.
12. Shipman made no attempt at physical examination of the dead woman.
13. Shipman informed relatives that no post mortem was necessary.

Inevitably, Fred Shipman's notoriety led to his image joining those of Jack the Ripper and Adolf Hitler in a TV commercial aimed at preventing teenagers from smoking. The thirty-second ad was screened on Britain's National No Smoking Day, March 14, for the Cancer Research Campaign, and was written by twelve-year-olds. It's tag line included a pile of cigarette ends and the slogan "The Biggest Serial Killer of All." Six boys from the independent City of London School came up with the idea, which beat 2,500 other entries in a national competition.

Eventually police conceded that they were investigating *every single* death certificate signed by Fred Shipman in Todmorden. A West Yorkshire police spokesman said: "Fol-

lowing publication of Professor Baker's report and continued media speculation, West Yorkshire Police is widening
its investigation to include all twenty-two patients' deaths
certified by Shipman during his time in Todmorden. West
Yorkshire officers will continue to work closely with officers from Greater Manchester Police. This process is likely
to take some time."

Then an inquest heard how Shipman certified the death
of a patient he had not seen for two months. Shipman was
called to the home of Mabel Shawcross on Stockport Road
in, Hyde on January 22, 1998, by police who had found her
dead after being alerted by neighbors. Police Constable Stephen Broadbent found the 79-year-old spinster sitting bolt-
upright in a chair, but when Shipman arrived on the scene,
he insisted he had not seen her for "a couple of months."
Then Shipman said that he could certify the death, and recorded that Miss Shawcross had died of a stroke.

A few days later another new inquest into an alleged Fred
Shipman victim heard how Shipman had once more been
callous when dealing with the relatives of a patient who died
in his clinic. Widow Bertha Moss, of Newton Hall Court,
Hyde, died in the doctor's treatment room during a check-
up in June 1995. Her daughter, Ann Whelan, told the coroner's court that Shipman said her mother suffered a heart
attack while his back was turned.

When she asked him why the relatively fit 68-year-old
had died so suddenly, he replied, "If her heart hadn't killed
her, she would have had to have her legs chopped off because of her diabetes. She would not have wanted to spend
the rest of her life in a wheelchair and be a burden." Mrs.
Whelan was upset by the GP's comments, but did not have
the courage to question him. "It was like he was shouting
at me," she later recalled. "Like he thought I was stupid. I
was very intimidated by him."

Shipman later noted on Mrs. Moss's cremation certificate
that practice staff were present when she died. But former
receptionist Jane Kenyon—who was alone on duty that
day—told the court that she was not aware of what had

happened, and Shipman had never spoken to her about Mrs. Moss's death. Coroner John Pollard recorded his twelfth unlawful killing verdict following the inquest.

Then the daughter of one of Shipman's victims announced that she was planning to sue the police after their initial, bungled investigation enabled the GP to continue killing patients. Kathleen Adamski was the daughter of Winifred Mellor, one of at least three people killed by Shipman after the police abandoned their first investigation.

She planned to seek substantial compensation if she could prove that she suffered posttraumatic stress as a result of discovering her mother's death and that it could have been avoided if the police had arrested Shipman earlier. Mrs. Adamski explained: "I am sick of the whole notion that doctors are untouchable. There have been many cases where the doctor has had previous problems, and Shipman had a previous drug conviction. Who else has this tremendous protection of reputation? Police officers can't have criminal records, and teachers are rigorously checked too. There are bad apples in every profession, including medicine. Now I am very, very angry. From what I have been told, it seems the police did not want to upset anybody, because it was such a sensitive issue. But we are talking about people dying unnecessarily. I think the police should have rigorously investigated it."

Greater Manchester Police responded: "We are entirely sympathetic to all the families involved in this case, particularly at this time." There really was little else they could say.

A few days later Kathleen Adamski announced that she'd changed her mind about suing. She decided that she wished to grieve in private and stopped her plan for action against Greater Manchester Police. But the fact remained that she had highlighted a situation that still needed to be properly addressed.

Soon after it emerged that a man who had survived Shipman's attempt to kill him could also receive a six-figure compensation award. Derek Webb, 58, suffered brain damage when the GP suddenly doubled the medication he was receiving to control epilepsy. Now, after ten years of legal wrangling and the rejection of an out-of-court settlement worth tens of thousands of pounds, Mr. Webb's family was at last on the verge of a full settlement.

Meanwhile, yet another inquest into one of Shipman's patients heard how pensioner Mary Wall, 78, had been playing energetically with her grandchildren the day before she died during a visit by Shipman, who'd recorded her death as coronary thrombosis. After hearing how the GP had phoned victim Ivy Lomas's niece, Elizabeth Lomas, to say that her aunt had died, coroner John Pollard concluded that Shipman's version of events was "extremely unlikely." Following the phone call, Lomas went straight to the widow's house in Werneth Avenue, Gee Cross, near Hyde, where she was greeted by Shipman.

Inside the house, Mary Wall was still sitting in her favorite armchair, fully clothed and "looking very peaceful—as if she had fallen asleep."

Shipman told Lomas that Mrs. Wall had been unconscious when he arrived. But later, Mrs. Wall's daughter, Eileen Morris, said that Shipman told her a different account. Shipman had informed her that Mrs. Wall had told him where to find her phone book in order to contact relatives after he had arrived at her house. Both women said it was unlikely that, as Shipman had claimed, Mrs. Wall had left her front door unlocked so he could walk in.

Coroner Pollard concluded beyond reasonable doubt that Mrs. Wall had been unlawfully killed by Shipman.

By this time—early spring 2001—some of the relatives of Shipman's victims were pressing harder for compensation. Criminal Injuries Compensation Board Chief Executive Howard Webber and members of his team even held a special meeting in Dukinfield Town Hall to talk to family members and answer questions. The meeting was organized by the Victim Support and attorney Alexander Harris, who represented many relatives of victims and suspected victims. Attorney Ann Alexander even said at the time: "We are delighted the board's chief executive has agreed to attend. Compensation has never been an important issue for many of the relatives, but it is important for those who believe Shipman may have murdered their loved ones to understand the compensation system."

In the second week of March 2001, there was a predictable outcry from the respectable citizens of Hyde when it was revealed that shooting of the TV movie about Shipman was taking place on their streets. Many of his victims' families were said to be appalled that the filmmakers had hired Shipman's actual Renault Espace van, which had become famous thanks to the one piece of TV news footage of the GP leaving his house shortly after the police investigation was finally made public.

Soon the people of Hyde were lining up to take a swipe at the TV film. Jane Ashton-Hibbert, whose grandmother was one of Shipman's victims, told her local newspaper: "It's just too soon. He was only convicted last year, and the wounds are still raw. There are many relatives of victims here who would have a heart attack if they saw James Bolam [the actor playing Shipman in the movie] walking down the street looking the spitting image of Shipman. Also, it would be very macabre to see him driving past in the car as he did on his way to kill."

Tameside Metropolitan Borough Council even sought advice from the Broadcasting Standards Commission to see if they could do anything to stop the project. But there seemed little chance that the film would be delayed, let alone canceled. "This is a matter of record, and it's a case that has fascinated the world. People want to know more about Shipman."

Leaders of the local Tameside council completely refused to help the filmmakers. They explained: "It was felt filming of this nature would be very distressing for local people." It then emerged that the producers of the Shipman movie were under so much pressure from local people that they'd switched many of the locations to a similar-looking town named Ossett, in Yorkshire, to avoid any embarrassing scenes with angry Hyde residents.

Meanwhile, chilling footage of Fred Shipman talking about caring for patients in the community instead of hospitalizing them was broadcast. This was the archive film the World in Action current affairs program shot in 1982—at a time when the GP is believed to have murdered up to thirty-five patients. Interviewed at the desk of his surgery in Hyde, Shipman seemed enthusiastic about a new type of treatment for the mentally ill. The film had first aired almost twenty years earlier, when Fred Shipman was regarded as a deeply caring and widely respected doctor. This time, the footage was shown on *Tonight with Trevor McDonald*. Shipman even talked about the need to "break down the barriers" between doctor and patient.

Police investigator Detective Chief Superintendent Bernard Postles said of Shipman's TV performance, "Anybody who has met him will see that he is a very confident individual, very able to put together a story quite coherently."

Dr. John Grenville, who was called as an expert witness during the Shipman trial, told *Tonight with Trevor McDonald*: "He certainly comes across as being very arrogant, and I'm sure that the only way that he could get through the trial was to think himself invincible."

By the beginning of the spring of 2001, more than £700,000 ($1.2m) had been paid out to relatives of Fred Shipman's victims—even though each payment did not exceed a £10,000 ($15,000) ceiling. A total of 160 people had made the claims in relation to seventy deaths. At least 120 awards had already been made, while about thirty were still under consideration. Only twelve applications had been rejected—relating to cases which both the police and Crown Prosecution Service had been unable to offer any evidence in support.

And the £10,000 ($15,000) sum handed out to relatives was reduced to £5,000 ($7,500) if more than one family member made a claim. Relatives were also offered an additional award of up to £20,000 ($30,000) for mental injury if they could show they were psychologically scarred by a death, but only a dozen applications of this type were ever made.

Meanwhile the chairman of the newly formed Shipman Public Inquiry promised to establish just how many victims the former Hyde GP claimed. Dame Janet Smith wrote to families of suspected victims and told them she would also consider the methods he employed and the period over which the killings took place. She added: "I will do everything possible to give an indication of whether a patient died from natural or unnatural causes."

The families of Shipman's numerous victims were promised a video link from the hearing so people in the area could "keep in touch" with the evidence, Health Minister John Hutton told Members of Parliament. He said: "We owe it to families and friends of victims to implement whatever steps are necessary to prevent a repetition of these terrible crimes."

In June 2001, Dame Janet Smith's public inquiry finally began hearing evidence at Manchester Town Hall. The day before proceedings got under way, coroner Dr. John Pollard called for reforms that would stop any future serial killing doctor in his tracks. Dr. Pollard admitted the current system was uncoordinated and provided insufficient safeguards to the public. He conceded that one of the main reasons Shipman got away with murder for so long was that not all deaths had to be reported to the local coroner. Even when they were, there was no centralized system that might identify emerging criminal patterns. Pollard said that a single organization should be set up for all aspects of the investigation and registration of deaths throughout England and Wales.

The new service would be headed by a legally qualified coroner and two deputies. In each area these officials would receive reports from registrars, plus a number of full- and part-time medical referees. Pollard explained: "For the future, not only would it be much more likely that all deaths requiring further investigation would receive the attention they require, but also the system could be interrogated to spot unusual patterns."

If the proposals went ahead, then the deceased's doctor would be required to provide a medical history, and it would no longer be legally possible for him or her to issue a death certificate without having examined the deceased post-mortem. But as one coroner said: "A very admirable list of recommendations. But in the case of more than 400 Shipman victims, it is all a little late . . ."

28

These days, Primrose Shipman does her shopping on Sundays when the supermarket tends to be quieter. That way there's less chance of her or her children being recognized. For that same reason, she hasn't been on a bus for two years. It's all part of her legacy as the wife of mass murderer Fred Shipman.

Since her husband was exposed to the world as one of the most deadly serial killers of all time, Primrose's life has changed forever. What she and her four children do not yet know is how long it will take for the finger-pointing and sly remarks to stop.

The victims of Fred Shipman extend well beyond those he actually killed. They include, of course, the families of his victims. But often forgotten are the families who have to live with the shocking fact that one of their number has joined a select criminal roll-call of infamy. Fred Shipman was responsible for more than 400 murders. The home where he escaped the pressures and guilt of his life as a doctor is now owned by another family. But in the community where the Shipmans lived, Primrose has lost many of her friends. They've stopped calling her at her new home. She's no doubt feeling lonely, and she must surely sometimes feel like shouting, "This has nothing to do with me!" But for the moment, her loyalty to Fred Shipman remains intact. As one friend explained: "All they've got is each other, and there's no way Primrose is going to let go after all they've been through together."

Following Fred Shipman's trial and its worldwide coverage, Primrose called up many of her friends and associates to tell them that she still believed her husband was innocent. In the small community of Whitby, Yorkshire, where she now lives, Primrose has long since learned to steel herself against outright abuse from some quarters, including passers-by—although it has to be said that on a few occasions, she has beaten a hasty retreat from a local shop when confronted by an angry crowd.

Primrose also receives at least ten anonymous letters a week, including the classic threatening paste-and-scissors notes using the print from newspaper headlines. "It's not so much what they say that disturbs Primrose," said one old Shipman family friend. "It's the fact that someone bothered, someone disliked her husband so much that they would cut up these newspapers." Ever since Primrose bought the house in Whitby, she's kept a very discreet distance between herself and her new neighbors. She has virtually no contact with anyone in the community. She thinks that many have already made up their minds what sort of person she is.

Today, two years after the trial's worldwide banner headlines and massive, global TV coverage, Primrose remains incredibly cautious about meeting new people. One of her few long-standing friends says that Primrose is determined to fight on, and one day hopes to clear her husband's name. She refuses to even slightly concede that he might be guilty of anything more than simply being a good doctor.

As for the Shipman children, Sarah, 32, now works in a ticket agency; Christopher, 28, is an engineer; 20-year-old David is a university student; and Sam, 18, is at agricultural college. All of them will no doubt be haunted by their father's evil deeds for the rest of their lives. But as Stephen West, son of serial-killing couple Fred and Rosemary West, recently explained: "The first thing you have to remember is that there's nothing you could have done to prevent it. You have a life that's as precious as anyone else's; you have to think you're number one, because no one else will think it of you.

"You can't forget about what happened, and if you try,

you will end up damaging yourself. I have spent a time each week when I have five minutes to myself just thinking about what happened. It makes you understand a little bit more each time."

Stephen West is, for the most part, remarkably well focused when he talks about his situation. He becomes less so, and is clearly emotional, when he addresses his feelings for his parents, the parents who killed so many innocent people. "I believe you can still love a person—your mum or dad—as detached from what they have done, but they are your parents, and it's so difficult to let go.

"People say to me, 'How can you still love them?' There's a fine line between love and hate anyway, and people shouldn't judge till they have had to live with something like this. You can't make yourself hate someone. If I have anything to thank my parents for, it's that I'm healthy and I'm alive. The Shipman family should know that things will get better."

Primrose and her children have seen their figurehead in the dock for mass murder. They've seen Fred Shipman taken off to prison. They've continued to back his plea of innocence totally. Even when the jury found him guilty, they refused to condemn him. They all saw him within twenty-four hours of that guilty verdict, and told him they would support him until their dying day.

There will not be a day in their lives when they won't be hit by the magnitude of what has happened. The Shipman family's image to the outside world is one of solidarity in the face of irrefutable facts. They have all become tougher and more cynical as a result of Fred Shipman's conviction, but then, that is how they survive. No doubt some of the Shipman children must have wondered if they inherited from their father any of his genetic predisposition to murder. But experts say there is no point in lingering on such thoughts.

Stephen West believes the Shipman children simply have to try to live as normally as they can, however hard that might be. He says: "I enjoy my job, and take a lot of pride in my work. Everyone needs something, whether or not they're the son or daughter of a mass murderer. And people won't appreciate you for stopping working. And they won't forgive you either. This kind of thing will never go away—but it can make you a stronger person."

However, psychologists warn that Fred Shipman's crimes will have an everlasting effect on his wife and children. Some believe the children will be unlikely to ever fully recover from their father's betrayal, and could even turn on Primrose as they try to make sense of his horrific double life. Consultant forensic psychologist Ian Stephen believes that Primrose, having married Shipman as a pregnant teenager and relied on him totally for the previous thirty-two years, will be feeling utterly alone for the first time in her life, and might see suicide as the only way out.

"She has lost the whole focus of her life," he explained. Stephen believes that Primrose's weight problems could well be a sign of long-standing depression. Her composed exterior, as she posed for photographers on the day after her husband's sentencing, was a typical sign of emotional shutdown. Now she must try to build a life for herself in the outside world, while still clinging to her all-powerful husband—a doctor whom many believe took the lives of more than 400 patients.

EPILOGUE

An extraordinary catalogue of errors allowed Fred Shipman to continue his orgy of killings undetected for more than twenty-five years. Many victims died because of the arrogance of Shipman's colleagues, who refused to believe the doctor's drug addiction could seriously impair his abilities as a GP. These blunders gave Fred Shipman a free run at turning murder into a full-time hobby. There were *seven* key areas that should have helped bring him to justice many years earlier:

1. **CRIMINAL RECORD.** Initially, police completely failed to check and see if Shipman had any past convictions, which would have uncovered his drug addiction in Todmorden.

2. **BMA CHECKS.** Investigators also failed to check the British Medical Association's file on Shipman, which it had held since that first conviction.

3. **DEATH CERTIFICATES.** Police requested from local authorities all death certificates relating to Dr. Shipman's cases over a six-month period. They only saw nineteen, when there was actually a total of thirty.

4. **VICTIMS' RECORDS.** Medical files on only fourteen of the first nineteen suspected victims were provided by the local health authority. Nobody even bothered to try to locate the missing five.

5. **SOFTLY SOFTLY.** The police were so oversensitive to the relatives of the victims that initially they failed to grasp the sheer numbers involved.

6. **RELATIVES.** Officers were reluctant to upset victims' relatives by interviewing them. Thus, vital information was not gathered quickly enough.

7. **PRESCRIPTIONS.** No checks were run on Shipman's prescription records, so the huge amount of diamorphine he was prescribing went unnoticed. Shipman was in fact the sixth highest prescriber of the drug amongst more than ninety local GPs.

Never has a story unfolded with such horror. The chilling conclusion of this book is that Fred Shipman may have murdered upwards of 400 patients. That is the number of unexplained deaths which occurred under his "care." He truly is amongst the worst serial killers in history.

For hundreds of families in Todmorden, Yorkshire, and Hyde, Lancashire, the nightmare continues. Did their loved ones die of natural causes? Or were they cold-bloodedly slaughtered by the doctor they trusted with their lives? Many will probably never know the truth. All they can be certain of is that for years, Shipman got away with killing, right under the noses of the authorities. The British government was finally forced to agree to a public inquiry after relatives of the victims successfully challenged its original, short-sighted refusal.

What I hope my book has established is how Shipman got away for so long with his career of mass murder. Why no one noticed what he was up to, and how slipshod medical checks and misplaced professional loyalties must share the blame. It surpasses belief that such systematic evil could flourish undetected and unchallenged for so long. The case of Fred Shipman has exposed a catastrophic failure in the British medical system.

Then there is Fred Shipman himself and the demons that drove him to commit such atrocities. Will he ever come to terms with the sheer scale of his murderous ways? In this book I've tried to unpeel the mind of Fred Shipman, his wife Primrose, and the life they led so quietly and so reservedly for more than thirty years. But Fred Shipman is not a two-headed monster, a freak show exhibit. On the outside he was a painfully normal middle-class family man. Some found him a tad boring, to put it politely. But inside his head, the darkest, most evil thoughts were taking shape from the day that his mother died.

He went on to murder many innocents, including a mother and daughter, two brothers and two sets of next-door neighbors. Two women died on the same day. Shipman claimed the lives of at least five patients at his clinic.

His crimes were connected to power and status. Accustomed to godlike adulation and authority, he easily slipped into the role of playing God. Soon his murderous desires became all-consuming, and the sick and elderly became the means of satisfying those aspirations. If many were close to death, then he believed he was doing them a favor.

Intriguingly, that was how prosecutors depicted the rationale which had driven another British medical killer, Dr. Bodkin Adams, a GP who lived in the county of Sussex, in the south of England. In the mid-1950s, Adams murdered at least twenty-one of his female patients, after many of them had changed their wills in his favor.

Bloated, balding bespectacled Adams, in his late fifties, had a taste for the good life. Wealthy elderly ladies made up the majority of his patient list. Adams's favorite type of treatment for many of these old ladies was a bottle of barbiturates and opiates. He prescribed such generous doses that many of them were soon addicted to the drugs. Most of his victims died through either barbiturates or Fred Shipman's favorite weapon, diamorphine, which Adams fraudulently prescribed to himself. The similarities with the Shipman case are chilling.

Many of Adams's victims expired soon after naming him as the major beneficiary in their wills. Just like Fred Shipman, Adams was finally brought to justice thanks to the curiosity of the relatives of one of his victims. Adams eventually found himself facing twenty-one murder charges at the infamous Old Bailey criminal court in London. Another batch of cases was lying in wait in case prosecutors did not succeed.

Adams argued that he had indeed contributed to his patients' deaths by giving them large quantities of painkillers so they could retain some dignity in passing. His attorney used the phrase "easing the passing" in open court. The jury shook their heads in understandable agreement. The end of his lengthy trial in 1957 shocked the nation, because the jury was unable to accept that a respectable doctor could commit such heinous crimes. The roly-poly medic seemed a bumbling, innocent character, and his victims had included some who were terminally ill. Less than an hour after retiring, the jury returned with a not guilty verdict. Adams survived, although he lost his license to practice medicine because of prescription irregularities.

The case of Bodkin Adams seemed to prove that doctors could literally get away with murder, providing they were careful, clinical and discriminating in their choice of victims. Whether this ever occurred to Fred Shipman, we will probably never know. Many believe that he was so sloppy in the execution of many of his murders that he is not in the same league as Adams, but with almost 400 deaths thought to be his handiwork, Shipman certainly managed to be far more prolific.

The most recent UK case of a murdering health expert before Shipman was that of nurse Beverly Allitt, convicted of the murder of four children, the attempted murder of three others, and grievous bodily harm of six more. Health services must accept responsibility for protecting patients from such individuals. The public cannot be expected to have confidence in a system that fails to detect the murder of a large number of patients over a period of years by a doctor or other health professional.

Of course, there is no standard blueprint of the rogue, Fred Shipman–type killer doctor, but there are a number of common denominators that connect each:

1. They do not usually start killing until middle age.

2. They abuse drugs, in particular diamorphine or its cognates.

3. They are brusque and acerbic in their manner.

4. They are arrogant with colleagues.

5. They can command extraordinary loyalty from those close to them.

6. Often self-made, they are over-conscious of their status as doctors.

7. They have a complete lack of empathy.

The many new revelations I have uncovered in the towns and communities where Shipman worked as a GP will add further anguish to those whose relatives died under Shipman's care, and may lead to fresh demands from some of them for a new public trial. That desire is a natural response to an appalling series of crimes. At the time of Shipman's original criminal trial, detectives were well aware of the potential number of his victims, but they chose to focus resources and attention on a limited number of murders in order to secure a conviction in court.

Fred Shipman now faces the rest of his life in prison; trying him for more than 350 other killings in order to pile life sentence upon life sentence would add nothing to his punishment. What is important is that the findings of the recent governmental report and my investigations are acted upon by the Shipman Public Inquiry, which is expected to last a further two years. It is a disturbing fact that the extraordinarily high death rate among Shipman's patients, especially elderly women, passed unnoticed by the health authorities for many, many years. If statistical aberrations in the performance of general practitioners are now to be routinely checked, this will show, more than any number of retrials, that the lessons of Fred Shipman's horrific crimes have been taken to heart.

The British government believed that by launching the Baker Inquiry and the public examination of all the Shipman

deaths they could strengthen the bond of trust between doctor and patient. Patients' protection seemed to be the key
phrase. But the truth is that the entire medical profession
needs to take a closer look at itself by examining the role
of the General Medical Council, under whose rules Shipman
remained a GP for years after his arrest. That seems to suggest that the GMC did not do enough to protect patients.
They also need to more closely examine the measures
needed to safeguard against the risk of a lone doctor committing long-term malpractice, as well as carefully review
the policies on the handling of controlled drugs by doctors.

But will we ever trust doctors again?

AN ANONYMOUS DOCTOR WRITES . . .

Britain's medical profession is split by the Shipman case because many believe that he may genuinely have considered himself an angel of mercy, putting old and sick people out of their misery before the pain of illness became unbearable. As an eminent cancer specialist, I know just how thin that line between encouraging death and treating pain can frequently be.

I've followed the Shipman case closely, and I can tell you I have personally 'killed' hundreds of patients with huge doses of morphine. But because they were suffering from cancer, no one has ever turned around and questioned my wisdom in administering those drugs.

So where do you draw the line? If one of my patients is obviously suffering both emotionally and physically, I often make that decision without any reference to their relatives if I feel certain that painful death is just around the corner. Does that make me a mass murderer?

And I am not talking about a couple of instances a year. I probably "kill" at least three or four patients a month. Of course, Dr. Shipman was in a different position from a cancer specialist, but he did work in an area dominated by the elderly and sick. I sometimes wonder if, when he first started killing, he genuinely wanted to prevent them suffering, but then became addicted to the thrill and power of death. Certainly, there doesn't seem to have been any sexual gratification involved. His motive may well have originally been a misguided conviction that he needed to ease the pain for these people, just in the way drugs eased the pain of death for his own mother.

Euthanasia may still be illegal in many countries but, quite frankly, it's being carried out every day of every week of every month of the year. In fact, most doctors will tell you it's better if it remains illegal, because then we don't get bogged down having to fill out silly forms like they do in Holland where euthanasia is legal.

You see, the Shipman case is a benchmark for many of us . . .

HYDE—THE AFTERMATH

Hyde, with its 35,000 residents, will for many years be associated with Fred Shipman's murderous habits. Like Hungerford, Gloucester, Dunblane and Bradford before it, the community has found itself unwillingly thrust into the spotlight, forced to deal with a notoriety they would rather not have. As David Hagg, assistant chief executive of Tameside Council, pointed out: "It has put the town in the spotlight, and that's been hard for many of them—but people are resilient, and I think they have ways of dealing with it. We would ask everyone to give them an opportunity to move on with their lives and deal with the shock and trauma they have been through."

Community psychologist Alistair Cameron believes the process of rebuilding a community in the wake of such a tragedy can take several years. "There were a series of killings which produce a series of emotions in the local community including anger and disbelief," he says. "The problem with a community is that no two people will have been affected in the same way. They may have known the victim, or they may have known the culprit, and these different experiences can divide a community at a time when it most needs to be united."

Dr. Lorraine Sher, a trauma psychologist from the Royal Free Hospital in London, said: "It is important that the community bonds together and shares its grief through counseling, or by attending a memorial service for the dead. Over time, the wounds will begin to naturally heal, but it is important that this process is not rushed. Remembering what has happened does not have to be a negative experience. Often the most poignant legacy of a horrific event is how it can bring people closer in a community."

Fred Shipman, once liked and respected by the people of Hyde, is now reviled across the community. From the ironically named Age Concern shop in Market Street to the doctors' waiting room opposite, the people of Hyde now dismiss Shipman as an outsider who was in partnership with the devil. They believe Shipman wheedled his way into the heart of Hyde and then tried to destroy it. Virtually everyone has a relative, friend or friend's friend at the heart of the Shipman affair.

Yet patients still wait to see their GPs with the same loyalty that they had before Fred Shipman was arrested. Dr. Raj Patel, who runs the nearby Brook clinic, is surprised by how little Shipman's crimes have undermined patients' trust in their GPs. He recently had an elderly patient who insisted on her GP giving her a Vitamin B12 injection rather than wait for the nurse. "Doesn't it worry you?" he asked. "No," she said. "Dr. Shipman was a very bad man who became a doctor, not a doctor who became a serial killer."

NOTES OF GRATITUDE

A leaden, dispassionate word like "Acknowledgments" for this section cannot begin to express the depth of my feelings for the many individuals who've made this book possible. I owe them my deepest and most heartfelt gratitude, and I know that many in Hyde would rather I didn't mention their names in print.

However, to my literary manager and great friend Peter Miller and my editor Anderson Bailey I say many thanks. Without them this book would never have happened. Their support and guidance has been very much appreciated. Then there is John Glatt, John Blake, Jo Holt, Bob Duffield, Fran Pearce, Dr. David Walker, Adrian Pomfret and all the family, friends and associates of many of Shipman's victims and his own family . . .

As Detective Chief Superintendent Postles explained shortly after Fred Shipman's incarceration: "It's the question everyone asks: Why? With each killing he usually turned up on spec, but we don't know why he targeted particular people. We were constantly questioning ourselves: Are we wrong? We tried to keep an open mind and be objective, but it was difficult.

"We considered all the possibilities: greed, revenge, sex. Money only appeared to be the motive in the Kathleen Grundy case. There was no evidence of sexual interference with any of the victims. Clothing, apart from a rolled-up sleeve, had not been touched.

"His finances showed nothing out of the ordinary. There was no evidence of him having an affair. The only clue is his attitude. He thinks he is superior, and wants to control the situation."

FRED SHIPMAN—A CAREER IN MURDER

DoB	14/1/1946
1965–1970	Leeds University Medical School
1970	Gained MBChB
July 23, 1970	Provisional registration with GMC
(Number 1470473)	
Aug 1, 1970	Pre-registration house officer
Jan 31, 1971	(surgery) Pontefract General Infirmary
Feb 1, 1971	Pre-registration house officer
July 31, 1971	(medicine) Pontefract General Infirmary
Aug 5, 1971	Full registration with GMC, number 140473
Sept 1972	Diploma in Child Health (DCH)
Sept 1973	Diploma of Royal College of Obstetricians and Gynecologists (DRCOG); Number A9640
March 1–	Assistant general practitioner,
March 31, 1974	Todmorden Group Practice, Todmorden
April 1, 1974	General practitioner, Todmorden Group
Sept 1975	Practice, Todmorden

1976   Convicted of dishonestly obtaining drugs, forgery of an NHS prescription, and unlawful possession of pethidine. He was fined on each charge and ordered to pay compensation to the local Family Practitioner Committee. These offenses were reported to the GMC, who told Shipman that if he offended again, these cases would form part of a subsequent hearing. Medical reports at that time said he was unlikely to offend again.

Dec 11, 1975 Break in practice, 1 year and 264 days

1977   Clinical Medical Officer, South West Durham. His responsibilities were reported as having been limited to examination of infants and advice about development.

Oct 1, 1977— General practitioner principal, Donnybrook House Group Practice, Hyde
Dec 31, 1991

1985   The GMC received a complaint alleging that Shipman had provided inadequate medical care to a young man who died from an undiagnosed illness. The complaint was referred back to the Family Practitioner Committee.

1989   A complaint was made that Shipman had prescribed the wrong dose of Epilem to a patient with epilepsy. The complaint was upheld, but there was no withholding from his remuneration. A civil case for negligence was pursued and settled for £250,000.

Jan 1, 1992— May 31, 1992	General practitioner principal, Donnybrook House, Hyde, operating as a single-handed GP
1992	A complaint for failure to visit was upheld.
June 1, 1992	General practitioner principal, the Surgery, 21 Market Street, Hyde
1995	A complaint about inadequate/ incorrect treatment was made, but the patient did not pursue the complaint.
Mar 24, 1998	Concerns about the excess number of deaths among Shipman's patients reported by local general practitioners to Stockport coroner
Sept 7, 1998	Arrested by Greater Manchester Police
Jan 31, 2000	Sentenced to life in prison after being found guilty of murdering fifteen of his elderly patients as well as forging Kathleen Grundy's last will and testament

They'd do anything to win their mother's love.
But would they kill their own sisters?

WHATEVER MOTHER SAYS...

A True Story of a Mother, Madness and Murder

Wensley Clarkson

Raising her five kids alone in a rundown section of Sacramento, Theresa Cross Knorr seemed like the ultimate survivor. But her youngest daughter, 16-year-old Terry, told police another story. According to Terry, Theresa—no longer the petite brunette she once was—had turned insanely jealous of her pretty eldest daughters and enlisted the help of her two teenaged sons in a vicious campaign against their sisters. Terry's gruesome tale tells how Theresa had drugged, handcuffed and shot 16-year-old Suesan, allowing her wounds to fester, until she ordered her sons to burn their sister alive. Next, according to Terry, her mother savagely beat 20-year-old Sheila and locked her in a broom closet, where she would starve to death. Here, in vivid detail, is the shocking account of Theresa Cross Knorr, a woman who might just be the mother of all murderesses...

AVAILABLE FROM ST. MARTIN'S PAPERBACKS
WHEREVER BOOKS ARE SOLD